Off the
Beaten Path®

maritime provinces

Help Us Keep This Guide Up to Date

Every effort has been made by the author and editors to make this guide as accurate and useful as possible. However, many changes can occur after a guide is published—establishments close, phone numbers change, hiking trails are rerouted, facilities come under new management, etc.

We would love to hear from you concerning your experiences with this guide and how you feel it could be improved and be kept up to date. While we may not be able to respond to all comments and suggestions, we'll take them to heart, and we'll make certain to share them with the author. Please send your comments and suggestions to the following address:

The Globe Pequot Press
Reader Response/Editorial Department
P.O. Box 480
Guilford, CT 06437

Or you may e-mail us at: editorial@GlobePequot.com

Thanks for your input, and happy travels!

INSIDERS' GUIDE®

OFF THE BEATEN PATH® SERIES

Off the Beaten Path®

FIFTH EDITION

maritime provinces

A GUIDE TO UNIQUE PLACES

TRUDY FONG

INSIDERS' GUIDE®

GUILFORD, CONNECTICUT
AN IMPRINT OF THE GLOBE PEQUOT PRESS

The prices, rates, and hours listed in this guidebook
were confirmed at press time. We recommend,
however, that you call establishments to obtain
current information before traveling.

To buy books in quantity for corporate use
or incentives, call **(800) 962–0973, ext. 4551,**
or e-mail **premiums@GlobePequot.com.**

INSIDERS' GUIDE®

Text design by Linda Loiewski
Maps created by Equator Graphics © The Globe Pequot Press
Illustrations by Carole Drong
Illustration of Grand Falls Gorge on page 27 from slide courtesy of
New Brunswick Tourism Department. Illustration of *Bluenose II* on page 115 from slide
courtesy of Nova Scotia Department of Tourism and Culture. All other illustrations from
photos by Greg Fong.
Spot photography throughout © J. A. Kraulis/Masterfile

ISSN 1542-5533
ISBN 0-7627-3524-4

Manufactured in the United States of America
Fifth Edition/First Printing

To Greg, companion of all
my significant voyages—
"The only railroad romance that ever lasted."

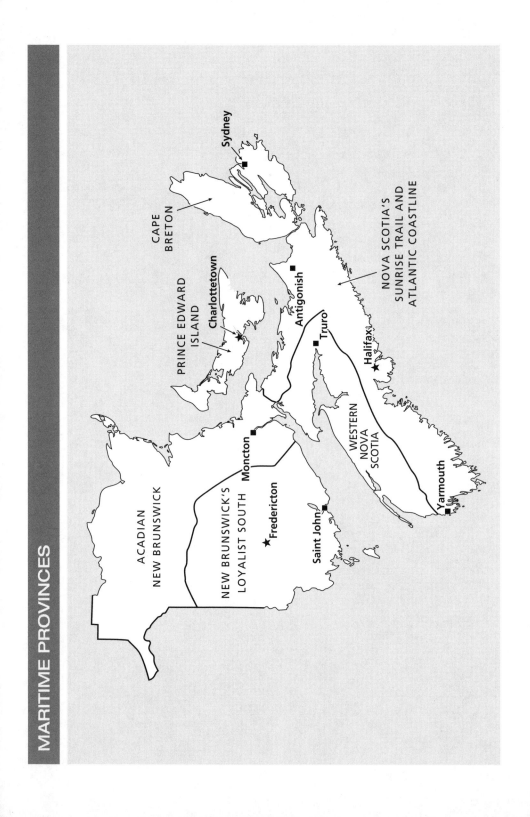

MARITIME PROVINCES

ACADIAN
NEW BRUNSWICK

NEW BRUNSWICK'S
LOYALIST SOUTH

★Fredericton

Saint John

Moncton

PRINCE EDWARD
ISLAND

Charlottetown★

CAPE
BRETON

Sydney

Antigonish

Truro

Halifax★

WESTERN
NOVA
SCOTIA

Yarmouth

NOVA SCOTIA'S
SUNRISE TRAIL AND
ATLANTIC COASTLINE

Contents

Acknowledgments

The following people have been wonderfully enthusiastic and informative and have inspired me with their special love of the Maritimes. I wish to thank them: Eleanor Mullendor, Lida Babineau, and Ronnie Doucet, Helen Sievers, Cathy McDonald, Randy Brooks, Carol Horne, Valerie Kidney, Doug Fawthrop, Bob Benson, Ann Godard, Margaret and Axel Begner, Nora Parker, Webb Burns, Alida Visbach, and Simone Larade.

All but two of the renderings in this book are drawn from photographs shot by my husband, photographer Greg Fong. The Nova Scotia Department of Tourism and Culture supplied the shot of the *Bluenose II,* and the Grand Falls Gorge illustration is from a shot supplied by the New Brunswick Tourism Department.

Introduction

My first real experience of travel in the Maritimes came as a result of a job on VIA Rail, the passenger-train service, which at that time left twice daily for Montreal from Halifax. I had graduated from college and was at loose ends when I took the job.

There were many opportunities to become familiar with the lay of the land as the train trundled by farms and woodlands, lakes and rivers. And with every stop the cultural and linguistic fabric would subtly change. Then as now, what struck me is the region's tremendous diversity, the vastness of the land, and the tiny communities that live in relative isolation from one another. Perhaps it is this isolation that has created fiercely independent peoples who are nevertheless able to extend exceptionally warm welcomes to outsiders. While exchange rates fluctuate and prices change, businesses close, and new spots open, there is an enduring quality about the Maritimes that keeps visitors coming back year after year.

Prices in this book are in Canadian dollars. If you are coming from another country, you will want to know the value of your currency compared with the Canadian dollar. To calculate conversions quickly, divide any Canadian price by the rate posted for your currency on that day.

Canada uses metric measurements for weight, distance, and temperature. In this book I've listed measures according to the U.S. standards and provided their metric equivalents in parentheses. Take note that all road signs in Canada are in kilometers, not miles. Posted speed limits of 100, often shown without a "km," translate to 62 miles per hour.

Dressing for weather conditions in the Maritimes means packing layers. Carry a windbreaker, which is good in fog or mist, conditions that occur in the Maritimes about as often as the tides. A warm sweater is a good item to pack even in the summer months, because Maritime temperatures often drop significantly at night. Sunblock is also a must. The cool sea breeze or overcast skies can fool you into thinking that the sun is not very strong, but even a hazy day at the beach can result in a severe burn if you don't take precautions.

I include several good hikes in each province. These were selected for the natural wonders that you may discover along the trails more than for their ease. That said, a good pair of walking shoes or, better still, hiking boots is a must. Hats are also a good idea, as is bug repellent in the countryside, particularly in the spring.

All three Maritime Provinces have taxes on consumer goods, some of which can be reimbursed to out-of-country visitors, with certain restrictions.

Nova Scotia and New Brunswick have a harmonized sales tax that blends both the provincial sales tax and the federal goods and services tax, or GST.

Prince Edward Island has these taxes, but in "unblended" form, which means it taxes fewer items than the federal government. But when the provincial tax is levied, it applies to the retail selling price of the goods, which already includes the GST. This means that the province's 10 percent is added to the price of goods after the 7 percent federal tax has already been added. If you do a lot of shopping, it's worthwhile to try to get some of that tax money back.

Visitors from outside Canada can receive rebates on taxes paid on goods intended for use outside Canada, if they are removed from the country within sixty days of their purchase. Exceptions to this rule are the taxes on tobacco and alcohol. You also can get rebates on short-term accommodations other than campgrounds or trailer park fees.

To get all that tax money back, present your original receipts to any participating duty-free shop or send them to Revenue Canada. You must fill out a form, available at most provincial visitor centers. Or write the Visitor Rebate Program, Revenue Canada, Summerside Tax Centre, Summerside, PE, C1N 6C6, Canada. Call (800) 668–4748 (in Canada), (902) 432–5608 (outside Canada).

If there is no duty-free shop at your exit point, you must have your receipts for goods stamped by a Canadian customs official before you leave the country. Also note that each receipt must total at least $50 (*before* taxes) to be eligible for the rebate.

Most museum admission prices in the Maritimes are quite reasonable, because many of these sites are government operated. If you plan to visit several national parks, it may be more economical to buy a season pass sticker for a flat fee rather than paying for each entry.

In some remote areas accommodations are quite limited, so I have listed several places you can call to reserve a room ahead of time to avoid a last-minute search. In a number of places I refer to Heritage properties. These are buildings or areas that various government bodies have determined to have significant historical connections. Having survived the plow and wrecking ball thus far, they have been designated by the government for future protection. Heritage properties are taxed at special rates, and the owners are assisted in restoration so that the sites may be preserved for future generations. The "Heritage" designation means that the property is preserved as much as possible in its original state. Scenic Heritage Roads on Prince Edward Island are old clay roads that appear exactly as they did one hundred years ago and offer the traveler an abundance of scenic beauty.

Every trip has to start somewhere. That said, my travel throughout the Maritimes seems to have happened consistently in a clockwise direction. Therefore, if your entry point into the Maritimes is not the same as the one at the beginning of this guidebook, merely search through the index for your starting point and follow the route clockwise from that point onward.

The Maritimes are full of hidden treasures— for the gourmet, the photography buff, or the artist. This book is intended as a compass, to help you make your own personal discovery of the wonders that Canada's east coast has to offer. *Bon voyage!*

Rates for accommodations (before taxes, per night)

Under $70	Standard
$70–$150	Moderate
$151 and above	Deluxe

New Brunswick's
Loyalist South

The first province you reach when entering the Maritimes by land is New Brunswick, with its vast, unpopulated interior full of rich timberlands and salmon rivers.

The first characteristic that will strike you is that the bulk of the population is distributed around the rim of the province. Next, you will notice that the province retains many native Indian place names. But certain areas, like the northwestern interior and the gulf coast, have a preponderance of French names, while the Fundy Coast and the Saint John River Valley feature many names of British origin.

These are clues to the character of New Brunswick. Overlaid on a land inhabited by people of the Maliseet and Mi'Kmaq (formerly spelled Micmac) tribes for thousands of years, today the province's linguistic fabric resembles that of Canada as a whole more closely than any other province: Roughly 34 percent of the population are French-speaking, with the remainder using English in their day-to-day communication.

New Brunswick is really two places in one: the French New Brunswick of the northwest and the north and east coasts, and the British Empire Loyalist New Brunswick of the Saint John River Valley and the Fundy shore. It is because of these two distinct characters, rather than any particular geographical

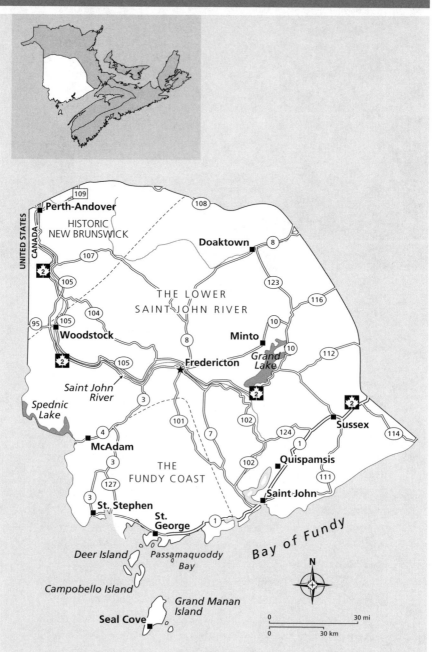

UNITED STATES

CANADA

109 Perth-Andover

HISTORIC
NEW BRUNSWICK

108

107

Doaktown   8

2

105

123

116

THE LOWER
SAINT JOHN RIVER

95   105   104

8   10

Woodstock   Minto

Grand
Lake   10   112

2

Saint John
River   105

Fredericton   2

Spednic
Lake   3

101   7   102   124   Sussex   2

4   114

McAdam   102

3   Quispamsis   1

THE
FUNDY COAST   111

127   102

3   Saint John

St. Stephen

St.
George   1

Deer Island   Passamaquoddy
Bay

Bay of Fundy

Campobello Island   N

Grand Manan
Island

Seal Cove   0   30 mi

0   30 km

reason, that we discuss New Brunswick in two separate chapters. The first, the Loyalist South, begins at the Maine–New Brunswick border, where Yankees and British Loyalists have lived cheek by jowl for two centuries.

The Fundy Coast

If you enter New Brunswick from Calais, Maine, you're struck by the fact that the national border runs right smack dab through the middle of town. In fact, Calais and St. Stephen natives have had such congenial relations that they refused to fight each other during the War of 1812. They still seem to form one community.

Upgrades in the New Brunswick highway system (now featuring large sections of twinned [divided] highway), have caused changes in exit numbers for certain areas. Repeat visitors to New Brunswick will want an up-to-date map to avoid confusion. The development of new highway and New Brunswick's growing popularity has caused a hotel-room shortage. Book rooms well in advance, or book early in the day. You can book rooms en route by calling (800) 561-0123.

Follow the TransCanada Highway (TCH) Route 1 to *St. Andrews by-the-Sea.* The signs will indicate St. Andrews long before anything much appears: The town is there, hidden behind trees. Watch carefully for the sign indicating Provincial Highway 127. Turn right here and drive toward the shore.

You will soon see a small sign pointing left and indicating *Ministers Island*, where you can visit the former *Estate of Sir William Van Horne,* the builder of the Canadian Pacific Railway. Note: If you would rather bypass

TRUDY'S FAVORITES

Beaverbrook Art Gallery,
Fredericton

City Market,
Saint John

Grand Manan Island

Harvest Jazz and Blues Festival,
Fredericton

Kings Landing Historical Settlement,
Fredericton

Legislative Assembly Building,
Fredericton

Machias Seal Island

Ministers Island

Roosevelt Cottage,
Campobello Island

Rossmount Inn,
Saint Andrews by-the-Sea

World's Longest Covered Bridge,
Hartland

Ministers Island and head directly to St. Andrews, simply continue east on Highway 127 (in the direction of Saint John).

To get to Ministers Island take the left turn, then turn right onto Mowat Drive, and take another left onto Bar Road. This will lead you to a barricaded bit of shoreline. A chart listing the times when people can visit the island is displayed there. In this area of the Bay of Fundy, the tides change the water level by about 25 feet. At high tide, the island is inaccessible by car, but at low tide a sandbar serves as the tail end of Bar Road.

A small sign indicates the times when guides will lead small contingents of cars to the island. Wait here rather than crossing the bar to the island on your own—without a guide, a barricade will prevent you from entering even during low tide.

When you first arrive on Ministers Island, you will see a small stone building, then a windmill and a massive barn—in fact, one of the largest in Canada. It was here that Van Horne kept his prized herd of Dutch cattle and his Thoroughbred horses.

agarrisontown

St. Andrews's strategic location on the New Brunswick–Maine border made it a garrison town of long standing. A fort once stood above the town on Barracks Hill. While some documents identify the fort as Fort Tipperary, today the earthen rampart and few cannons that remain are generally referred to as Barracks Hill.

Although neither New Brunswick nor Maine wanted any part of the hostilities, the War of 1812 necessitated the construction of further fortifications, including batteries and blockhouses rimming the coastline, to serve as protection against marauding American privateers. Today only St. Andrews Blockhouse National Historic Site on Joe's Point Road (888–773–8888) remains.

Everything about William Van Horne was meticulous. Not only did he have the entire milking area washed—along with every cow—after each and every milking, but he also ordered a fresh layer of sawdust to be put down in the barn every night. To complete the task, the farmhands had to draw the Van Horne coat of arms in the sawdust! The barn also contains a lovely old carriage, which looks like it is still awaiting horse and driver.

Van Horne had his country house built on the other side of the island using sandstone cut from the shore. Its massive rooms are full of mahogany paneling and post-and-beam supports. The drawing room alone is as large as the average modern bungalow. There are fifty rooms in the house; seventeen of these were bedrooms. In the billiards room is a 6-by-12-foot billiards table crafted for Van Horne in London.

Carriage at Van Horne Estate

Van Horne was an avid and skilled painter. Some of his finest paintings hang in the National Art Gallery in Ottawa. He created them at night in a huge, circular stone bathhouse overlooking Passamaquoddy Bay. A massive lamp was hung from the ceiling to illuminate his work. The property included several heated greenhouses. Van Horne's eight gardeners were able to produce peaches weighing as much as two pounds each. Even when Van Horne lived in Montreal, the dairy products and fruit from his estate were sent via Bar Road to a waiting train, to be delivered the next morning to him.

Sadly, after Van Horne's daughter died in 1941, the property remained empty for many years until it was sold to a succession of speculators, all of whose plans to turn it into a lodge fell through. More than 600 pieces of Van Horne's original mahogany furniture were auctioned off by one group of investors just three days before the province declared it a protected historic site. Even though today the building is emptied of nearly all its furnishings, it is still an amazing place and well worth checking the tide tables to schedule a visit. Call (506) 529–5081 to inquire about tour times. Admission is $5.00 per person.

After leaving Ministers Island, return to Highway 127 and drive east (in the direction of Saint John) for a few minutes. To your left will be a sign indicating the ***Rossmount Inn,*** a Provincial Heritage building. Even if you don't stay here, plan to drop by to eat something so that you can soak up some of the Old World atmosphere inside.

There are so many pieces of pure Anglophile magic here that you'll swear you are in a manor house in England. In the front hallway, rich with mahogany paneling, banisters, and stairway and carpeted with Persian rugs, is a chair used by the King of Belgium during the Queen of England's coronation in 1952. The tables in the dining room are decked out in the finest English bone china and silverware, while the lamps are Tiffany. Reservations can be made by calling (506) 529–3351 or faxing (506) 529–1920. Rates for nonsmoking rooms are moderate.

This part of New Brunswick has long been the haunt of Ivy League types, who sail all summer long from one island to the next. Franklin D. Roosevelt learned to sail in this area. The waters of the bay are quite calm, and each island is unique and appealing.

Continuing along Highway 127, you will find exquisitely preserved St. Andrews by-the Sea. Still oozing with charm, St. Andrews was founded by United Empire Loyalists from nearby Maine in 1783. It was laid out in a grid pattern common in New England towns of that era.

Streets were named after royal personages to leave no doubt about the political stripe of the town's founders. There are King Street, Queen Street, Princess Royal, and Prince of Wales Streets. Prosperity came from selling lumber and wooden ships to Mother England and fish to the West Indies.

trivia

The fronds of the ostrich fern, which is native to New Brunswick, are commonly called "fiddleheads" when they appear in the spring and are a much-loved delicacy.

The idea of packaging heart-shaped boxes of chocolate for Valentine's Day originated from the Ganong Brothers, Limited, in St. Stephen, New Brunswick.

Some of the old houses were actually disassembled in their original locations in Castine, Maine, moved by barge in 1783, and reassembled here.

Downtown St. Andrews offers marvelous possibilities for puttering and sight-seeing. Some of its quaint historic houses date back to the province's early days. Of note is *Sheriff Andrews House,* an authentic Loyalist home built in 1820 by Elisha Andrews, the sheriff of Charlotte County. Situated on the corner of King and Queen Streets, the house is maintained in mint condition. The home was taken over by the province in the late 1980s and meticulously restored. It has undergone few alterations since its original construction. It features nine period-furnished rooms depicting domestic life in the old seaport. Rooms have working fireplaces, and one of its most appealing features is the huge stone hearth in the basement, typical of Loyalist houses of the time. The basement "keeping room" also contains beehive ovens and a pantry. The cooking fireplace is kept going all summer long for visitors, who are invited by the costumed guides to enjoy some refreshments while exploring the house. Guides also demonstrate early cooking and hand-work techniques. The house is open mid-June to late September, from 9:30 A.M. to 4:30 P.M. Monday to Saturday, and from 1:00 to 4:30 P.M. Sunday. Admission is free. For information, call (506) 529–5080.

Now that you are in New Brunswick, you may as well check out some of the seventy-odd "kissing bridges," or covered wooden bridges, that span the many woodland rivers, particularly on old logging roads. Although picturesque, they can be quite tricky to find without detailed directions. The best approach is to work in a visit to a couple of covered bridges en route to somewhere else, with a slight detour onto a secondary road that will take you near a bridge.

The purpose of covering bridges was to keep them from wearing out too soon. Uncovered wooden bridges last an average of ten years; covered ones last eight times as long. Surprisingly, it's not the snow that does the damage, but the sun and rain. It is because of the romantic opportunities they offered that they came to be called kissing bridges. Crossing the bridges by horse and buggy or horse-drawn sleigh (in winter the bridge flooring was covered with snow so that sleighs could pass through) must have taken some time. If the horse was experienced and reliable, a romantic young couple could leave the driving to their four-legged friend and take advantage of the momentary privacy and darkness afforded by the covered bridges.

Among these seventy bridges is the so-called **Covered Bridge Number Four,** which spans the Digdeguash River, near McCann. You can reach it by turning off Route 127 onto Route 760 at Rollingham.

The next stop is **Deer Island,** which is reached by the Deer Island L'Etete Ferry, off Route 1 at St. George. Take Route 772. Departures are frequent, and the ferry is free. The crossing takes about twenty-five minutes and is quite pleasant, especially on a sunny day when a cool breeze is blowing across the calm waters of Passamaquoddy Bay. The ferry lands at Lambert's Cove.

TOP ANNUAL EVENTS

Times for these events vary, unless specified. For full details, contact the **New Brunswick Department of Tourism** at (800) 561–0123.

Acadian National Day,
Acadian Pioneer Village and Saint John
(August 15)

New Brunswick,
Summer Music Festival, Fredericton
(mid-August)

Harvest Jazz and Blues Festival,
Fredericton (second week of September)

Atlantic Balloon Fiesta,
Sussex (mid-September)

On Deer Island, take the left fork in the road. This will take you past Richardson, where you can join a *Cline Marine, Inc.,* boat for a whale-watching cruise. For information, call (800) 567–5880 or (506) 747–0114, or fax (506) 747–2287. The boat operates from mid-June to October. Cost is $50 for adults, students ages thirteen to eighteen, $30. Even in September and October the ship sails once a day (normally at 12:30 P.M.), so you won't be too late to watch the whales if you plan your day right. At this time of year the cruise sometimes leaves earlier to accommodate large groups or collect passengers from other ports. For details, check out www.clinemarine.com.

Pass Richardson and continue to follow the shore road until you reach the Eastport/Campobello Ferry dock just before the *Deer Island Point Park.* If you have timed the tides right, enter the park to get a close-up view of *Old Sow,* the biggest natural tidal whirlpool in the Western Hemisphere, just offshore, opposite the Deer Island Point Park campground, to the right of the dock.

You must be on site three hours before high tide to see Old Sow do its thing. If you are too early, relax and await the forces of nature at the picnic area here at the park.

The ferry ride from Deer Island to *Campobello Island* takes forty-five minutes. It's privately run, so expect to pay $14.00 for a car and driver plus a $3.00 fee for every passenger in your vehicle, to a maximum of $20.00 per car. Children under twelve years of age go free. Campobello is beautifully located on the Bay of Fundy. It's easy to see how it grew into a summer retreat for yachtsmen and Harvard grads.

If you desperately want to drive to Campobello Island through the United States but are in Canada, point your Pontiac south for the Maine border and get onto U.S. Highway 1 from Calais, heading south in the direction of Machias. When you get to Whiting, turn left and head to Lubec on Route 189. In all, you'll drive about 50 miles on highways south of the border. A round-trip by land involves two border crossings, with possibly time-consuming customs inspections—one to get out of St. Stephen and into Calais, another to pass from Lubec to Campobello. You may want to take the boat to the island and drive back or vice versa so that you can see the lay of the land but not take as much time as a round-trip drive.

You can also visit Campobello by boat. Cline Marine of Deer Island makes regular stops here during its whale-watching outings.

After passing through customs onto Campobello Island, take Route 774 and continue along for 1.4 miles (2.4 km). Here you will find *Roosevelt Cottage,* one of a complex of several cottages that now are often used for conferences and meetings. Clustered next to one another facing Lubec, Maine, across the water, the cottages and surrounding acreage are part of the *Roosevelt Campobello International Park.*

Roosevelt Cottage, Campobello Island

President Franklin D. Roosevelt spent many summers here. This is where he learned how to sail before he contracted polio at age thirty-nine. He eventually moved into a bedroom downstairs, just down the hall from his office. Everything in the house has been kept just as it was the last time Eleanor Roosevelt visited the cottage, right down to two massive megaphones left standing in the entrance to the dining room. (They were used to call the children in to eat.) Along with other memorabilia, you can see the flags presented to Roosevelt when he won the presidency. They now flank his desk.

Be sure to visit the house to the right of Roosevelt Cottage, which is part of the same complex. Graced with a roomy wraparound sunporch made from logs, its living room's oval-shaped picture window treats visitors to a perfectly composed view of Lubec across the water. For details on Roosevelt Campobello International Park, call (506) 752–2922. Admission is free. Donations are welcome.

Also on the island you will find *Herring Cove Provincial Park.* It has a beach where you can enjoy the bracing water of the Bay of Fundy. The park also encompasses an active beaver pond and some breathtaking cliffs overlooking the sea. For information on the Herring Cove Provincial Park, call (506) 752–7010. The park is on Route 774.

Before you leave Campobello Island, take advantage of the handy *Campobello Welcome Centre,* which can book accommodations for you in other parts of the province at no charge. It is recommended that those planning to go on to nearby Grand Manan Island take the time to book a room while still on Campobello. Campobello Island's tourist information center is just inside the Canadian border, next to Canadian customs, just a stone's throw from the bridge to Lubec. It is open mid-May to mid-October. For information, call (506) 752–7043.

If you are in the mood to visit a remote, unspoiled place, *Grand Manan Island* is the ticket, but you can't easily get there from Campobello. The best route is via the ferry, which leaves from Blacks Harbor, southwest of Saint John. Sailings are frequent, and you pay only to get off Grand Manan, not on it; the cost is $29.75 for a car and $9.95 for the driver and each adult passenger. Children ages five to twelve pay $4.95; children under five ride at no charge.

At the junction of Routes 785 and 776 on the mainland, take a right. Within five minutes you'll approach the ferry. Plan to take your car, since Grand Manan is quite large. The trip to Grand Manan is lengthy—roughly one and a half hours—and on breezy days you'll need either your sea legs or an antiseasickness pill or both, because Grand Manan is all by its lonesome out in the Bay of Fundy, and the seas can be much rougher than landlubbers expect of a bay. (On the ferry are pictures of the vessel being tossed so wildly by the seas that one end or the other is completely out of the water.)

The ferry docks in **North Head.** If you get there before noon on Saturday, you can visit the island's farmers' market, which is about 0.5 mile (1 km) from the ferry dock. For details and information on the Grand Manan Island ferry, call (506) 662–3724. Ferries sail up to seven times a day from both the island and the mainland during high season.

When you plan to leave the island, you can now reserve a spot on the next morning's ferry, taking some of the uncertainty out of departure times. Apart from this small change, little else has been altered since I first visited Grand Manan (except that the island now has a few stop signs; and once a year, for a half hour during the Rotary Days Festival at the beginning of August, Grand Harbour has its own traffic jam).

At that time of year, with so many former residents returning to visit family and such a small number of inns, you will have a very hard time chancing upon accommodations, so reserve ahead. Also remember that August is prime whale-watching time; romance is in the water, and mating activity takes place.

North Head is also the best place to get a look at the remains of the phenomenon that caused the island to come into being in the first place. Somewhere around 380,000 years ago, the ground folded up and formed the island out of massive igneous rock. At North Head you can still see where the folding happened if you take the hike that begins at North Head's pier. It is marked by an incredibly understated sign announcing hole in the wall and indicating a pathway. This path leads to a rocky stretch of coast where the highlight is a rock formation with a massive hole in it. The hike is roughly 2 miles (3 km) long and takes about an hour round-trip.

Turning left off the ferry dock, proceed down Route 776. You will almost immediately spot a number of pretty little houses that have been converted to bed-and-breakfast establishments. The **Compass Rose** offers a good view of the wharf and tiny North Head fleet.

The Compass Rose has undergone a number of renovations since Nora and Ed Parker took over the two adjacent Heritage houses in the mid-'90s. They built a sunroom dining room that stretches from one house to the other and faces the harbor, giving a lovely view. They switched the rooms around so that each has a private bath, more space, and more luxurious touches. Their top room has a fireplace and king-size bed.

Guests are served a traditional English breakfast. During lunch and suppertime, the Compass Rose features fresh local seafood specialties like lobster Newburg, pan-fried lobster, and the chef's own pasta stuffed with lobster. The menu also features scallops either panfried with ginger or in coquilles St.-Jacques. Chef Holly Morse, who gets rave reviews, is formerly of Montreal but is married to a Grand Manan fisherman. The quaint restaurant has only eight tables, so make reservations to avoid disappointment.

Rates are standard to moderate. For reservations call or fax at (506) 662–8570 or visit www.compassroseinn.com. It is open from the end of May to the beginning of October.

Note the local paintings on the walls of this establishment; many are framed in sea-weathered old planks and bits of driftwood. This type of framing is very characteristic of Grand Manan's artists. One such frame trims a lobster still life at Compass Rose, which was painted for the previous owner as partial payment for a room.

Since Grand Manan is such a picturesque island, complete with quaint fishing communities, stunning sea vistas, lighthouses, and a bird sanctuary, it is a magnet for artists.

Isolated as it is, there are a number of pleasant places to stay on the island, but you put yourself at risk if you do not reserve a spot before your arrival. The poshest digs on Grand Manan are in North Head at the *Manan Island Inn Ocean Side,* which has a three-and-a-half-star Canada Select rating. Rates are moderate. Call ahead to reserve a room at (506) 662–8624.

The *Shorecrest Lodge,* in the same community as Compass Rose, trails the aforementioned spa by only a star, has similar rates, and includes breakfast in the bill. This waterfront property is wheelchair-accessible and also has accommodations for the visually impaired. For information, contact Mr. and Mrs. Andrew Normandeau at Shorecrest Lodge, North Head, Grand Manan, NB E0G 2M0. Call (506) 662–3216, or e-mail at shorecrestlodge@yahoo.com.

This area of North America's east coast is located on the migratory path of many species of birds, and the island's isolation has ensured their continued presence here. One of the neighboring islands is *Machias Seal Island,* a bird sanctuary. The island is home to puffins (which look like small penguins in casual attire), razorbill auks, arctic terns, and other birds.

From mid-June through the first week of August, you can take a guided tour to the island and watch the puffins being their adorable selves from an arm's length away, since you will be concealed inside blinds. You can arrange this trip through your place of lodging, but be sure to do so well in advance, because only a limited number of people are allowed on the island per day.

There are five lighthouses on Grand Manan, pictures of which show up on scenic calendars with impressive regularity. It's easy to see why: Every corner of Grand Manan seems like a promontory at the end of the known universe, and land's end seems to be around every corner. Check out *Swallowtail Lighthouse* in particular if you want to get a feel for the rugged isolation of the island.

If this is still not far enough away from the crowds, you can take a short (and free) ferry ride to *White Head Island* (population 178). Ferries departing Ingalls Head run every hour from 7:00 A.M. to 4:30 P.M., but the schedule for the ten-car ferry is not cast in stone. The 7:00 A.M. crossing is "on demand," and it's a good idea to let them know the day before if you want to get started that early. In the late afternoon there is about a three-hour gap after the 4:30 P.M. crossing. If demand exists, one more ferry sails around 7:00 P.M. The crossing takes twenty minutes. The boats also wait until the mainland ferry docks in case there will be more passengers.

White Head is a great place for hiking and biking and has a lighthouse, and two completely beautiful and empty beaches for that Robinson Crusoe experience.

Grand Manan has two provincial parks, both along Route 776. The park in Castalia includes a picnic and rest area. Farther along Route 776, take the second left turn after the community of Grand Harbor to visit *Anchorage Provincial Park.* Here you can hike, recreate, or take advantage of the camping facilities, including fully serviced sites. The park includes a migratory bird sanctuary. For information on both parks, call (506) 662–7022.

Anchorage Provincial Park is just a stone's throw from *Seal Cove,* which is reached by taking the left turn off Route 776 after the park. Seal Cove, at the southern tip of the island, is a photographer's dream. Once in the village turn left and follow the signs to the breakwater to get some beautiful shots. (Plan to arrive with lots of film as there isn't much chance of stocking up in Seal Cove.) Viewed from the water's edge, Seal Cove is dotted with well-tended,

trivia

In 1885, in response to the danger of disease transmission by new immigrants, Saint John became the location of the first quarantine station. At the time, immigrants who were ill could potentially spread dangerous diseases, such as smallpox, typhus, cholera, and influenza.

Getting a Good Look at Puffins

Grand Manan Island offers the ideal opportunity to get a rare look at the common *Atlantic puffin*. Many of these adorable creatures are found on Machias Seal Island, which is about 10 miles (16 km) from Grand Manan.

Puffins are sometimes referred to as "bottlenoses" or "sea parrots" because of their colorful beaks. They are compactly built at about 12 inches (30 cm) tall, with three webbed front toes. The birds are happy campers in the Bay of Fundy, where they feed by diving for marine organisms. Getting a good look at a puffin is a challenge since they live along isolated seacoasts and on islands in the northern oceans, where they nest in colonies of as many as 50,000. This is quite a hopeful sign, because the common Atlantic puffin was once threatened with extinction in this region and in the United States. Puffins from colonies in Canada were used to reestablish breeding colonies in Maine. The common Atlantic puffin is one of three species in the world.

Machias Seal Island has roughly 1,000 nesting pairs of puffins (along with thousands of pairs of arctic terns, and hundreds of common terns, and razorbill auks). The puffins usually nest in burrows or caves, and each female lays a single white egg.

Sea Watch Tours operates the only Canadian tour vessels that are permitted to land on Machias Seal Island. When I visited the island with Sea Watch, I was glad that my boots had a good tread because we had to walk across some slippery, seaweed-covered rocks to get onto the narrow island. Once ashore, our group was greeted by a warden of the Canadian Wildlife Service, who led us to a series of enclosed blinds, permitting us to hide from the birds. The puffins came within 3 feet (0.9 meters) of us. Bring an extra roll or two of film. The pictures you'll get will be incredible.

You can arrange a tour with Sea Watch by calling (506) 662–8552, or by e-mail at: seawatch@nbnet.nb.ca.

Bear in mind that access to the island is very limited. Only twenty-five people a day are permitted to land, six days a week. There are several Machias Seal Island tour possibilities. Note that viewing the puffins on the island itself costs $75, whereas going around the island in a 16-foot skiff is $55 for ages twelve and older, $35 for younger children. (Plan ahead, if possible. While most of the shore spaces are booked by late April, there are still a few spaces left for shore access in late July and August.) Tours to Machias Seal Island run from mid-June until mid-August. Whale-watching and birding tours, ($50 per adult and $30 for children under twelve), operate from mid-July until the end of September.

neatly shingled and painted herring-smoking facilities. They look like a new cottage development. To the left of the smokehouses is a pleasant beach for strolling, beachcombing, or swimming.

At Seal Cove you can join a group of whale watchers with **Sea Watch Tours,** a company operating from the southernmost pier in the village. To get there, stop next to the two churches of the community and turn onto the road directly opposite. Follow this lane to take you up to the last pier on the cove. To book ahead with Sea Watch, call (506) 662–8552.

The Lower Saint John River

Back on the mainland, take Provincial Highway 776 until you reach the turnoff for the TransCanada Highway (TCH) "Route 1," headed east to Saint John. If you wish, you can take a small detour onto Highway 790 at Lepreau. Continue until you reach the Little Lepreau Road. Take a slight detour to see the covered bridge that spans the Little Lepreau River, overlooking a mill pond. This road is closed to traffic but is wonderfully scenic. After the little detour, backtrack to the TCH and continue east to Saint John.

Saint John is a good place for antiques hunting, because this is where the Loyalists did their shipbuilding. If you are eager to look at some pieces, emulate the locals and scan the newspaper for auction notices.

In the days of wooden ships, mahogany was prized because its density made it ideal as a ballast in the hull of the ships. Shipbuilders would discard their mahogany "scraps," which craftsmen quickly gathered up to use in the making of furniture. Now that mahogany is so valuable, their work is quite a find.

You might want to stay at a Heritage inn in Saint John to enjoy many old-fashioned antique niceties, like four-poster beds and huge mahogany chests of drawers, all in a charming inn that happens to be run by one of the province's finest chefs. The *Dufferin Inn and San Martello Dining Room* are operated by Axel and Margaret Begner, who ran a hotel and restaurant in Germany for a decade. Axel, a European-trained master chef and pastry chef, has been cooking for more than thirty years. The restaurant is the sort recommended by other chefs; with dishes like Bay of Fundy Cake, done with crab, scallops, salmon, and lobster, and Grand Marnier crème brûlée, you can be certain that you won't be bored with the selection.

trivia

In 1896, while visiting Canada's first mental asylum, in Saint John, New Brunswick, Harry Houdini (the famous escape artist) obtained his first straight-jacket and formulated his idea for freeing himself from it.

The Begners came to Canada years ago and renovated and restored the home of J. B. M. Baxter, a former premier and chief justice of the province. Be sure to visit the inn's library, where you will find a wealth of information on Saint John. Environmentally friendly and fully renovated, the inn also offers the occasional organic cooking class for groups or individuals. I recommend calling ahead for information or booking.

To get to the inn, travel to **Saint John** west on Route 109. Turn left onto Market Place just after crossing the bridge. Take a right turn onto Saint John Street, and continue along this street for 5 blocks, by which time the road will be called Dufferin Row. The inn is at 357 Dufferin Row. Room rates are moderate. Dinner runs about $40 per person for the set menu, plus drinks and taxes. For a reservation, call (506) 635–5968, or e-mail duffinn@nb.aibn.com.

The Dufferin Inn is just down the street from the **Carleton Martello Tower,** a stone battery built during the War of 1812.

Martello towers originated in the Mediterranean, where they were used as watchtowers. One such tower in Corsica allowed so stiff a resistance to its British attackers in 1793 and 1794 that the idea of using these lookouts for coastal defense caught on in a big way. During the Napoleonic Wars, the British built more than a hundred Martello towers.

The flat roof of the Carleton tower was meant to hold two twenty-four-pounder guns and two twenty-four-pounder carronades. It never was armed for the War of 1812—by the time the tower was finished, the war was over. Some guns were installed in 1866, when a group of Irish-American Fenians threatened to capture British North America in a quest for Irish independence. Inside this particular tower you will see a barracks restored to the 1866 period and the powder magazine to its 1840s appearance. From June to mid-October, the tower is open daily from 9:00 A.M. to 5:00 P.M. Admission is $3.50 for adults, $3.00 for seniors, and $1.75 for children. Families are admitted for $8.75. For more information call (506) 636–4011 in season.

While in Saint John you may want to visit the **City Market.** The building was constructed by famous shipbuilders, who also built one of the world's fastest sailing ships, the Marco Polo. The market has had a charter since 1785 (along with Saint John itself) and is the oldest farmers' market in Canada.

The City Market is a large, open space, made possible by the post-and-beam ceiling. Take a picture of this ceiling; when you get it developed, hold it upside down. Then you will see how the builders solved the problem of supporting a roof this size without a lot of braces: It's actually the upside-down hull of an old-time sailing ship!

The entrance to the market on Germain Street has been spiffed up to include a new glassed-in foyer and a spot for eating. The City Market is located at the corner of Charlotte and Germain Streets. It is open year-round, Monday to Thursday from 7:30 A.M. to 6:00 P.M., Friday until 7:00 P.M., and Saturday until 5:00 P.M. Closed Sunday. Admission is free.

If you proceed just past this market, you will soon come upon a park and then the old Loyalist graveyard, with markers dating back to the 1780s. The buildings along these streets and in the vicinity of Market Square are largely older buildings with intricate brickwork. You can hail a horse-drawn carriage to check out the downtown core if you want a different perspective. If you want to stay in downtown Saint John, you might want to check out the classy *Parkerhouse Inn* at 71 Sydney Street. It's an elegant three-story Victorian town house with nine guest rooms and all the posh trimmings that will leave you raving about the place. Prices are moderate; reservations are required. To make a reservation, call (888) 457–2520 or (506) 652–5054; fax (506) 636–8076.

Just twenty minutes' drive outside of town, at the *Irving Nature Park,* you'll see harbor seals frolic at a location where more than 240 different species of birds have been spotted. To get there, take exit 119 A-B off Route 1 onto Bleury Street, turn right onto Sand Cove Road, and drive 1.2 miles (2 km) to the park. For details, call (506) 653–7367. Bring binoculars, sturdy hiking boots, and plenty of insect repellent. Admission is free, but remember that the park closes at dusk. Exercise caution on some trails along the ocean side; the occasional rough wave can give you quite a soaking.

Now turn inland along the river valley to Welsford, on Route 7. Adjacent to Route 7, on Cochran Road, about 1 mile (1.6 km) south of the community, you can admire a covered bridge over the Nerepis River. Then return to Route 101 north.

Inland on Route 101 you can see three more covered bridges without too much trouble. Exit Route 101 in Hoyt and turn onto Hoyt Station Road. There you will see *Back Creek Bridge Number Two* (Hoyt's Station).

Farther along Route 101, turn off onto Mill Settlement Road until you reach North Mill Settlement Road—here you will find spanning the South Oromocto River another bridge called the *South Oromocto Number Two Bridge* (Mill Settlement).

Continuing on Mill Settlement Road, you will come across Boyne Road. At this point, turn right and continue until you reach the *South Oromocto Number Three Bridge,* also called the Bell Bridge. From Boyne Road, return to Route 101 and proceed toward the town of Fredericton.

Once you've puttered around historic *Fredericton,* walked under the city's elms, and had a look at the Victorian and Queen Anne homes, you will not find it at all surprising that many places here display the British flag. The United Empire Loyalists who came to New Brunswick left the same sort of indelible British stamp found in former outposts of the empire like Belize, Malaysia's west coast, and India.

Fredericton is a wonderful town for strolling around, particularly because driving in the downtown is quite tricky. Many of the streets are one-way—with no prior indication until you come to an intersection and find youself facing the wrong way down a one-way street.

When you arrive in Fredericton, drop in first at the city hall tourist office, which is right downtown on Queen Street (next to the water). Here you can get a three-day tourist parking pass, available to any out-of-province vehicle. This entitles you to park in the lot behind City Hall or at any meter without paying a cent— or getting a ticket.

Turn left when you leave city hall. You will soon come to the old garrison, now the *York-Sunbury Historical Society Museum.* Between this onetime officers' quarters and the guardhouse is a parade ground in typical colonial British style, around which "soldiers" in period costumes march in traditional fashion.

Adults pay $3.00 and student pay $1.00 for admission to the garrison museum, which houses a collection of artifacts associated with the early Loyalist pioneer days, from the early regimental ornamentation of Colonial officers to memorabilia from the first World War. You can witness the changing of the guard at 11:00 A.M. and 7:00 P.M. (all to the sound of bagpipes, so you will know it's starting from a long way off) from Tuesday to Saturday in July and August. The Officers' Square is also used for free evening concerts on Tuesday and Thursday during the summer months.

The garrison museum's second floor is home to a giant stuffed frog. He was already big when he hopped into the life of his owner, Fred Coleman, in 1885, but at his death eight years later—after a good deal of overindulging on buttermilk, rum pudding, and June bugs dipped in honey sauce—he weighed in at forty-two pounds (18 kilograms).

Just beyond the parade ground is a lighthouse that's now a gift shop down on St. Anne Point. It has a large wooden deck where people can relax and enjoy the river views. In front of this is a charming riverfront walkway, *Waterloo Row.* On warm summer nights people stroll along the river while the odd houseboat and its occupants look on from offshore. A number of speedboats tie up here, giving access to the downtown for people up- and downriver.

trivia

"Only in Canada, you say?" is the typical television ad for Red Rose Tea. It is in fact a very typical Canadian tea, and the flagship product of T. H. Estabrooks Company of Saint John. By 1900, Red Rose Tea—a blending of teas from at least three different plantations—had won adherents from all over Canada and abroad, and it sold in excess of two million pounds annually.

Proceeding in the same direction, away from city hall, you will eventually come to a must-see attraction: the **Beaverbrook Art Gallery,** which has a huge painting by Salvador Dali and several of his smaller works. The gallery has quite an extensive collection of art, including a number of paintings by Cornelius Krieghoff, J.M. Turner, John Constable, and Thomas Gainsborough. There are some works by the Group of Seven, Canada's most famous group of artists.

trivia

The father of nature photography was George T. Taylor of Fredericton, who began work in 1856, thirteen years after Canada's first photo studio was established. Many of his photographs show remote corners of New Brunswick.

You will also find a number of Graham Sutherland studies of Winston Churchill. Commissioned by the British House of Lords and House of Commons, Sutherland's definitive portrait was presented to Churchill as an eightieth birthday gift. Both Sir Winston Churchill and Lady Churchill hated the portrait. After its presentation, it was never allowed to be seen again. Within a year Lady Churchill reportedly destroyed it. The gallery is at 703 Queen Street. Call (506) 458–8545 or (506) 458–0970. The gallery is open daily June 1 to September 30 from 9:00 A.M. to 6:00 P.M. Monday to Friday, 10:00 A.M. to 5:00 P.M. Saturday, and noon to 5:00 P.M. on Sunday. Admission is $5.00 for adults, $4.00 for seniors, and $2.00 for students.

The art gallery is named for William Maxwell Aitken, who became Lord Beaverbrook. He was born in Ontario but grew up in Newcastle (now Miramichi). He served in Britain as the minister of aircraft production during World War II, but he is chiefly known as a "press baron" and famous for the empire he created from The Daily Express newspaper. The name Beaverbrook is forever connected to the Fleet Street newspapers in England.

One other building you must get a look at before leaving Queen Street is the **Legislative Assembly Building,** the seat of the provincial government, which is across the street from the gallery. This particular Colonial sandstone building dates from 1882, when it was constructed to replace an earlier edifice destroyed by fire. The whole structure, including its fittings and furnishings, cost $120,000 in the currency of the 1880s. (At that time, a typical annual salary was $300.) It is constructed in the Second Empire style, with a mansard roof and corner towers.

There is no mistaking just which empire mattered when this was built. Perched like some daring stuntman in the exact center of the facade is a statue of Britannia with her trident. Other Colonial reminders are inside: Portraits of King George III and Queen Charlotte flank the throne in the chamber. (The province was named after George III—when New Brunswick was separated from Nova Scotia in 1784, it was named for his family's ancestral seat, Brunswick in Germany.) Admission is free.

In this area of New Brunswick, the British Loyalists almost completely supplanted the Acadian settlers, and there is no stronger evidence of this than the city's old architecture.

If you're looking for a nice place to eat in downtown Frederiction, there are two possibilities along Queen Street, a stroll much favored by visitors. Try *The Regency Rose Cafe* at 608 to 610 Queen Street for excellent seafood crepes, as well as salads and soups. Or, visit the *M&T Deli* at 602 Queen Street for deli sandwiches and bagels. This friendly spot will even supply the picnic basket and blanket if you want to take your lunch to the park across the street.

Two blocks farther away from the water and a block east is *Christ Church Cathedral*, on Church Street. To get there on foot, follow Queen Street as it rounds the point for another block or so past the legislature building.

The outside masonry was recently touched up, so the cathedral sparkles like new. This is an impressive Gothic church, a copy of St. Mary's at Snettisham, England. The cornerstone was laid in 1845, with construction completed in eight years. This was the first entirely new cathedral foundation on British soil since the time of the Norman Conquest in 1066.

In July and August, you may join a free guided tour of the cathedral on Monday to Friday from 9:00 A.M. to 6:00 P.M., Saturday from 10:00 A.M. to 5:00 P.M. Sunday visits are limited to the afternoon, from 1:00 to 5:00 P.M. For details call (506) 450–8500.

If you happen to be in Fredericton in the second week of September to admire the glorious fall foliage of the "city of elms," you can enjoy the *Harvest Jazz and Blues Festival.* For specifics on this annual event, call (888) 622–5837 or (506) 454–2583. This is the largest jazz and blues festival east of Montreal. You can check the entertainment lineup by visiting www.harvestjazz andblues.com.

A pleasant stand of virgin forest can be found at *Odell Park,* just outside the downtown core. Take Smythe Road headed away from the water and turn left just after Dundonald Street. You will then be at one end of the park, wedged between it and the Fredericton Exhibition Grounds. The park is quite extensive (388 acres, or 175 hectares), so plan to spend at least a full morning or afternoon roaming around here. The park also contains a picnic area and a children's zoo.

There are beaches in the vicinity, including one at Killarney Lake, 5 miles (8 km) from Fredericton on the Killarney Road. Fairly close by, a covered bridge spans the Keswick River, at Stone Ridge. It is roughly 4.5 miles (7.2 km) off Route 104 on the Morehouse Road, going north from Fredericton.

If you are staying in Fredericton overnight, consider checking in at the *Carriage House Inn,* which is located on University Avenue, 2 blocks from the Beaverbrook Gallery and the legislature building. The former home of a mayor and lumber baron, the cozy inn is a lovely mahogany-accented Victorian. Rates are moderate. Breakfast is included, and laundry facilities or services are available on site. Pets are welcome, and the inn has nonsmoking rooms. (You can still light up on the lovely porch.) For reservations call (800) 267–6068 or (506) 452–9924.

A twenty-minute drive outside Fredericton is the large hydroelectric *Mactaquac Dam,* the building of which flooded a sizable chunk of woodland almost four decades ago. From the town, get on the TCH Route 2 headed west, and turn off onto Provincial Highway 105 at the Mactaquac turnoff.

There is a beautiful provincial park here with a good golf course and a warm beach along the edge of the lake created by the dam. The cost per vehicle entering the park is only $3.50 for the day. As you dip your toes into the lake, consider this: The entire area was once a forest, submerged under the water now for thirty-seven years. The buildings that used to be where the lake is now were moved to an area twenty minutes away: They became *Kings Landing Historical Settlement.*

To get there from Mactaquac, return to Highway 105 and drive for a minute or two until you reach the turnoff for TCH Route 2. Head west in the direction of MacAdam. Fifteen minutes later a series of signs will direct you to Kings Landing.

The settlement is authentic right down to the cow pies in the field. More than one hundred costumed residents and seventy authentically restored buildings re-create a United Empire Loyalist settlement dating back to the first century following the American War of Independence.

These living-history lessons are always lots of fun, but Kings Landing is also quite historically accurate. The assistant curator told me that when the houses were moved to their new locations, they were even oriented in exactly the same way as they were on their previous site. If a house was built on a sloping hill with a kitchen in the basement, with one side of the lower floor exposed, that was exactly how it is set up on its new location.

Visitors leave their cars at the reception-center building and then walk along a dirt road to the old-time settlement, so no sign of the modern world is evident. A horse-drawn cart helps with the commute to the village; you'll see youngsters in costume hitching a ride on this cart, or weeding the gardens and doing other chores.

These young people are participants in a program that allows them to stay at the settlement for five days, living life exactly as it was lived in the early nineteenth century. The program, called Visiting Cousins, accepts kids from nine to fourteen years old and costs $330 a session. Family Kin is for children twelve to fifteen who have visited previously. Seniors can also get into the act in the $575 Elderhostel program. Day programs allow short-term visitors to spend their time learning crafts and doing nineteenth-century chores. If you want to take historic authenticity to its fullest extent, you can have a genuine Victorian wedding, using a rented reproduction wedding dress (or have your own made to order by expert staff). The cost of these weddings runs less than $2,000, but you need to do some advance planning, including finding clergy or a justice of the peace who will do the deed. For details on any of these living-history holidays, contact the staff well in advance.

trivia

New Brunswick is home to 10 percent of the world's covered bridges.

At the blacksmith shop you can watch a skilled craftsman turning out tools to be used in the settlement's other enterprises—hooks for holding logs at the sawmill, for example.

The cooper I watched making wooden buckets has it down to a science, slowly carving out the perfect curve in each slat so that a group of them will result in a round, airtight bucket. Eight hours of work will give you a bucket worth forty cents, he notes—"A good day's pay."

The settlement includes a sawmill with the largest functioning waterwheel in Canada. I watched a log being maneuvered into position for cutting, a process that took a good half hour.

If you are interested in sampling some of the early settlers' homestyle cooking, drop by the ***King's Head Inn*** for lunch. (There are also benches outside.) After lunch, hitch a ride on the horse-drawn cart outside the door of the inn back to the reception center.

For more details on the various programs, or to make a reservation at the King's Head Inn, call (506) 363–4999 or fax (506) 363–4989; write to Kings Landing Historical Settlement, Prince William, NB E0H 1S0; or visit www.kings landing.nb.ca. Admission is $14 per adult or $34 for a family.

Just after this settlement is ***Lake George Park,*** about 7 miles (11 km) off Route 2 west on Route 259, or 8 miles (13 km) north of Harvey on Route 636. There is a lovely beach here.

Whether you find yourself in Prince William, Kings Landing, or Lake George, when you want to resume your travels, return to the TCH via Route 2 and drive northwest to Pokiok. It is about 13 miles (21 km) north of Prince William. From here you can cross the Saint John River (it's quite narrow at this point), turn right at the fork in the road at the end of the crossing, and proceed to Nackawic and then Millville, about 9.5 miles (15 km) farther on.

Turn left onto Route 104, then left onto Route 585. To see the ***Nackawic Siding Covered Bridge*** that straddles the Nackawic River here, take the exit to Nortondale, just north of the main road. Then return to Route 585 and in about a half hour you will come to ***Woodstock,*** which is at most a twenty-minute drive from the Canada–U.S. border. Woodstock is a pretty little town for stretching your legs (and for shopping when the currency exchange rate favors it). Communities that straddle the border in this area are at the mercy of changing fiscal policies and monetary fluctuations, so businesspeople on both sides of the border find themselves suffering periodic downturns due to the drop in their neighbor's dollar.

To view yet another covered bridge, turn back onto Route 2 and head south toward Meductic. Just before Meductic you will see a sign for Benton. Turn right here and continue until you reach the Benton Village Road. Here, the covered ***Benton Bridge*** crosses the Eel River, which also serves as the county line for a while along its meandering path.

Now return to Route 2 and head north past Woodstock to ***Hartland.*** As if you haven't already seen enough of covered bridges, now you come to the granddaddy of them all, the ***world's longest covered bridge,*** at 1,282 feet (391 m) in length. Imagine the possibilities for clandestine romantic interludes presented by a kissing bridge that took a horse a good quarter hour to traverse. The bridge remains a popular site to this day, long after automotive breakdowns and drive-in movies replaced it as a lovers' hot spot. To the east of Hartland you will come to the Becaguimec River system and a collection of yet more picturesque covered bridges.

Places to Stay in New Brunswick's Loyalist South

FREDERICTON

Carriage House Inn
University Avenue
(800) 267–6068
(506) 452–9924
fax (506) 458–0799
Victorian charmer.
Moderate.

GRAND MANAN

Compass Rose
North Head
(506) 662–8570
fax (506) 662–8570
Standard to moderate.

Manan Island Inn
Ocean Side North Head
(506) 662–8624
Walking distance to
whale-watching.
Moderate.

Shorecrest Lodge
North Head
(506) 662–3216
Birdwatcher's paradise.
Moderate.

SAINT JOHN

Dufferin Inn
357 Dufferin Row
(506) 635–5968
fax (506) 674–2396
For gourmets and
antiques lovers.
Moderate.

The Parkerhouse Inn
71 Sydney Street
(888) 457–2520
(506) 652–5054
fax (506) 636–8076
Moderate.

**ST. ANDREWS
BY-THE-SEA**

The Algonquin
184 Adolphus Street
(506) 529–8823
(800) 441–1414
fax (506) 529–4194
Deluxe.

Rossmount Inn
Highway 127
(506) 529–3351
fax (506) 529–1920
Moderate.

Places to Eat in New Brunswick's Loyalist South

FREDERICTON

M&T Deli
602 Queen Street
(506) 458–9068

The Regency Rose Cafe
608/10 Queen Street
(506) 455–2233

GRAND MANAN

Compass Rose
North Head
(506) 662–8570
fax (506) 662–8570

PRINCE WILLIAM

King's Head Inn
TCH Route 2, Exit 253
Kings Landing Historical
Settlement
(506) 363–4999

SAINT JOHN

Dufferin Inn
357 Dufferin Row
(506) 635–5968
fax (506) 674–2396
Authentic gourmet
experience.

**Grannan's Seafood
Restaurant and Oyster Bar**
1 Market Square
(506) 648–2323

Il Fornello Restaurant
33 Canterbury Street
(506) 658–6027

**ST. ANDREWS
BY-THE-SEA**

Rossmount Inn
Highway 127
(506) 529–3351
fax (506) 529–1920
Victorian touches in
charming dining room.

ST. GEORGE

**Granite Town Hotel and
Country Inn**
79 Main Street
(506) 755–6415
Great fresh salmon.

Acadian New Brunswick

The Upper Saint John River

As you drive inland along the Saint John River Valley, you will gradually enter the land that has been home to the Acadians for more than 300 years, despite massive population upheavals. One historian noted that because of the great distance from the French capital at Port Royal, the Acadian French, who lived in these parts long before the British takeover in 1755, had no real force of law, and yet they managed to maintain societal order purely through their sense of community.

Uprooted in 1755 from their homes, they were determined to return to this independent way of life, so much so that many Acadians deposited along the Eastern Seaboard spent years finding their way back to Acadia, only to discover that their lands had been taken over by the English. They then settled informally along the coast and in the northern interior of New Brunswick.

Without external structure or governmental endorsement, they managed to keep their language, traditions, and culture intact. They remained loyal to their identity even though the boundaries of Acadia could never be shown on a map.

ACADIAN NEW BRUNSWICK

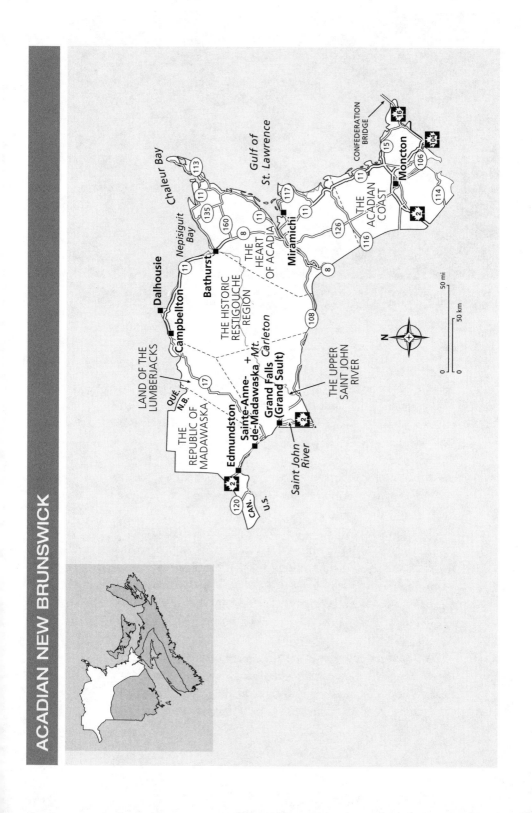

The first major stop along Route 2 in Acadian New Brunswick is *Grand Falls,* noted for a set of gorges and a series of falls that, step by step, descend a total of about 1 mile (1.6 km). If the weather has been dry, Grand Falls is not quite as spectacular as in rainy seasons. But periodically the people who run the electrical generating station situated at the falls let a backlog of water go, so be sure to check when the gates are due to be released if you want to see the falls in their full glory. A pontoon boat offers an interesting alternative for viewing the falls close up. Trips depart from the Falls and Gorge campground, which also offers a combination

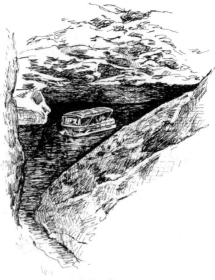

Grand Falls Gorge

camping/boat rate. You get one night at a campsite and the boat tour for a fee of $45 per couple or $50 per family. To book ahead, (which is highly recommended), call (877) 475–7769. The campgrounds are open from mid-June to mid-September.

The massive rock face through which the water flows is, in itself, quite something to see. At night it is illuminated with colored lights, making for a surreal spectacle.

An interpretive center at the power station has a scale model where tour guides explain exactly how the generator functions. Called the *Malabeam Reception Centre,* it is named for a young Malecite Indian maiden. According

TRUDY'S FAVORITES

Acadian Historical Village,
Rivière du Nord

Cap-Pelé Beach,
Shediac

Forestry Museum,
Kedgwick

Hopewell Cape

Miscou Lighthouse,
Miscou Island

New Brunswick Botanical Garden,
Saint-Jacques

Sackville Waterfowl Park,
Sackville

The waterfall,
Grand Falls

to Indian legend, the young girl was captured by Mohawks. Forced to head an expedition of Mohawks who intended to attack her village, the girl instead led all of them to their doom over the gorges of Grand Falls. The center, off Front Street, which doubles as a tourist office and reception, houses an interpretive display of the dam. Teamed with this, and a 1.2-mile (2-km) pathway away, is the Centennial Park on Chapel Street. Along with the usual amenities of a municipal park (free admission), you will have the opportunity to enter **La Rochelle Visitor Centre,** which leads to a series of 253 steps down the side of the falls. Admission is $3.00 for adults, $1.00 for children, or $7.00 for a family. The most scenic part of the trail lies at the bottom of a deep, 0.9-mile (1.5-km) gorge carved out by the falls. Bug repellent is a good idea, and footing can be slippery in damp weather.

trivia

In 1982 Grand Falls was officially declared bilingual and given a name in both English and French. Its French name is Grand Sault.

The *Baie de Chaleur*—Chaleur Bay— means "Bay of Warmth" in English.

The three-pointed hats worn by the Loyalists were called "tricornes."

This is a region of fertile farmland. The biggest crop here is the potato, which New Brunswick produces in greater abundance than any other province in Canada. Grand Falls holds an annual potato festival at the beginning of July and crowns a "Miss Potato" to preside over the festivities.

If you think that a small center like Grand Falls doesn't have nightlife, then think again. Indeed, the town is noted for it in the region. The main drag in town is particularly wide, since it was used at one time for military parades. Once those spectacles ended, the wide street was turned into a divided boulevard with a park running down the middle, complete with gazebo and a few old pieces of military hardware. On hot summer nights all Grand Falls seems to show up, walking or driving down this street. In winter, however, it's cold in Grand Falls, and there are no real nightlife hot spots to warm lingering travelers.

If you are staying in the neighborhood for any length of time and are feeling a bit restless, drive from Route 2 to Route 108 and then on to **New Denmark.** (Note, however, that you must follow the signs for Plaster Rock, since New Denmark does not figure prominently on the maps.) This is a trek of 10 miles (16 km) on secondary roads, but the scenery, provided by the lush potato farmlands and the distant hills, is well worth the time and effort.

This is the site of Canada's first Danish community. The area was settled by Danes in 1872. They had been assured that it was good farmland, but they discovered after they arrived that it was woodland that had to be cleared by manual labor. The small *New Denmark Memorial Museum* recounts their story and displays a collection of century-old dolls and porcelain from Copenhagen. Next door you will find *Immigrant House,* which depicts the life of the early settlers. For information call (506) 553–6724. Admission is free, and donations are welcome. The museum is open Monday to Saturday from 9:00 A.M. until 5:00 P.M. and from 2:00 until 5:00 P.M. Sunday.

Since the settlers were farmers who stayed in the area for many years without moving around, many residents of this area over age fifty still speak Danish.

The Republic of Madawaska

About 34 miles (57 km) northwest of Grand Falls on Route 2 is *Edmundston,* the commercial hub for this neck of the woods. Across the Upper Saint John River is Madawaska, Maine. The residents of these communities cross the border the way other people cross the street. The flow of workers in lumbering and related industries has caused the area to develop a distinctive character of its own, regardless of which side of the border its occupants live on. This is the *Republique de Madawaska,* named for the river that flows from across the Quebec border and into the Upper Saint John River.

Here the Upper Saint John serves as a border between Canada and the United States. Not many people today realize that during the last century, there was considerable wrangling about where the border actually fell. When it came to this particular area, the line was moved around so much that in 1827, a man by the name of John Baker erected a flag in protest and declared the land the American Republic of Madawaska.

The name has stuck, and the memory of John Baker lives on in the form of Baker Brook and Lac Baker, wedged in the tiny strip of land between Maine and Quebec. As for John Baker, he was sent to jail for treason. Today you can visit a park at *Lac Baker,* which has picnic facilities, a nice beach, and lots of water sports.

This area has become a major gateway to New Brunswick from Quebec, Maine, and upstate New York. It is lush agricultural land that can get quite hot in summer. Combine these—a flow of visitors from all over the region and excellent growing conditions—and you have the ideal location for a botanical garden.

In *Saint-Jacques,* just off TCH Route 2 and only 6 miles (10 km) south of the Quebec border (and ten minutes' drive north of Edmundston) is the *New Brunswick Botanical Garden,* opened in 1993. Over a meticulously groomed seventeen-acre (seven-hectare) site is a garden planned by the expert consultants to the Montreal Botanical Garden, including noted landscape architect Michel Marceau.

The site now consists of eight separate gardens and two arboretums, or tree gardens. Hidden under the shrubbery are small outdoor speakers, which broadcast classical music deemed appropriate for each specific garden. For example, Mozart sonatas for piano complement the rose garden; perennials invite up-tempo works by Handel, Bach, and Vivaldi; and the lake and gazebo areas have more tranquil compositions by the same musical greats.

There are more than 30,000 annuals and 850 rosebushes of more than fifty varieties. A total of 80,000 plants are divided into the Rose Garden, the Garden of Annuals, the Garden of Perennials, the Garden of Economic Plants, the Alpine Garden, the Shade Garden, the Garden of Rhododendrons, and the Flowery Brook. Trees are arranged into the Arboretum of Coniferous Trees and Deciduous Shrubs and the Arboretum of Deciduous Trees and Coniferous Shrubs. Nature has been coaxed into submission here: Boulders were rearranged and water pumped in to create a miniature waterfall in the style of Grand Falls, complete with gorges. There are also several ponds.

Avid gardeners take note: Although the greenhouses are closed to the public, they'll be opened to gardeners who make the request to look around. A snack bar and gift shop are on site. Admission fees are $4.75 for adults, $4.25 for seniors and students, $2.25 for children ages seven to twelve. Children younger than six enter for free, and families are admitted for $11.75. For information call (506) 737–5383.

The parking lot for the botanical garden is directly behind the ***Antique Automobile Museum.*** Along with other unusual cars, here you can get a look at the Bricklin, a failed automobile design that enjoyed a brief heyday in the

1970s when New Brunswick's premier, Richard Hatfield, threw his support behind a would-be entrepreneur who briefly established his factory in the province. Open year-round. Admission is $3.75 for adults and $3.00 for children ages six to eighteen. For details call (506) 735–2637.

This area is part of a provincial park called ***Les Jardins de La Republique,*** which has the usual recreational and camping facilities and a supervised, heated pool. Nearby is the ***Petit-Témis Interprovincial Park,*** which you can access from the botanical garden. This linear park is a cycle path 80 miles (130 km) long that takes bicyclists into Quebec, along the shores of Lake Temiscouata and the bank of the Madawaska River. The trail reaches the town of Cabano and then continues on to Rivière du Loup.

If you've driven as far north as Saint-Jacques, you're going to have to return to the outskirts of Edmundston via Route 2 and continue on this same stretch of highway to Saint-Léonard. Then you can get onto Trunk 17 and head to Kedgwick. (From Saint-Jacques to the Saint-Léonard exit is 32 miles [56 km]—not that much of a detour to enjoy the beautiful botanical garden and cycle path.)

Land of the Lumberjacks

Almost as soon as you leave Saint-Léonard, you'll be surrounded by dense forest, the trees so much alike that they appear to have been cloned from the same original seedling. In fact, these trees were planted at the same time after the area had been intensively logged.

The first large community after Saint-Léonard is ***Saint-Quentin.*** When a railway was built between Saint-Léonard and Campbellton, this little community sprang up. It was originally named Five Fingers, after a brook of the same name. After a logging company operating there caused the community to swell in size, it became Anderson Siding, named for the head of the Canadian National Railroad. (The "Siding" part of the name was common to any area where sawmills operated.) In 1919 the town was renamed again, this time to commemorate the Canadian victory in Saint-Quentin, France, during World War I.

The town's location in the middle of densely wooded New Brunswick seems incongruous with its chief claim to fame: Saint-Quentin is home to the biggest annual western festival in eastern Canada. Apparently, you can't get more country-and-western than Saint-Quentin; even the streetlights are festooned with cowboy boots as the town puts its best foot forward for its shindig, culminating in a weekend-long rodeo, including cowboys from the United States, western Canada, Quebec, and Ontario. Held the second week in July, it

Mount Carleton Mini-Excursion

I'm recommending this trip only to outdoor types who also have a car with a powerful engine, fully functioning radiator, and reliable brakes. This is a lengthy, arduous drive through wilderness, with no handy service stations in sight. If your radiator overheats, it's a long, lonely walk back. Just after Saint-Quentin, fill your gas tank and check your oil, and then turn onto Highway 180 and drive 27 miles (43 km) to the entrance of **Mount Carleton Provincial Park.**

Mount Carleton Provincial Park is the province's largest and wildest park, encompassing 43,000 acres (17,427 hectares) and Mount Carleton, the highest mountain in the Maritimes. The park includes stands of spruce, fir, and yellow birch; wild blueberries; mountain cranberries; and lots of wildlife.

Stop at the entrance to get extensive maps and information about camping and hiking opportunities along the 36 miles (60 km) of trails. Most of the hikes take between two and four hours and form loops that culminate in mountain peaks. The Mount Bailey Trail is the easiest of the lot, the Mount Carleton Trail takes you to the top of the highest peak and includes access to a backcountry camp, and Sagamook Trail is the most scenic.

Note: While the trails provide gradual assent, there are points where you will be above the tree line and you'll need a warm windbreaker. Pack a whistle (in case you get lost), high-energy snacks, matches, a first-aid kit, a compass, and plenty of water. It is also a good idea to pack a couple of Sterno canisters to quickly heat up some food.

You will see spectacular scenery: sweeping vistas of mountain peaks, beaver ponds, and beautiful Nictau Lake. The trailhead of the most scenic trail, the Sagamook, is conveniently located near **Mount Carleton Lodge,** where you can refresh yourself and soothe your feet. If you decide to stay the night, the lodge has cabins and canoes to rent. Prices are standard. To reserve a cabin call (506) 235–6040.

There are a number of campsites as well, some more rustic than others. Phone (506) 235–0793 for details. There are no reservations for campsites; it's a first-come, first-served basis. Serviced sites are $11.00 weekdays to $14.00 on the weekend. Wilderness sites are only $9.00, but they have no showers or flush toilets. Caution: The park's wildlife includes bears, who will be attracted to the scent of any food left carelessly lying around. If you don't want a sleepless night, keep all foodstuffs locked in your cooler, inside your vehicle.

When you've finished visiting Mount Carleton, you can backtrack to Saint-Quentin via Highway 180 and then rejoin Trunk 17E, turning in the direction of Campbellton.

also features concerts, a powwow, and a parade. Free camping is available for serious cowboys, but reserve early. To get an idea of the east-turned-west, you can check out their Web site at www.festivalwesternnb.com. Take your French/English phrase book with you.

An interesting outdoor excursion possibility is located near Saint-Quentin. Leave Trunk 17 at the exit for Kedgwick River and take the smaller Collector Highway 265. It is here that you will find the rustic cabins of the **Centre Echo-Restigouche.** The facilities are of excellent quality, with some of the cabins large enough to accommodate up to eight people. For details on ecoadventure packages that the facility offers, or for reservations, call (506) 284–2022. Rates are moderate.

If you don't detour to the Kedgwick River, you'll continue along Trunk 17 to **Kedgwick.** After you pass through what appears to be almost all of this community, you will see a sign marked MUSÉE FORESTIER. This is the **Forestry Museum,** formerly known as the Heritage Lumbercamp. It provides a detailed look into the lives of lumberjacks before the introduction of modern tree-harvesting methods.

The complex includes a number of log cabins built under the direction of old-time loggers. The tour of the complex begins with a short film in which lumberjacks and storytellers recount their experiences in the woods from the nineteenth century to the 1960s. You will quickly see that the life of a lumberjack was extraordinarily hard. Your understanding of the logging industry will be enhanced by the old tools and other artifacts that have been donated to the complex by people who worked in the industry.

Before you leave the camp, be sure to look at the original 1937 snowmobile, the manufacture of which launched industrial giant Bombardier. It's a fascinating machine, fully enclosed and constructed of wood. And glance at the wall of the museum's main reception building. A forty-pound (nineteen kg) salmon is mounted here, a fitting example of why the area is a favorite among anglers and outdoorsmen. A small admission is charged. For information, call (506) 284–3138.

To resume your drive, continue east on Trunk 17.

1937 Snowmobile at Kedgwick Forestry Museum

Life of a Lumberjack

The life of a lumberjack, or logger, was often complicated by the rules of the forestry companies. For example, they issued the men cleated boots for working in the woods. "If a logger decided to quit," said one old-timer, "then he had to walk 30 miles (48 km) through the woods without his work boots."

Beds were made of soft tree branches, collected fresh every Sunday. The loggers were sometimes crammed so tightly into the bunkhouse that they had to sleep two in a bed. To make sure there were no complaints about the food, the men were obliged to remain silent at the table.

Work was especially hazardous at the time of the log drives downriver. To loosen up the logs, they sometimes blasted them with dynamite. Drivers also rode on top of the logs, poking at trapped ones with sticks. Every year, loggers died while driving logs downriver. Some drowned and some were too close when the dynamite went off.

A particularly tough job was held by the person who manned the lookout towers, deep in the woods. In the area of Kedgwick, there were three lookouts who would immediately notify others of any sign of fire. Each lookout tower was manned by a single person, who stayed there alone, twelve months of the year.

If you are interested in knowing more about the old-time logging camps, I suggest you see the award-winning feature film Mon Oncle Antoine, made by a noted Quebec cinematographer.

The Historic Restigouche Region

Just before you reach Campbellton, you will see a turnoff for Matapédia, Quebec. After this point be on the lookout for Atholville and one of the province's most popular ski slopes: *Sugarloaf.* Even if you are here in the summer, this slope is noteworthy: You can take the chairlift to the top and then slide down on a luge course made of cement. The view from the top of Sugarloaf is quite spectacular, well worth the $3.50 for the chairlift ride to the top.

Now continue on to *Campbellton.* It's a pretty little town, a gateway to Quebec. Just before the bridge across the river to Quebec, on the right-hand side, is a fountain, the centerpiece of which is a statue of a giant salmon, *Restigouche Sam,* promoted as "the largest salmon in the world." The fountain is surprisingly elegant, considering that it is dominated by a 28-foot (8.5-m) metal fish that appears to be in the throes of being reeled in by a giant angler.

The street where you will find this is Salmon Street. You can guess what the town's claim to fame is.

Campbellton has managed to maintain its rail connection, though many other communities in the region have lost theirs. The passenger service passes

Restigouche Sam

through six times a week, with its next stop Matapédia in Quebec. Railway lore abounds about the train from Halifax to Montreal and the many times that it literally was "frozen in its tracks." (You knew that expression had to come from somewhere!)

You can relive some of the old railway glory at the **Train Station Museum,** next door to the tourist information center, to the left of the exit to the bridge to Quebec. Outside the museum are an old locomotive and caboose in mint condition.

To the right of this turnoff, just down from the giant salmon fountain, is a lighthouse that has been turned into a youth hostel. The lighthouse is small and not that interesting, but the hostel offers a rare opportunity to spend the night in a lighthouse. The doors are closed every day from noon until 4:00 P.M.

Just to the left of the tourist information center and to the right of the giant salmon fountain as you face the river is Andrew Street. The **Galerie Restigouche,** easily found by looking for the rather large statues at the front, houses a collection of regional, national, and international exhibitions year-round. To get to the gallery, drive 8 blocks up Andrew Street from the harbor. The gallery is on your right. For information call (506) 753–5750.

Campbellton was once the site of a native village. Over the centuries the Restigouche natives were gradually pushed farther north. Today the Restigouche Nations live on the other side of the water, in Quebec.

thelegendof sugarloaf

Indian legend has it that Sugarloaf was once a giant beaver, which was turned into the mountain by the Mi'Kmaq god Glooscap. The beaver had angered the god by building a dam that prevented the salmon from swimming upriver to spawn. In anger, Glooscap destroyed the dam and turned the beaver into a ski hill. While he was at it, he cut the other beavers down to size, turning them into the small creatures they are today, as opposed to the mythic giants they once were.

Few people realize it, but the final battle in which the English gained control of Canada from the French was fought just off these shores in 1760.

After the Battle of the Plains of Abraham in 1759, when Quebec City fell, the navies of the two countries met just outside Campbellton (then Restigouche) at a point about 3 miles (5 km) east along Route 132, on the Quebec side of the border. It is now a national historic site designated by a humble marker that belies its significance. As you drive there you pass through native lands at Pointe-à-la-Croix. These are the Restigouche Mi'Kmaq who used to live on the New Brunswick side of the bay.

fiddleheadfans

Since the late 1700s, fiddleheads have been a popular source of food for New Brunswick's Mi'Kmaq and Maliseet natives. About forty-seven tons of the elegantly curled, edible wild ferns are picked and commercially processed here each year for sale in local and international markets. Nutritionally similar to asparagus, fiddleheads are loaded with vitamins A and C, niacin, and riboflavin, and are high in potassium and low in sodium, making them ideal for low-salt diets.

It is a short drive from Campbellton to **Dalhousie.** Follow either TCH Route 11, which bypasses Dalhousie, or Highway 134, which takes a more meandering route into Dalhousie and then back out to River Charlo, where it connects to Route 11 again. From this point they become one road, following the coast along **Bay Chaleur.**

If you want to putter around the area of Dalhousie, try the Chaleur Phantom, which offers both nature cruises and scenic cruises, depending on the time of day. The 50-foot (13.2-m) boat is also available for private charters. It operates from late May to the first week in October.

The morning nature cruises offer close-up looks at seals, eagles' nests, the occasional whale, and a multitude of bird life, including black cormorants. The afternoon cruise involves sight-seeing, such as trips to the Bon Ami Rocks and possibly some points on the Quebec side, and Heron Island, which is now the home of thousands of birds (and was at one time the home of nineteen human families).

The cruise itineraries vary, so it's best to ask if your particular trip will take you to the sites you want to see. Tickets are $15 for adults. Tickets for children are half price. For details or to reserve a trip, call (506) 684–4722.

Just outside Dalhousie is a beach with the longest natural sandbar in North America. Blue herons fish inside it. Locals call it the **Eel River Sandbar** or Eel River Beach, but it's marked on the map as Charlo, which apparently has another beach that runs into the sandbar. To reach it you must get on Highway 380. This minor road connects to Highway 134 in a rather confusing way, so be sure you are headed east. Incidentally, as you drive from

Dalhousie to Eel River Sandbar via Highway 134, you will be passing through a native community.

The day I dropped in to check out the Eel River Sandbar, the beach was the meeting place of 3,500 Boy Scouts from all over the region. (Apparently, there are a lot of Scout camps in the vicinity.) A madhouse, you say? Near the food concession, perhaps, but the beach is sufficiently long that at the other end there was no sign of a crowd.

The beach is a bit on the pebbly side, so beach sandals will come in handy. Several other pleasant beaches are along this coast. Most of them are not visible from the road, however, so you need to be armed with a map. Unlike Nova Scotia, where roads follow the coast and lighthouses and beaches are self-evident, roads in New Brunswick are almost always a bit of a way from the shore. A new nature touring opportunity is available at Eel River Sandbar, courtesy of the local First Nations band. They now offer the state-of-the-art Tesnegeg tour boat, from mainland New Brunswick and Quebec to **Heron Island.** This is home to more than 180 species of birds and offers 12 miles (20 km) of interpretive trails, sixteen traditional farm settlements, screened gazebos, a lookout tower, and six lookout platforms. Daily trips are limited to 500 people to ensure that Heron Island is preserved in its pristine state. The island also features camping facilities, some near nesting sites. Two-hour trips are $25 for adults. Discounts are available for seniors, students, and children. For details call (506) 684–9870. To preview the tour, visit www.heronisland.ca.

stuckonthevia railline

During our youth, both my husband and I worked on the VIA Rail service, which ran from Halifax to Montreal. On one of its midwinter runs, the train became stuck between Matapédia and Campbellton for three days, because the track was so buried in deep snow. Once supplies and fuel ran out, passengers were kept warm with blankets and fed takeout that was brought in by snowmobile from nearby Matapédia. The train often came up against other obstacles, such as moose on the tracks.

One beach that is not so hidden away is at Jacquet River Campground on Highway 134. The beach is accessible through a small provincial park, entrance to which costs $1.00 per vehicle. **Fenderson Beach** is behind the campground, down a small hill. The water here is quite shallow and therefore warm enough for even the fussiest swimmers. From this point, on a clear day, you can see across the water to Quebec. The stretch of land up and down the coast from this point appears as unbroken wilderness. This cozy little campground has 31 sites and costs $16 for a semi-serviced site.

The next major urban center is **Bathurst,** which you can reach by either TCH Route 11 or Highway 134, the more scenic of the two, which also passes several more beaches, but you won't get much of a look at them from the road. Be sure to visit the **Nicolas Denys Monument** on Main Street, overlooking Bathurst Harbor.

This Nicolas Denys was quite a busy chap. In the 1650s he established a fur-trading post in the then-virgin territory of Cape Breton (see Cape Breton chapter). When you visit Cape Breton, you'll see a small museum dedicated to and named for Denys along the side of the St. Peter's Canal. In Miscou you'll pick up Denys's traces, and here, somewhere in Bathurst's Gowan Brae Golf and Country Club, he is believed to be buried.

After his exploits in Cape Breton, this native of Tours, France, was made governor of the entire gulf region of New France, from Cape Breton to the Gaspé Region of Quebec. Denys wrote one of the first classic works on the people of Acadia, a century before the Expulsion, which uprooted them from their homes in Nova Scotia and left them scattered throughout the eastern seaboard and Louisiana.

Because of the instrumental role he played in bringing over settlers, Denys is credited with giving the region its distinctive Acadian flavor, with its mixed population of fishermen, fur traders, and farmers who were expert in farming the marshlands. (Many of the latter came from an area of France with the same kinds of marshlands, farmed for centuries by their ancestors.) In 1654 Denys and his wife set up housekeeping at Pointe-aux-Pères, at a site that later became the golf course. He died there in 1688.

If you continue along the Acadian Coastal Route, also known as Route 134, you will come to **Daly Point Reserve,** just on the other side of Bathurst. This consists of 3.75 miles (6 km) of walking trails leading through more than one hundred acres (forty hectares) of salt marsh, forest, and old farmland that is gradually reverting to its wild state. It is a great spot for nature lovers. Thousands of Canada geese stop by here during their fall migration, and the ringlet butterfly, found in only four saltmarshes in the world, can be seen here.

There are five trails and two paths, with the latter requiring more stable footwear. Scenery varies from a large gulch, which you cross on a footbridge, to twisting woodland paths, to the tamer boardwalks of the salt marsh trails. Bring plenty of bug repellent.

You won't get out of this region without hearing references to the phantom ship. (Recall that the tour boat in Dalhousie is called the Phantom.) For centuries people have claimed to see a ship on fire, far offshore. Skeptics argue that it is an optical illusion. The rest claim that it's the ghost of a ship lost long ago in battle.

The Heart of Acadia

From the Daly Point Reserve, continue on Trunk 11 until you reach the outskirts of Caraquet. The drive should take about an hour; the road follows the coast quite closely until after Grande-Anse. When you reach a small community called Rivière du Nord, a sign on the right-hand side of the road will indicate the **Acadian Historical Village.**

This is far more than just a historic re-creation of an Acadian village. Many of the fifty buildings are actual restored Acadian homesteads from the 1800s, gathered into one village along with artifacts of bygone days and some carefully constructed replicas. There are also a blacksmith shop dating from 1865, a school from 1869, and a reproduction of a Neguac cobbler's shop, circa 1875, where moccasins were the specialty.

The wonderful thing about this site is that all contact with the modern world has been kept at a minimum so that history is a living thing. Here the costumed guides illustrate life as it was lived by Acadian settlers from 1780 to 1890. A close look at period clothing reveals the skills of bygone days: Buttons made of wood or bone fasten hand-loomed clothes dyed the color of berries. You'll see the home of a Scottish administrator whose powerful position in the community gave him the poshest accommodations. He even had a grandfather clock and other imported furniture. Most of the other villagers lived in rough-hewn houses the size of a modern family's single-car garage, with rugged plank floors and simple furniture made by the occupants.

A boat awaits repair in front of one dwelling, while the lady next door sweeps her steps with a broom made by whittling a young birch trunk. Elsewhere in the village you can watch as men split cedar to make roof shingles. Throughout the summer, activities follow the pattern traditionally followed in an Acadian village: There are gatherings or working "bees" of various sorts, and occasionally visitors can see a whole milling "frolic" taking place.

farming the marshlands

Early Acadian settlers were experts in cultivating marshes. They built dikes and reclaimed land from the sea on their coastal settlements.

Like farmers of the Dutch lowlands, the Acadians kept their feet dry by wearing wooden clogs, called sabots in French. The name was once linked in France to a group of insurrectionists, hence the origin of the word *sabotage*.

Acadian marshlands are fertile places, and today Acadian entrepreneurs export their coastal wetland's abundant peat moss to gardeners worldwide.

Milling frolics, like barn raisings, were the early settlers' way of turning a tedious task into a fun event so that as many participants could be roped into the job as possible. A parade with all the equipment usually started the day. Next, the homespun cloth, often close to 50 yards long, would be soaked in soft lye soap and water in troughs made from hollowed-out tree trunks. Using long wooden pestles, the cloth was then beaten by a half-dozen men until softened. The men would sing songs to maintain the rhythm. Since the cloth was usually made from wool or flax, it was very coarse until it was softened and, essentially, preshrunk in a milling frolic. The payoff for all the hard work was a big feast prepared by the women and a party that lasted well after midnight. Milling frolics were still held in the early part of this century.

On the Acadian National Holiday, which falls on August 15, the staff re-creates a turning point in the history of the Acadian people: It is 1884. Actors, including one playing Rogersville founder Father Richard, debate the future of Acadia. (Father Richard instigated a number of "National Conventions" between 1881 and 1905 which helped to establish a common voice for the Acadians.) Finally, after much discussion, they agree on the priest's suggestion and choose a flag, an anthem, and a patron saint, strengthening their identity and creating a rallying point for cultural pride. Admission to the village is $14.00 for adults and $9.00 for children six to eighteen years of age; children under six enter free; families pay $34.00. After Labour Day, most of the costumed guides return to life in the twenty-first century and admission drops to $17.00 for a family and $7.00 for individuals. If you want to take historic re-creation seriously, you can now stay at the village in the **Chateau Albert,** modeled after a Caraquet hotel, which was built in 1907 but burned down in 1955. In 2000, the exact replica was built using the original blueprints that survived the fire. Details like wide pine-board halls, exposed wooden beams, and claw-foot tubs add to the authentic feel. The hotel has fifteen spacious guest rooms. But, in keeping with its historic theme, there are no television sets or fax machines. However, they do have Acadian-style musical entertainment during authentic suppers.

Packages are available from the end of June until the last week of August, which include a room for two nights, tickets to the dinner show, and two breakfasts, for $243 per person, based on double occupancy. To make a reservation call (506) 726–2600, or visit www.villagehistoriqueacadien.com.

Near the entrance to the Acadian Historical Village is a privately run wax museum, the **Musée de Cire d'Acadie.** This museum features eighty-six figurines in twenty-three different vignettes relating to the early life of the Acadians. The figurines were made by the same people who make wax models for Disney World. The developers of the museum have taken "lifelike" to its fullest extent. When you walk in front of the cabin of a ship carrying settlers to Acadia, for

Rappie Pie (*Pâté à la Râpure*)

Why not try rappie pie when visiting Acadian communities or **La Paneterie,** a snack bar at Le Pays de la Sagouine? This soul-satisfying variation of a chicken pot pie is featured on menus in French as pâté à la râpure. In case you want to make it at home, the following is a good, all-purpose recipe.

10 pounds potatoes, peeled

1 chicken, 3 to 4 pounds

6 cups chicken stock

1 teaspoon dry thyme

½ teaspoon ground, dry bay leaves

½ teaspoon poultry seasoning

2 tablespoons salt

1 tablespoon pepper

1 medium onion, chopped

8 strips of bacon, finely chopped

1. Place the peeled potatoes in a bowl and cover with cold water (so they retain their color) until needed.
2. Rinse the chicken and simmer it in a pot of water, along with all the seasonings.
3. After 1½ to 2 hours, the meat will fall away from the bone. Remove the meat and cut into pieces. Leave the water and the chicken bones to simmer until needed. This will be your chicken stock.
4. Grate the potatoes ten at a time. Then squeeze them in a cloth bag until all moisture and starch are removed, and set aside this liquid. Remove from the bag, and cover the grated potatoes with a wet cloth.
5. Measure the liquid squeezed from the potatoes. This will be the amount of chicken stock required. Discard the liquid.
6. Strain the chicken stock. Place squeezed potatoes into a large pan. Add the stock and stir slowly to remove all lumps. The potatoes will look like jelly.
7. Cover the bottom of a well-greased lasagna-style pan with half the potatoes. Then arrange the chicken pieces, chopped onion, and 2 chopped slices of bacon. Cover with the remaining potato mash and top with the remaining bacon. Bake at 400°F (182°C) for 1½ to 2 hours, or until crust forms on top.

example, it heaves just like a ship on the high seas. The museum is open daily from 9:00 A.M. to 7:00 P.M. For information call (506) 727–6424. Admission is $18.00 for a family or $7.00 for adults, $6.00 for seniors, and $5.00 for children.

Caraquet seems to be a mecca for Quebecois tourists in search of the picturesque. You will find hints of the Quebec urban landscape that seem quite out of place here, including a club with exotic dancers, and Quebec-style restaurants.

Check out the ***Crêpes Bretonne*** restaurant, in nearby ***Paquetville*** (the birthplace of noted Acadian folksinger Edith Butler). This village is reached by turning onto Highway 325 directly after the Acadian Historical Village, before Caraquet. Paquetville is near the junction of Highways 135, 325, and 340. To get to Paquetville after leaving the Acadian Village, turn west on Highway 325, then south onto Highway 135 for a short distance, which leads to the main intersection at the center of town. Here you will find New Brunswick's largest church, St.-Augustin, and nearby, Crêpes Bretonne, at 1085 Ruc du Parc (Park Street). The food served is typical of the Brittany-style crepe places in Quebec City: meat or seafood and vegetables, served up in a cream sauce and then rolled in a thin French "pancake."

From Paquetville you can go on to Caraquet, where you may stay for the night. Or you can drive on to the junction with Highway 355, where you must turn left at the intersection and then right at Junction 217 to go in the direction of ***Shippagan*** via Highway 113.

There is an excellent natural harbor in Shippagan, which on the map looks almost like a collection of islands. In fact, the land is so low-lying that much of the area is covered in peat moss—so much so that they even have a peat moss festival, Le Festival de Tourbe, during which time they crown a peat moss queen and throw a big party. Peat moss is a big industry now, due to the growth of home gardening. You'll be able to tell when you're in peat moss territory, because the area seems unusually flat and boglike.

At the tail end of Shippagan you will come to a causeway that will bring you to ***Île Lamèque.*** This is quite a picturesque island, popular with Quebecois because the region boasts several beaches with relatively warm water, due to their location in the shallow, narrow Chaleur Bay instead of right out on the gulf.

Once you get there, stay on Highway 113 and drive along the northern side of the island. Soon you will see a small coastal village in which the church of ***Ste.-Cécile*** hosts the annual ***Lamèque International Festival of Baroque Music.*** Despite its remote location, the festival features authentic period instruments and musicians from all over the world. Constructed in 1913, Ste.-Cécile is noted not only for its wonderful accoustics, but also for its "naive" interior decor, executed in vibrant colors, the intensely painted handiwork of two artists.

A unique event for Canada, the festival confines its musical programming to works of the Baroque period (1600–1750). It offers concerts, brunch, conferences, and even boat tours at prices ranging from $10 to $35. An award winner as the best cultural event in New Brunswick, it's a bargain. One of the highlights includes performances on a spectacular Casavant organ. You can check out concert details by visiting http://festivalbaroque.acadie.net. Keep your French/English dictionary handy. I am convinced that one of the reasons this festival is an inside secret is that very little information is available in English. The French-language twin of CBC, La Société Radio-Canada, records and rebroadcasts these performances nationally.

Because the area's accommodations could easily get filled to the limit during the concert series, reserve a room in advance if at all possible. The closest accommodations to the concert are found in the neighborhood of Lamèque. Try *L'Auberge des Compagnons,* a relatively new hotel at 11 Main Street. It has sixteen rooms and is right downtown, close to the beach, and fifteen minutes by car from most of the musical performances. Reserve by phone at (506) 344–7762, or by e-mail at auberge@nbnet.nb.ca. Breakfasts are included in the price. Rates are deluxe.

The village where you will find Ste.-Cécile is called Petite Rivière de l'Île. It ends just a short distance from the connection to *Miscou Island.*

Miscou is now connected by a bridge, which makes this summer paradise slightly more accessible. Still, its relative isolation lends it a bit of a Robinson Crusoe effect. The island is beautiful, as unspoiled as anyone could want. There are five beaches here.

The best one is located by taking the marked turnoff to *Miscou Island Camping,* just before the road turns abruptly right and leads to the lighthouse. The beach is accessed by a privately run campground. The parking fee of $2.50 entitles you to day use of the campground's facilities. The rate for overnight camping, with all hookups, is $19 to $20. There are no lifeguards, and the big waves and strong current are quite hazardous. The water is warm and the beach is well worth the drive to the island.

Be sure to visit *Miscou Lighthouse,* the oldest functioning wooden lighthouse in the Maritimes. It overlooks a pristine natural setting, with miles of sandy shore. For a small fee you can climb to the top.

Once there, look out toward the flatland to see the site of a Russian pilot's crash landing back in 1939. He was attempting to make the first solo transpolar flight from Moscow to New York when he ran into difficulty. He attempted to land on what appeared to be a good makeshift tarmac, but it turned out to be a peat bog, unfrozen, and the plane was destroyed. He did, however, officially make it across the polar ice cap—alive and without too much wear and tear on his body.

This is the most incredible place I have ever seen for beachcombing. The beach in front of the lighthouse is covered in driftwood of all sorts—so much so that you won't want to swim here. Try the beach at the campground to take a dip.

Slightly fewer than 900 people live on Miscou Island. The French spoken on Miscou and Lamèque dates back to the era of the first Europeans in Canada, so you will have a chance to brush up on your Balzac.

Miscou's remote location has always been its biggest selling point. In the era of New France, it was favored as the ideal location for the illegal fur trade, since it was so far away from Port Royal.

Its proximity to a rich fishing area drew French fishermen here as far back as the early 1600s. Among the early entrepreneurs to invest time and effort in the island was Nicolas Denys, who had a post here before moving on to Cape Breton and then becoming governor.

Miscou, unfortunately, is only a summer paradise. In the winter it is blanketed by heavy snow, lashed by the bracing winds of the gulf. You'll notice that few trees attain much height.

After returning to Île Lamèque, take Route 113 until you reach exit 217. This is a fork in the road: Haut Pokemouche lies to the north. Turn left, heading south toward Pokemouche, and follow Highway 11 until you reach Miramichi, comprising the former communities of Chatham, Newcastle, and Nelson-Miramichi.

In the midst of all this Acadian culture you will suddenly come upon an area of considerable Irish settlement, so much so that **Miramichi** is the site of an **Irish Festival on the Miramichi.** Held in mid-July, this is the first and largest Irish festival in Canada. It features traditional music, culture, and entertainers from Ireland. Some recent innovations include a "cyberpub," where a local pub links to a pub in Ireland. Nighttime admission is $14. The main festival venue is the Lord Beaverbrook Arena, directly under the Miramichi water tower. Festival details can be found by visiting www.canadasirishfest.com.

After Miramichi you have the option of taking Route 11 south as far as Kouchibouguac National Park or driving along the coast on a pretty stretch of highway called Route 117. The reward of this latter course is an unsullied stretch of coast culminating in **Pointe-Sapin,** where you can snuggle up with nature. If you wish, you can camp or enjoy solitary stretches of beach here.

Pointe-Sapin is a charming Acadian village. The residents hold the Festival du Bon Pecheur ("Festival of the Good Fisherman") each mid- to late July, purely as a local thing.

The village is at the northern, coastal entrance to **Kouchibouguac National Park.** The protected dunes of the shoreline stretch like a long arm the length of the park. Along with watching rare-bird life along the grassy dunes of Kouchibouguac, you can hike on any of ten trails; rent canoes, bikes, or paddleboats; or swim in lagoons holding the warmest saltwater north of Virginia.

Much of the shoreline of this park is protected wilderness hosting a variety of rare flora and fauna, including the piping plover. There is an active beaver dam in the park, which always makes for fascinating viewing, and along the coast you can spot harbor and gray seals. For details call (506) 876–2443.

After leaving the national park, you will be traveling south on Route 11 until you reach exit 42. Turn into a small town called *Sainte-Anne-de-Kent,* along a smaller highway, Rural Route 505. This village offers a unique opportunity to mix shopping, learning, and grooming at a combination museum and specialist soap shop. (Say that twice rapidly!) *The Olivier Soapery and Soap Museum of Canada* is a provincially run museum that demonstrates the traditional art of soap making and displays objects from history that were dedicated to personal grooming products and their manufacture.

They also manufacture their own line of mild biodegradable skin solutions, created from pure essential oil extracts of plants and flowers. Some of the shampoos, milk baths, therapeutic oils, and creams are specifically designed to treat skin disorders. And, of course, some are just to pamper yourself, naturally. They make great gifts for the people who stayed home on this trip. The museum is open from May to September daily from 10:00 A.M. to 8:00 P.M. They hold demonstrations five times a day. During winter months, the museum is open from 9:00 A.M.to 5:00 P.M.

After the museum, return to Route 11 by backtracking to exit 42 and continue south to Bouctouche.

worthmentioning

The Miramichi Folksong Festival is one of North America's longest-standing folk festivals, dating back more than forty years. So, it's not really off the beaten path, but it does offer a range of traditional and contemporary folk music in a pleasant, seaside community. In addition to the fiddlers and singers, there are dance performances. Entertainers come from across the continent to this event timed for the first week in August. For details on the performers, call (506) 623–2150.

The Acadian Coast

Bouctouche is the birthplace of two of New Brunswick's most famous natives: billionaire K.C. Irving and writer Antonine Maillet. Maillet's play La Sagouine ("The Cleaning Woman") won the highest acclaim possible in the French-speaking world, but its biggest impact by far is the fact that audiences have been unable to separate fact from fiction and are convinced that *la sagouine* is a real person. So, on the nearby *Île-aux-Puces,* reached by boardwalk and footbridge, you can enter an entire alternate universe devoted to her, entitled

Le Pays de la Sagouine or the "Land of the Cleaning Lady." Think of this as a 3-D play where you get to participate. By the time you've finished a meal of Acadian *poutine râpées, pâtés à la viande, poutines à trou,* and *chicken fricot,* and listened to some typical Acadian music and old-time storytelling in local French, you will have a hard time distinguishing fact from fiction yourself. Prices are moderate. For details, call (800) 561–9188 or (506) 743–1400.

Farther south along Route 11, in *Shediac,* the thing to do is visit *Cap-Pelé Beach.* The water is consistently wonderful here, and the sand goes on forever. All summer long it's a good bet for a swim because it is situated along a very narrow and shallow stretch of the Northumberland Strait, which causes the water to be warm.

Shediac has also laid claim to the title of "World's Lobster Capital," and while I've heard that before, only in Shediac will you have the opportunity to climb all over a gigantic lobster sculpture, situated along the village's main drag, overlooking a small inlet.

If you feel the need for an urban break, turn inland again on Route 15 west to *Moncton,* a surprisingly cosmopolitan and thoroughly pleasant little city, where the population is almost evenly divided between French and English speakers and bilingualism is a way of life. As a result, many nationwide services have gravitated to the area, adding to the dynamic feel of this cozy place.

Whether you are in Shediac or Moncton, you now must make a crucial decision: whether to explore the rest of New Brunswick's Fundy Coast, go on to Nova Scotia, or head for Prince Edward Island. Here are the three alternative routes:

1. If you are headed toward Nova Scotia, be sure to stop first in *Sackville,* New Brunswick, for a visit to the *Sackville Waterfowl Park.* Sackville is right in the middle of the migratory path of millions of birds, particularly ducks. For years the early Acadian settlers tried to turn the Tantramar Marshes into farmland, draining it for the purpose, but to no avail. Eventually the town decided to flood an area and allow the ducks their way. The result is the fifty-five-acre (twenty-five-hectare) park, which has earned the town its reputation as the "Bird-Watching Capital of Atlantic Canada."

   Extending right up into the community, the park provides an amazing close-up of airborne wildlife. The park is crisscrossed with boardwalks, giving easy access to the wetlands. Guides are available to take visitors on a tour and explain the intricacies of the ecosystem, which includes rare species of wildflowers and birds. A guided tour costs $5.00 for adults, $3.00 for children.

A Visit to Sackville Waterfowl Park

There are now 160 different species of birds in the **Sackville Waterfowl Park,** according to Tracy Cole, our guide and wildlife biologist. She greets our group with her bird book in hand. "I know eighty species that I can identify, but I need help with the rest," she explains.

Part of the park is built on an old rail line that has been torn up and replaced by gravel trails. Boardwalks crisscross the old Acadian pastureland. Remaining are apple trees, now hundreds of years old, and basket willows, which early settlers used for weaving household goods.

The wild snapdragons growing here were used to make an ointment for bee stings and mosquito bites. In a thicket of the shrub spirea, so dense the locals call it "hard hack," we find yellow warblers hiding out.

Unfortunately, decades ago European settlers brought purple loosestrife to this country, and it has been crowding out other plants ever since. Until recently, the park workers would periodically try to eradicate the loosestrife by hand. A few years ago the park switched to the newer tactic of releasing several hundred mating pairs of a small weevil, which feed off the weed.

Much of the water in the park is covered by duckweed, which feeds almost all of the species of ducks that live here. The park's residents include mallards, green-wing and blue-wing teals, gadwalls, wigeons, ring-necked ducks, and pied-billed grebes.

The area is also visited by osprey. To encourage a mating pair to set up house, the park constructed an "osprey tower," which looks like a telephone pole rising out of the water, with a platform on top.

Amid the reeds you may see a muskrat. From a cluster of bulrushes comes a high-pitched squeak. It's from a bird called the sora rail, completely camouflaged by the bulrushes when its beak points skyward. Once it drops its beak, it looks like a small chicken.

Although the area is marshland, we weren't plagued by mosquitoes. A large number of tree swallows have been established in the park to keep the bug population down.

Sackville itself is a great town for aimless puttering: It is the home of Mount Allison University, which includes a well-recognized art college. Over the years it has become a magnet for artists, and the community's gift shops provide many good art-collecting opportunities for out-of-town visitors.

Just before the border with Nova Scotia you will come to **Fort Beauséjour** in Aulac. You will find this on TCH 2, in the heart of the windswept Tantramar Marshes. The fortress was the site of a major turning point in the history of New Brunswick: It was here that the British defeated the French and gained a toehold in the territory of New Brunswick. Here you can see earthworks, shaped like a five-sided star, and underground portions of the fortifications. The fort, which is a National Historic Site, has outdoor paintings depicting scenes from early battles. Admission is $3.50 for adults, $3.00 for seniors, $1.75 for youths, and $8.75 for families. For details, call (506) 364–5080.

2. To get to Prince Edward Island from Shediac, take Provincial Highway 15 until you connect to the TCH 16, just a short distance from the link to P.E.I. The road is well marked.

3. If you are sticking to New Brunswick, then point your Pontiac south from Moncton along Route 114 until you reach **Hopewell Cape,** where the Petitcodiac River widens out to Shepody Bay. This is the site of the **Flowerpot Rocks,** which give a nature walk an added appeal. Actually chunks of land created by erosion resulting from the action of the Bay of Fundy's tides, these sandstone rocks tower above you at a height of four stories when the tide is out. At high tide, though, the site is unimpressive, and you'll wonder what all the fuss is about. This is the fate of sightseers along the Bay of Fundy—everything depends on the tides. The average difference between high and low tide is 36 feet (11 meters). When tides are low, you'll get a one-time chance to walk on the ocean floor.

   Hopewell Rocks Park is now triple its original size and has several large parking lots at the entrance. Nearby is a modern shop and dining complex, where you can get a decent meal for roughly $10 to $15 a plate. The setting is very nice, and while outside seating on the viewing decks may be very breezy, the inside tables still offer a good view of the Bay of Fundy. The complex includes an interpretive center with displays of the ecology of the area and a multimedia exhibit. The souvenir shop here has a wide selection of gift items.

   When you are ready for your hike among the Flowerpot Rocks, a shuttle will take you to the starting point, where you will descend a series of stairs to the ocean floor. After you're finished, take advantage of the hoses provided to scrub down your muddy footwear (as much as possible). This is a good place to take rubber boots with good tread or, failing that, the kind of Velcro-strapped sandals favored by kayakers. Admission to the park is $7.00 for adults, $6.00 for seniors, $5.00 for children ages five to eighteen, and $18.00 for a family.

   The most dramatic way to see the Flowerpot Rocks is by kayak with a naturalist guide from **Baymount Outdoor Adventures.** The two-man kayaks are extremely stable and handle much more easily than canoes, so they can be used even by novices.

Kayaking around the rocks takes some forethought and timing, since the Flowerpots are flooded roughly two hours before and after high tide. Tours are timed to coincide with the tide's peak, so call ahead to book a spot. For $55 per person, Baymount provides the seaworthy with basic instruction, the use of sea kayaks, and a three-hour guided tour. To book a kayak and instruction, call (506) 734–2660.

For about two weeks, starting at the end of July, between one and two million semipalmated sandpipers make their way here to double

Paddling among the Flowerpots

Baymount Outdoor Adventures tour guide Richard Faulkner takes groups to the Flowerpots twice a day in the summer, to coincide with the times when the rocks are flooded.

I take off with a group early in the morning, while the air is still and cool, a faint mist rising above the chocolate water of Shepody Bay. Because the sun has not yet heated the water, there is little breeze and no discernable current to contend with. Still shrouded in fog, the early-morning Flowerpots seem to hover in a cloud. Up close, the purple-hued, iron-oxide-tinged rocks look as if handfuls of granite were thrown at wet clay, which hardened into a wall.

These are called "conglomerate rocks," made of rock fragments that over eons have been compressed together. The conglomerate rock came from the Appalachian Mountain range 250 million years ago: First, the earth's plates shifted, creating vertical fractures in the rock. Then, water from melting glaciers eroded and caused the separation of some rock from the mainland. The Flowerpots themselves weren't carved out until the last ice age, about ten thousand years ago. They were eroded by the tides of the Bay of Fundy, which sculpted them at the base to look like elegantly formed pottery.

One of the first big rocks is Lover's Arch, through which kayaks easily pass. We continue to weave in and out of the rocks, for a total distance of roughly 1 mile (1.6 km). In the distance a peregrine falcon swoops down over and over again, apparently in search of small shore birds.

After close to an hour, we round the point. From here we see Shepody Mountain and Grindstone Island, 7 nautical miles (11.3 km) away.

Later, as the water moves roughly 450 feet (137.1 m) offshore, tiny mud shrimp burrow into the silt-covered floor of the bay. These are the food of the semi-palmated sandpiper, a small gray-and-white shorebird that makes the upper Bay of Fundy its one stop on its migration from the Arctic to Surinam, on the northern coast of South America.

their weight, before a marathon five-day flight. Hopewell Cape is their one stop on an annual journey from the Arctic to Surinam, a country on the northern coast of South America. They shift around every few days, but with some luck and good timing, you may get a look at the dramatic sight of a mass migration. Says kayaking guide Richard Faulkner, "It's nature. So we don't promote and advertise and guarantee, because the birds may have a different plan that day."

During a recent migration, kayakers were surrounded by hundreds of thousands of the gray-and-white birds—a flock so thick that the bright yellow boats were invisible to one another, even at distances as close as 30 feet (9 meters).

Bear in mind that the tides here can take you by surprise. The change in water height can be sufficient to leave you stranded if you are not careful. Plan ahead by consulting a tide table (widely available in New Brunswick).

After Hopewell Cape you can return to Route 114 and drive to Riverside-Albert, where the highway joins Route 915 and continues on to Alma, where you can experience *Fundy National Park,* on the Bay of Fundy. There is an outdoor pool here filled with water that is pumped in from the bay and heated. While you swim you can catch some stunning views of the bay, but the area is otherwise quite isolated. Admission to the swimming pool is $3.00 for adults, $1.50 for children, or $7.50 for a family. Season passes are available to campers. From here you can continue through the park on another stretch of Provincial Highway 114 until you reach TCH Route 2 a few miles outside Sussex. For details call (506) 887–6000, or fax (506) 887–6008.

If you happen to be in Sussex and the vicinity in the early fall, you will notice a large number of hot-air balloons overhead; balloonists hold a festival here annually. After Sussex you can return to Saint John via Route 1; now you will have done a complete circumnavigation of New Brunswick.

Places to Stay in Acadian New Brunswick

BATHURST

Keddy's Le Chateau
80 Main Street
(506) 546–6691
Moderate.

CARAQUET

Chateau Albert
14311 Route 11
Acadian Historical Village
(506) 726–2600
Time travel included in price.
Moderate.

GRAND FALLS

Best Western Près du Lac
TCH, Route 2
(506) 473–1300
Standard.

HOPEWELL CAPE

**Hopewell Rocks Motel
and Inn**
Route 114
(at the entrance to Hopewell
Rocks Park)
(506) 734–2975
Stunning setting.
Standard.

KEDGWICK

Centre Echo Restigouche
Route 17
(506) 284–2022
Nature in surround-sound
(pack repellent).
Moderate.

LAMÈQUE

**L'Auberge des
Compagnons**
11 Main Street,
(506) 344–7766
auberge@nbnet.nb.ca
Deluxe.

MIRAMICHI

**Rodd Miramichi River
Lodge**
1809 Water Street
(800) 565–7633
In the heart of anglers'
paradise.
Moderate.

SACKVILLE

Marshlands Inn
55 Bridge Street
(1 mile from TCH)
(800) 561–1266
(506) 536–0170
Historic.
Moderate.

Places to Eat in Acadian New Brunswick

All feature fresh Atlantic
seafood in addition to the
usual fare.

BOUCTOUCHE

**Auberge Le Vieux
Presbytère de
Bouctouche**
157 Chemin du Couvent
(506) 743–5568
Delicious regional cuisine;
excellent wine list.

HOPEWELL CAPE

The Log Cabin Restaurant
Route 114
(at the entrance to
Hopewell Rocks Park)
(506) 734–2110
Spectacular view.

MIRAMICHI

P. J. Billington's
1 Jane Street
(506) 622–0302
At the water's edge.

MONCTON

Cy's Restaurant
170 Main Street
(506) 857–0032
In charming heart of town.

Wharf Village Restaurant
exit 488 off TCH 2 or
Route 126
(506) 859–1812

PAQUETVILLE

Crêpes Bretonne
1085 Rue du Parc
(near Highways 135 and 325)
(506) 764–5344

SHEDIAC

**Fisherman's Paradise
Restaurant**
Main Street
(off exit 37 on Route 15)
(506) 532–6811

Prince Edward Island

Prince Edward Island

The descendants of the original settlers on Prince Edward Island (P.E.I.) have clung so tenaciously to their traditional ways and manner of speech that you will find yourself imagining that you are in Ireland, Scotland, or Brittany.

It isn't such a stretch of the imagination: Initial European settlements of French Acadians were followed by waves of Irish farmers and Scots. All of them have come to think of P.E.I. as the center of the universe—so much so that anywhere else is referred to, vaguely, as "away," and people from anyplace out of the province are said to "come from away." And Prince Edward Island is simply referred to as "The Island." Even when those words are spoken aloud, you can tell they are in capital letters. A lot has changed for the visitor to Prince Edward Island over the past few years. The Island's section of the Trans-Canada Trail, known locally as the Confederation Trail, is complete. So is the "fixed link," now called the Confederation Bridge. The bridge makes shorter visits or even day trips possible, whereas before, visitors might have to factor in a half day's wait for a spot on the ferry. If you take day trips into account and plan to target

PRINCE EDWARD ISLAND

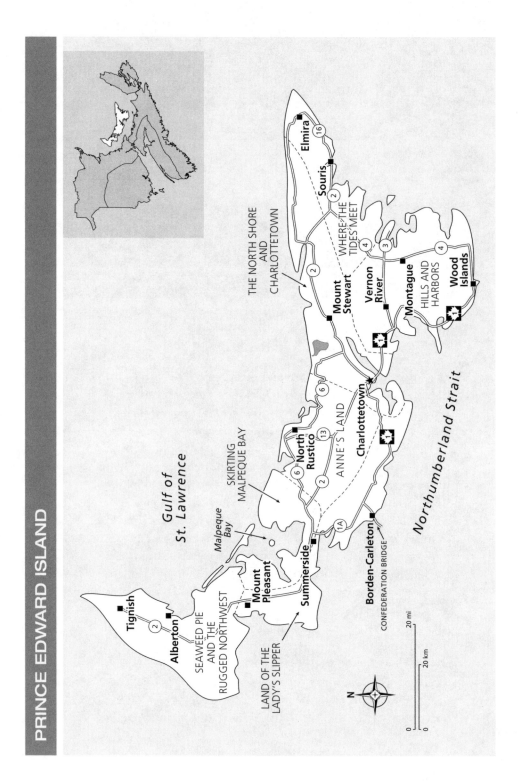

Gulf of
St. Lawrence

Malpeque
Bay

SKIRTING
MALPEQUE BAY

THE NORTH SHORE
AND
CHARLOTTETOWN

Elmira

Souris

WHERE THE
TIDES MEET

Mount
Stewart

Vernon
River

Montague

HILLS AND
HARBORS

Wood
Islands

North Rustico

ANNE'S LAND

Charlottetown

Summerside

Mount
Pleasant

LAND OF THE
LADY'S SLIPPER

Tignish

Alberton

SEAWEED PIE
AND THE
RUGGED NORTHWEST

Borden-Carleton

CONFEDERATION BRIDGE

Northumberland Strait

N

20 mi

20 km

areas farther afield, you can still enjoy the quaint countryside and outdoor lifestyle of this picturesque province.

The key to getting off the beaten path in Prince Edward Island is to concentrate your travel at the two end points of The Island, thereby avoiding the outrageously popular tourist attractions clustered around the home of famous author Lucy Maud Montgomery and the sites related to her fictional heroine of *Anne of Green Gables*. First published in 1908, the book that made this red-haired orphan famous is in its hundredth printing and has now been translated into dozens of languages. It holds cult status in Japan, where its place on the school curriculum and the spunky character of its heroine have guaranteed its supremacy in the hearts of young Japanese women. Thousands of Japanese make an annual pilgrimage to the Cavendish area of P.E.I. every summer.

Cavendish Beach is undoubtedly spectacular, but if you are looking for Anne, you may find her hard to spot among the legions of Japanese honeymooners, the bus-tour groups, and the visitors to Ripley's Believe It or Not! Museum and the many amusement parks. Since The Island has forty beaches to choose from, a good strategy is to aim for one of the less-frequented beaches. But if you are determined to visit Cavendish, try to get there before school closes at the end of June or, alternatively, go near the end of August. To ensure that you'll be able to find lodgings at this popular spot, book ahead by calling (888) 268–6667. Now you can also book online at www.gov.pe.ca/visitors guide/reservation/index.php3.

A little farther along, however, and you are in the countryside that spawned the heartwarming series of Anne books that made The Island famous. Take particular note of the Scenic Heritage Roads, which dot the various

TRUDY'S FAVORITES

Basin Head,
(museum and beach)

Cap-Egmont Bottle Houses,
Cap-Egmont

Confederation Centre of the Arts,
Charlestown

Dalvay by-the-sea,
Grand Tracadie

The Dunes Studio Gallery,
Brackley Beach

**Elmira Railway Museum and
Confederation Trail,**
Elmira

Mill River Golf Course,
Woodstock

Victoria by-the-Sea

counties of P.E.I. These are characterized by the deep-red clay (not so scenic in spring thaw or after several days of rain) and the pastoral countryside that has remained unchanged by the modern world. It is a constantly changing canvas: at times, all deep green and red clay; later in the summer, fields of purple and white potato flowers, ripening corn, and yellow hay.

trivia

The interior chamber of a lobster trap is often called a "bedroom" or "parlor."

In 1813, P.E.I.'s lieutenant governor devised a solution to a chronic coin shortage by permitting the use of Spanish silver coins, which had the centers punched out. The "holey money" was to be accepted at face value. They were pulled from circulation quickly, however, because of rampant counterfeiting.

If you fly over The Island, you'll be struck by the impression that you are looking at a diagonally pieced crazy quilt, boasting many shades of green and topstitched in the deep-red clay.

If you are traveling to Prince Edward Island from New Brunswick, you will be taking the 8-mile (12.9-km) *Confederation Bridge.* This is one of the engineering marvels of the world, currently the longest bridge to traverse ice-covered saltwater and the longest span in the Western Hemisphere. Fares are $39.00 per car and $44.50 for recreational vehicles. A free shuttle bus transports pedestrians and cyclists at regular intervals. Major credit cards are accepted at the toll booths. The crossing takes ten minutes. Tolls cover a round trip to and from the island and are paid for upon departure from the island.

From the town of Borden-Carleton it is only a short drive to the attractions in the western end of the province, while the east is quite accessible from Wood Islands.

Since the entire distance from one tip of P.E.I. to the other is only 180 miles (288 km), and the landscape is either flat or gently rolling, it is the perfect place to take a bicycle tour. This can last a few hours on a rented bike or for the entire holiday on your own trusty steed.

Added to this are the many country bed-and-breakfast inns and farm vacations that make slow-paced travel particularly appealing. Most important (for cyclists of my caliber), you're never very far from a rest stop, a scenic view, or the next village.

When The Island railway was closed down, it was decided to convert the abandoned rail lines to combination bike paths and hiking trails, which are used by snowmobilers in the winter. The many train stations left behind serve as rest areas for outdoor enthusiasts using the rails-to-trails. With the opening of the Confederation Trail and P.E.I.'s reputation as the ultimate bike-holiday locale, the number of bike-rental companies has grown to over two dozen. This means that you can take day trips from several locations on the trail or select from a wide range of departure points, without having to bring your own bike. The shared-use walking and bike trail runs from one tip of the province to the other, a total of 169 miles (270 km) from Tignish to Elmira, with additional branch routes bringing the total length of trail to 219 miles (350 km). There is even a link to the Confederation Bridge in Borden-Carleton. (You can't bike on the bridge, but a free shuttle will take you and your bike across.)

The same thing that makes cycling so wonderful in P.E.I. makes giving road directions a hazardous business. The Island consists of farmland from one end to the other, dotted with little communities, so the entire province is covered with a spider's web of roads. Since it is crescent-shaped and as narrow as 4 miles (6.4 km) across at one point, there are a half dozen ways to get anywhere—great for cyclists. If you don't like where you are, you can always take the next left and traverse the width of the entire province in less than twenty minutes.

We recommend one of two strategies for getting off the beaten path in P.E.I. Either follow the route we have mapped out in a clockwise direction from Borden-Carleton, with it located at six o'clock on the dial; or follow the same route in reverse from the Wood Islands ferry landing, on the southeastern

TOP ANNUAL EVENTS

Victoria Playhouse Summer Festival,
Victoria by-the-Sea
(end of June to end of August);
(800) 925–2025
www.victoriaplayhouse.com

P.E.I. Bluegrass and Old-time Music Festival,
Rollo Bay (second week in July);
(902) 569–4501

Souris Regatta,
(second week in July);
(902) 687–2157 or (902) 687–3835

Annual Rollo Bay Fiddler's Festival,
(third weekend in July);
(902) 687–2584
(902) 687–3464

Rendez-Vous Rustico,
(fourth weekend in July);
(902) 963–3252

Bluegrass Festival,
Orwell Corner Historic Village
(fourth Sunday in August);
(902) 651–8510

70-Mile Coastal Yard Sale,
Wood Islands and vicinity
(last weekend in September);
(902) 962–3242

end of the province. If there is something you want to bypass, simply detour onto one of the many rural routes that crisscross the province.

Land of the Lady's Slipper

Once in Borden-Carleton, if you so much as blink, you risk missing a charming little fishing village just fifteen minutes from the ferry landing. Therefore, even though I've mapped out a tour of The Island's western end first, I am going to suggest that you make one small detour east as soon as you arrive.

Simply because of its out-of-the-way location between the two arrival points, few explore the many and varied charms of the tiny unspoiled fishing village of *Victoria by-the-Sea.* Established along a British Colonial-style grid pattern, it is quite compact, which makes for pleasant strolling. Just park your car and drift around.

What Victoria by-the-Sea has to offer is 4 square blocks of quaint little nooks and crannies, cafes, and a theater (*The Victoria Playhouse* presents popular theater nightly all summer). You would be pleasantly surprised at the caliber of the entertainment that turns up in this tiny seaside village theater. To check its season's offerings, visit www.victoriaplayhouse.com. Summer performances are seven nights a week at 8:00 P.M.; on Sunday there is also a 2:00 P.M. matinee.

trivia

Cars were banned from Prince Edward Island early in the 1900s as a "menace to life and property." While people drive cars all over the island now, strictly speaking, they are against the law.

The *Studio Gallery,* on a lane to your right as you walk up from the shore, displays the work of a number of local artists, etchings, oils, and acrylics—some representational, some surrealistic. There are also pottery, antiques, craft and quilt shops, and other appealing stores. You can't miss anything by simply wandering around this tiny village. The wharf has now been spruced up to house a restaurant and shops, but the winds have so far kept the outdoor deck from being a favored dining spot.

The little harbor's lighthouse is also home to the *Victoria Seaport Museum,* where you can chat with the students who run the museum and catch up on the local scene. This is the second-oldest lighthouse on P.E.I., and photographs of some of its most reliable keepers are displayed here—one man put in fifty years on the job. The lighthouse exhibits navigational aids from the 1920s, including a kerosene lamp used in the range light for many years. You can climb to the top to see the modern light or just check out the harbor from the second floor. Admission is free, though donations are welcome.

The village boasts several beaches as well as a lobster pound, meaning a good supply of fresh lobster at the local eating establishments. You can also watch chocolates being made at *Island Chocolates.* The shop sells a variety of locally produced and specialty jams. Island Chocolates also offers its own brand of cocoa and specially blended coffees and teas designed to go well with chocolate. It also has Titanic-shaped chocolates and even chocolate-scented candles, which owners Ron and Linda Gilbert promote as "a calorie-free experience." Call (902) 658–2320.

The village's foremost accommodations are an inn dating back to 1900. The *Orient Hotel* on Main Street is one of the last two original hotels operating in P.E.I. (The establishment is now part of a network of Heritage inns in Atlantic Canada.) There are six guest rooms (all with private bath) and cable television. Cycle tourists take note: There is storage for bicycles. For a reservation, call (800) 565–6743 or (902) 658–2503. A full breakfast is included in the room rates. Prices are moderate. Visit www.theorienthotel.com or contact by e-mail at stay@theorienthotel.com.

After enjoying Victoria, turn west and backtrack the fifteen minutes toward Borden-Carleton and the western end of The Island.

If you want to skip Victoria by-the-Sea or leave it to the end of your stay on The Island, then turn west immediately after leaving the ferry. Turning west will take you briefly to *Summerside* and from there to the small fishing villages and cozy beaches of the western end of the island.

In the nineteenth century the economic mainstay of Summerside was its shipbuilding industry. You can relive some of that era at *Spinnakers' Landing,* which offers an opportunity to explore an interpretive center showing the shipbuilding techniques of the early 1800s. While the development is recent

Summerside's Fur Industry

The silver-fox fur industry in Summerside began to boom in the late 1800s and reached its peak in the 1920s. Breeding pairs of the top-quality foxes were even traded for houses; one pair fetched an outstanding $35,000 on the open market. At its height the industry constituted one-sixth of The Island's economic base, bringing wealth to many Summerside furriers.

The Island was the site of the first successful fur farm in the world, beginning in the 1870s with the capture of a pair of wild black foxes. A little more than a decade later, experimentation finally resulted in a successful breeding program. The results of these early studies form the basis of all current fur-farming methods in the world. The industry continues to this day with just over sixty fur farmers on the island.

rather than historic, the harborside shops stock a variety of crafts and gift items. Harbor cruises can be booked on the spot. In front of the shops is a play area that includes a jungle gym in the shape of a boat. On the morning I visited, flocks of children were playing tug-of-war while their parents explored the shops. Spinnakers' Landing has now become a venue for free concerts several times a week over the summer, usually Friday, Saturday, and Sunday nights from 6:00 P.M. to 8:00 P.M. There is also a bike rental location set up here during the summer.

Also along Summerside's shore you will find the **College of Piping** at 619 Water Street East. This is a place for people who want to learn to play the bag-pipes like a real Highlander—or at least look like one. In addition to crash courses in pip-ing, the college gives frequent free concerts and demonstrations of Highland dance by the little ones. You can also deck yourself out in full Highland tartan at the Celtic Gift and Highland Supply Outlet. To obtain a course calendar and events schedule, write to the college at 619 Water Street East, Summerside, PE C1N 4H8. Call (877) BAGPIPE, or visit www.collegeofpiping.com.

trivia

Prince Edward Island has dropped the provincial sales tax on clothing and footwear, cutting their cost by 10 percent. If you're itching to replenish your wardrobe, this can give added appeal to the commute across the bridge.

Summerside streets are graced with stately old homes that recall a time of wealth and ease. These date back not only to the years when it was the center of The Island's shipbuilding trade, but also to when it was the focus of the lucrative silver-fox industry. That era is depicted in charcoal drawings, photographs, and folk art at the **International Fox Museum and Hall of Fame,** 286 Fitzroy Street, 3 blocks back from the harbor. For details about the museum, call (902) 436–2400. Admission is free, but donations are accepted.

Fifteen minutes' drive west on Route 11 from Summerside will take you to **Mont-Carmel,** site of **Le Village de l' Acadie,** 1 mile (1.6 km) past Our Lady of Mont-Carmel Church. The route is marked by a logo depicting the lady's slipper, a typical island flower, for which Lady Slipper Drive (Route 11) is named. If you chance upon one of these flowers, don't pick it—it would take thirteen years for a new flower to grow in its place!

The first European settlers on The Island were Acadians, settlers from France's Atlantic coast. While many were exiled shortly after the British won pos-session of The Island, a number escaped into the woods with the help of native peoples and then quietly reestablished normal lives. The Acadian presence is still significant, with 17 percent of the Island residents descendants from these first European settlers.

In the center of the Le Village de l' Acadie complex is an open-air "theater," painted with massive murals depicting scenes from the early life of the Acadians. Among them is the story of Evangeline, the now-famous Acadian heroine who was separated from her husband on her wedding day. The real Evangeline became a nun in Philadelphia and was reunited with her husband on his deathbed, many years later. The village is open daily from 9:00 A.M. to 7:00 P.M. from June to mid-September. Admission is $4.00 for adults, half price for children ages six and older, and free for children under six. Call (800) 567–3228.

The restaurant ***Étoile de Mer*** serves traditional Acadian fare. These include such hits as *pâté à la râpure,* a potato pie popular throughout Acadian regions, and Quebecois specialties like *poutine*. During the summer the restaurant has a dinner theater. Call (902) 854–2227 for hours and reservations.

Just 3 miles (5 km) farther west down Route 11 (Lady Slipper Drive) from Mont-Carmel, you will come to Cap-Egmont, home of the ***Cap-Egmont Bottle Houses,*** the masterpiece of a stellar attempt at recycling.

You must not pass up the chance to consider at length the single-mindedness of someone who collects and then cements together 25,000 glass bottles to form buildings. Originally the work of the late Edouard T. Arsenault, a retired fisherman, the structures include a spectacular little chapel complete with altar and pews, a six-gabled house, and a spacious tavern.

The original inspiration for the project came from a bottle house on Vancouver Island, but that climate was far more benign during the winter. Much of the original complex had to be restored because of the impact of The Island's

Cap-Egmont Bottle House

severe winters on the unique building materials. Two of the three structures have undergone major repairs. Arsenault's family is carrying on his tradition and keeping the kids busy at the same time. Using more than 2,000 bottles, grandson Etienne added his own giant bottle to the site.

Hobbyists in particular will love this place, if for no other reason than to reassure themselves that they have yet to get truly carried away with their obsession. The three bottle houses and the gardens, which at their peak feature more than fifty varieties of flowers, are open daily from 10:00 A.M. to 6:00 P.M. In July and August hours extend from 9:00 A.M. to 8:00 P.M. every day. Admission is $4.00 for adults, $1.00 for children ages six to sixteen. Admission for groups can be arranged by calling (902) 854–2987. In the off-season, phone (902) 854–2254. There is also a gift shop on site with a variety of P.E.I. memorabilia. Some unique souvenirs include blown-glass articles and ornaments made from recycled bottles.

Seaweed Pie and the Rugged Northwest

Continuing along this sparsely populated stretch of shoreline will take you to the black-and-white **West Point Lighthouse,** located in the **Cedar Dunes Provincial Park.** This is the only functioning lighthouse in Canada that also serves as an inn. Built in 1875 and operated by the Canadian Coast Guard, this is one of The Island's tallest lighthouses, measuring 69 feet (21 m). It now includes a museum and gift shop. The museum holds maps, tools, logbooks, and a collection of other artifacts that recount the story of The Island's lighthouses and the era of sailing. Here you can read about the fascinating characters who ran the light, among them "Lighthouse Willie."

Admission is $2.50 for adults, $1.50 for children, but if you stay as an overnight guest, your visit to the lighthouse is free.

There are nine rooms for overnight guests, including one in the lighthouse tower. All guest rooms have private baths, and two have whirlpool baths. The rooms have been decorated to re-create the era of the lightkeepers, with old-fashioned touches and handmade quilts. Considering the incomparable view and the opportunity to fall asleep to the hypnotic lapping of the waves, you really ought to call ahead for reservations; call (800) 764–6854 or (902) 859–3605. Rates are moderate. Write for more information to West Point Lighthouse, O'Leary, RR2, PE C0B 1V0, or visit www.westpointlighthouse.com/local.htm. The lighthouse is located on Route 14. The inn is open from the third weekend in May (the Victoria Day weekend) until the end of September.

"Lighthouse Willie"

Lighthouse Willie held the job of lighthouse keeper from 1875 to 1925, never missing one night of work in fifty years. He was the father of eight children and ran a farm 1.5 miles (2 km) away. During the summer the family came to stay at the West Point Lighthouse, and his wife brought a beautiful organ there for entertainment. After passing through many family hands, that organ has been restored to its original lighthouse location.

This site offers even more. The 1.5-mile (2-km) long, white-sand beach at Cedar Dunes Provincial Park is quite lovely and well enough off the beaten path to offer a quiet respite from civilization. The park is protected by legislation because of its environmental significance. The ***Cedar Bog*** contains a fragile ecosystem that you can explore through guided nature trails and the interpretive program. There is a provincial government campground here, and they loan out recreational equipment. Sites are $19 and $22 per night.

While visiting the park and lighthouse, you can also satisfy your urge for souvenir collecting at the ***West Point Lighthouse Craft Guild,*** located to the right of the lighthouse. The shop features work by several local artisans and is open from 10:00 A.M. to 8:00 P.M. in July and August; from 10:00 A.M. to 6:00 P.M. in June and September.

This end of the province has wonderfully pristine fishing villages and presents a wealth of photographic opportunities. The coastal villages, which are particularly appealing, are clustered along the western end, where Irish moss is a big source of income. Fishermen harvest this seaweed, which is then processed for its carrageenan, a substance used in the making of ice cream and other food products. Depending on which way the wind is blowing, you will see the moss being harvested either by boats that skirt the shoreline, by men raking it by hand, or by men using horses to gather it up.

At ***Miminegash,*** at the intersection of Route 14 and Route 152, you can learn all about the industry in the ***Irish Moss Interpretive Centre,*** which is fronted by ***The Seaweed Pie Cafe.*** The interpretive center is open from 10:00 A.M. to 7:00 P.M. daily. Admission is $1.00. Stop by and have seaweed pie. I'm serious. Eating seaweed pie is like getting your ears pierced: Regardless of how you feel about it at the moment, you'll be happy with the results. More accurately called Irish moss pie, it is something like a custard or cream pie with a graham-cracker crust and a fruit topping. Since the custard is made from the same substance that is used in the manufacture of ice cream, it's really not bad at all. Take note: unlike the interpretive center, the Seaweed Pie Cafe is open from 11:00 A.M. to 7:00 P.M. Monday to Saturday, Sunday from noon to 8:00 P.M. (902–882–4313). If you get out of your car and walk along the coast north of Miminegash, you'll notice men riding along this shoreline on horseback, pulling what looks like a primitive plow. These are Irish moss harvesters who have switched from the usual method of harvesting on foot. Using horses overcomes the rougher waves and terrain of this end of The Island.

"wouldyou believe?"

The gathering of Irish moss is a surprisingly lucrative career. One man waiting to unload his truck at the "plant" mentioned that his truckload took four days to gather and was worth $1,800.

The image of The Island is one of pastoral splendor and potato fields, so the terrain at the far western tip of the province is more rugged than most people expect.

If you continue north on Route 14 after Miminegash, you will soon come to a village called **Skinners Pond,** childhood home of folk singing legend Stompin' Tom Connors. Although he was born in Saint John, New Brunswick, he was adopted into the Aylward family of Skinners Pond, P.E.I., where he lived until he started hitchhiking across Canada at age fifteen. Eventually he wrote and recorded twenty albums chronicling this country's common man and his life experience. Stompin' Tom received the Order of Canada, and despite his scanty early education he now holds an Honorary Doctorate of Law degree from St. Thomas University.

His childhood home in Skinners Pond is marked by a guitar-trimmed sign outside the tiny school he attended before hitting the road.

Continue north to the rock reef of The Island's northern tip and the historic **North Cape Lighthouse** at **North Cape.** A wide rock reef extends along the shoreline for 1 mile (1.6 km) offshore; on warm days people will wade around in the shallow water as far back as they can get, trying to take pictures.

You will not be able to enter this functioning lighthouse, but it's still worth dropping by for the view. Just as you drive up to the lighthouse, you may notice the whirligigs to your left. They mark the location of the **Atlantic Wind Test Site.** The twirling structures dotting the heath are gigantic wind turbines that are being tested and evaluated for use in harvesting the wind's energy.

The interpretive center at the North Cape Lighthouse includes a video explaining the work of the wind-power laboratory. Guides will answer questions, but the actual lab is closed to the public. Admission to the center is $2.00, which includes an aquarium where you can see local aquatic species like lobsters and mussels. The center is open from 10:00 A.M. to 6:00 P.M. from late May to mid-October. In July and August hours extend from 9:00 A.M. to

8:00 P.M. Upstairs, the **Wind and Reef** restaurant serves delicious (and very fresh) seafood. It is open from late May until the second weekend in October. Sunday to Friday, it's open from 11:30 A.M. to 10:00 P.M., Saturday from 11:30 A.M. to midnight. For a reservation call (902) 882–3535.

From here turn south again, but this time take the left fork onto Route 12, where you will come to some utterly unspoiled fishing villages, including Kildare Capes, Judes Point, Tignish, and Anglo Tignish, as well as the wonderfully uncrowded beaches of Fisherman's Haven and Jacques Cartier Provincial Park. Fisherman's Haven, between Tignish Shore and Kildare Capes, has picnicking facilities.

There are a fine beach and accommodations at the **Jacques Cartier Provincial Park.** On a blazing hot day in August, you'll see perhaps a dozen people at this lovely spot. The water is quite warm here, and the atmosphere is low-key.

While in **Tignish** visit the **Parish Church of St. Simon and St. Jude,** which has a large pipe organ dating back to 1882. Its pipes are up to 16 feet (5 m) tall. The church is a large brick building located at the corner of Maple and Church Streets, near the intersection with the highway.

Its chief historical significance lies in the fact that the organ is a product of the first French Canadian school of organ construction. It is the largest of four tracker-action organs built by the famous Louis Mitchell of Montreal. These pipe organs with huge bellows were operated by a team of two men who pumped air during the performance. Control of the organ was achieved with foot pedals. Many of these organs were either altered to electropneumatic instruments or destroyed as modernity and technology cut a swathe through tradition. This is the only one of its kind outside Quebec that is still intact. Only after most of these large pipe organs were gone from the face of the earth did musicologists, recalling the era of Bach, begin yearning for a return to a purer form of organ music.

The sound of the pipes is greatly enhanced by the neo-Gothic vaults of the church. Legends abound about the arrival of the organ in such an out-of-the-way community. One such story holds that it arrived by accident, and it was only when it was uncrated on the church lawn that a decision was made to keep it. Its assembly cost $2,400 at the time. Today it is considered priceless because of its historical significance, but its projected replacement cost is estimated at roughly $100,000.

You can indulge your passion for sublime music if you happen to be in the neighborhood on a Sunday. There are occasional concerts at other times as well. Because there is not always someone available at the church, you can check concert times by calling the parish house at (902) 882–2049.

Just behind this church is a bed-and-breakfast that was once a convent. It is now called the ***Tignish Heritage Inn.*** There is lots of space for travelers. Although this one-time nun's cloister was built in 1868, it has been considerably revamped; seventeen rooms have their own private bath and shower.

The convent was built so that nuns from Montreal could come and teach in the area. It became a residence for the nuns and was the site of instruction until 1966. It was then used purely as a residence for the sisters until it closed its doors in 1991. When it was taken over in 1993 by a nonprofit group called Tignish Initiatives, careful attention was paid to the preservation of the original structure. Organizers received a 1994 Architectural Preservation Award from the board of governors of the Prince Edward Island Museum and Heritage Foundation. Rates are moderate, with a continental breakfast included. For information or to reserve a spot, call (902) 882–2491 or write to P.O. Box 398, Tignish, PE C0B 2B0.

Just south of Jacques Cartier Provincial Park is ***Alberton,*** the one-time western terminus of The Island's defunct railway, now reborn as the Confederation Trail. From here you can take a deep-sea fishing trip for a reasonable fee ($20 for adults, $15 for seniors and children). There are numerous boats for hire on The Island. In Alberton try ***Andrew's Mist Deep-Sea Fishing,*** which is government-inspected. It is operated by Captain Craig Avery. Equipment is supplied free; you get to keep your cleaned, filleted, and bagged catch. For more information call (902) 853–2307.

trivia

In World War I Canadian soldiers fought alongside the British. The first Allied pilot to shoot down one of Germany's bombers was Wendell W. Rogers, a native of Alberton, P.E.I.

Apart from potatoes and fictional heroines, the rolling green farmland and deep-red soil of P.E.I. have also given birth to a number of excellent golf courses. These are affordable, accessible, and a big hit with visitors and residents alike.

A number of championships have been held on The Island's golf courses. According to Golf Digest, the most challenging course in Atlantic Canada is the ***Mill River Golf Course.*** It was the site of the 1994 Canadian Women's Championship. It was also a stop for the 1997 Canadian Pro Tour, Prince Edward Island Montclair classic. Mill River Golf Course is ranked among the top one hundred public and resort courses in Canada. You can reach it from Alberton by turning south on Route 12 and exiting to Highway 136 south.

Bounded by beautiful stands of hardwoods and spruce, this course features a series of spring-fed ponds down the eighth fairway. Golfers who goof and get their ball in the water are invited to take a drink of the spring water. The greens fees are $42 to $60. You can book ahead at (800) 235–8909 or (902) 859–8873.

Mill River Golf Course is near a Scenic Heritage Road. When you exit the golf course onto Highway 136 east, travel to Fortune Cove. Here you can take the clay Heritage Road by turning right and driving southeast until you reach Highway 142. At this junction, turn left and drive east.

You can't be on Prince Edward Island without paying homage to the potato, which grows so well in The Island's rich red soil. If you are interested enough in the Garden Province's sustaining crop, turn right instead of left at the Highway 142 junction and drive for about twenty minutes down Highway 142 until you reach O'Leary, home of the ***Prince Edward Island Potato Museum.*** It holds a unique collection of antique farm machinery, a community museum, and an authentic one-room school, as well as interactive displays and a sculpture of a giant potato. Admission is $5.00 per person, $12.00 for a family. Visit its Web site at www.peipotatomuseum.com.

Skirting Malpeque Bay

At the time of the European settlement of Prince Edward Island, the Mi'Kmaq of the area were nomadic, hunting game and fishing over a wide range. They settled for only short periods of time in any one area, as the seasons dictated. The white settlers, on the other hand, set about clearing the land and divided it up into lots for farming, establishing a system of ownership completely foreign to the Mi'Kmaq. As more land was cleared and fences built, the population of wild animals diminished. The Mi'Kmaq way of life was imperiled.

Finally, Sir James Montgomery, a wealthy British landlord, gave them the use of ***Lennox Island,*** rent free. By 1800 a missionary had persuaded some of them to live year-round on the island. Seventy years later, after much petitioning of the government and several attempts to resolve the land issue, Lennox Island was purchased for the Mi'Kmaqs. It lies just north of Route 12. You can visit the Band Council Complex on Lennox Island to get an idea of the history of the fifty or so families who still make Lennox Island their home. This band was the first in Canada to convert to Christianity. These indigenous people have just started giving a mixture of light to in-depth exposures to their culture, including traditional food, craft demonstrations, and adventure tourism and ecotourism information. The area features showers and facilities for weary hikers. Admission is $2.00. It is open year-round, from 10:00 A.M. to 6:00 P.M. Monday to Saturday in the summer. On Sundays, it opens at noon. Off-season hours are by appointment. For details, call (866) 831–2702 or (902) 831–2702.

Lennox Island also offers a 24-hour sea kayaking adventure that includes a paddle to a secluded beach, where you set up camp and eat a delicious dinner. Afterward, the beach is yours! The next day you explore the shallow waters and natural scenery of the gulf and bay side of Hog Island. Guides provide the kayaking instruction, and safety and comfort gear as well as a delicious breakfast and dinner (including P.E.I. jams, bread, cheeses, and local oysters, mussels, or lobster. Tours depart and return at noon. Advance booking is advised. Contact Mi'kmaq Kayak Adventures at (877) 500–3131 or (902) 831–3131. Cost is $370. There is also a small craft shop.

If you continue driving east along Route 12, you will see an exit to a secondary road, Route 167. Take this exit and you will soon reach a beautiful, pastoral little village called *Tyne Valley,* population 200.

Here you will find *The Doctor's Inn and Organic Market Garden,* operated by Paul and Jean Offer. The "inn" part of the place is a bed-and-breakfast establishment, making use of the charming former home of the village doctor, built in 1860.

For the environmentally conscious, the Offers provide a number of activities, from gardening to gourmet meals. One of their most popular features is a five-hour workshop on the cultivation and use of organic herbs, the intricacies of organic gardening, composting, and safe and effective insect control.

Nonguests may dine by reservation, with meals a mix of health-conscious, international, and classical cuisine. Although the menu choices are limited, the restaurant has been recommended in a number of national publications. Paul and Jean Offer say, "The gardens provide most of the items for our dinners and also guarantee the freshness we have become noted for." They are open year-round. It's a small place, so try to book ahead by calling (902) 831–3057, or check the Web site at www.peisland.com/doctorsinn. Rates are standard.

If you aren't up to a five-hour workshop, opt for a free informal tour of the two-acre market garden. Organized tours are set for 1:00 P.M. Sunday and Wednesday, from late June to September. If you roam around in the garden, take note of the red "balls" on the fruit trees; these are highly effective sticky insect traps that eliminate the need for bug spray.

While in this charming little hamlet, be sure to check out *Shoreline Sweaters Lobster Pattern,* just a minute's drive farther down Route 12. This is the birthplace of P.E.I.'s answer to the Fair Isle sweater: the copyrighted motif features stylized lobsters on pure Island-spun handcrafted wool.

The results are charming and subtle. Designer Lesley Dubey has often had to point out the lobsters in the complex motif, variations of which are found in cardigans, crew necks, and shawl-collar pullovers. "Once people realize it's really a little lobster, they really like it more than if it was a big lobster sprawled across their back or chest."

The cardigans are graced with pewter buttons decorated with little lobsters. Other creations include sweaters with lady's-slipper and lupine designs.

The shop also sells other craft items, including weavings, baskets, and their own wildflower honey. "We keep bees and have customers who spend summers here, then come and get a supply to take home." The nectars are gathered by "overwintered" bees, which make their honey from the profusion of wildflowers that make Tyne Valley particularly idyllic. Call (902) 831–2950.

Leaving Tyne Valley via Route 12, you will be skirting *Malpeque Bay,* with its many fishing communities. If you continue along Blue Heron Drive, you will soon find yourself at the far eastern end of the bay, at a fork in the road and the village of *Kensington.* From here you have the option of visiting gardens or large-scale models of castles, or backtracking and visiting both. There are also a fine beach and campground at the mouth of Malpeque Bay.

If you take Route 101 to Burlington and then turn right onto Route 234, you will come to *Woodleigh Replicas and Gardens.* Large-scale replicas of castles provide hours of fun in the middle of the countryside. Walk amid small versions of York Minster Cathedral, Scotland's Dunvegan Castle, and the Tower of London and never get out of breath. These replicas reach the height of an NBA basketball star and cover a thirty-three-acre (thirteen-hectare) country garden setting. Some of the little castles have interesting replicas inside. The Tower of London portion, for example, which comprises several of the towers where the famous and infamous were kept in dungeons, also houses a set of "crown jewels." The chopping block where two of Henry VIII's wives lost their heads is reproduced outside.

Colonel Ernest Johnstone, the gentleman who built these replicas as a retirement project, passed away in his eighties, just five years after he completed the "Temple of Flora," which opens on the gardens. Woodleigh is now more than forty-five years old and sufficiently successful that it has spawned the creation of another family venture: The *Kensington Towers and Water Gardens,* in nearby Kensington. Admission to Woodleigh Replicas is $8.50 for adults, $8.00 for seniors, $7.00 for youths, and $4.50 for schoolchildren. Call (902) 836–3401.

Just in front of Woodleigh, you will see a marking for a Scenic Heritage Road. This is Millman Road, which is a handy shortcut to Route 20, also known as Blue Heron Drive.

Farther along Blue Heron Drive, you'll come to Malpeque itself and then to *Cabot Beach Provincial Park.* The park has small beaches and is far enough off the tourist trail that it is a pleasantly quiet spot for camping. Its two quiet campsites are far from the maddening crowd that congregates during the tourist high season at Cavendish. These red-sand beaches are opposite each other across a sheltered bay and offer warm water and an unhurried rest only a few miles north of Summerside. The beaches—indeed, the entire shoreline—have a shelf of hard clay upon which bathers can walk from beach to beach, pausing along the way at sheltered spots where the water is bathtub-warm.

This was the location for the filming of the popular Canadian television series Emily of New Moon. Part of the filming required a schoolhouse, so the former Fanning School, built in 1794 and named after Governor Fanning, was restored and moved to Cabot Beach. Unique because it was a two-story schoolhouse, the building remains in Cabot Beach's day-use area. It's open daily 10:00 A.M. to sunset during the summer.

Because they are both small campsites, it is advisable to book in advance, especially during the high season. For information call (902) 836–4142 for Twin Shores, (902) 836–8945 for Cabot Beach.

Anne's Land

Past Darnley Basin and headed east you will soon come to **Park Corner,** still on Route 20. Several sites in this village recall The Island's famous author, but in a sedate way as compared with the tourist draw near Lucy Maud Montgomery's fabled home in Cavendish. These sites are less hectic alternatives if you happen to be an "Anne fan."

The first one that you will come to is the **Anne of Green Gables Museum at Silver Bush.** Silver Bush (so named by Montgomery) was the home of the writer's aunt and was built in 1872. The place remains much as it was in Montgomery's time. Because the author was married in the parlor, young Japanese couples often arrange with the owner to tie the knot here, but otherwise the house is not a slick, professionally assembled museum but, rather, a cozy old home. There is a little tearoom for visitors as well as wagon rides on site. When you peek at the lovely old bedsteads and furnishings, it isn't hard to understand why Montgomery said her ideal home would be an exact duplicate of this.

The farmhouse overlooks the pond for which she coined the name "The Lake of Shining Waters." Admission is $2.55 for adults, 75 cents for children. Open daily in July and August from 9:00 A.M. to 5:30 P.M., it closes one-half hour earlier in June and September. October hours are 10:00 A.M. to 4:00 P.M. For details, or to ask about group rates, call (800) 665–2663. You can also visit the Anne of Green Gables Society at www.annesociety.org.

After you leave this museum, the little pond will be on your left. Just after passing over a little stream, you will come to the next "Anne site."

The **Lucy Maud Montgomery Heritage Museum** was the home of Montgomery's grandfather, an Island senator. Still owned by the family, the house has been turned into an "attraction." It holds many family heirlooms and is largely unchanged since the time of the author's frequent visits, which she wrote about in her journals. Admission is $2.50 for adults. Call (902) 886–2807 or (902) 886–2752 for more information.

Just after passing Park Corner and continuing along Route 20, you will come to **French River,** a picturesque fishing community overlooking New London Bay. Apart from the photographic possibilities, you are directly across the water from Prince Edward Island National Park, which comprises several seemingly endless beaches, and the majority of the sites relating to Anne of Green Gables.

A small village called **Stanley Bridge** is a good place to stay if you want to visit the Cavendish area. Located at the junction of Routes 6, 224, and 254, the village is a mere 5 miles (8 km) west of Cavendish. Here you will find the cottages and country inn of **Stanley Bridge Country Resort.**

worthseeing

Certainly not off the beaten path is a visit to the birthplace of **Lucy Maud Montgomery,** beloved author of the *Anne of Green Gables* books. The cozy white and green Victorian house overlooks New London Harbour. The period decor and furnishings include memorabilia and scrap books from the author's life. Her wedding dress is also on display. She is so esteemed by the Japanese, that thousands make a pilgrimage to this cultural icon's birthplace annually. The house is found at the intersection of Routes 6 and 20. Open daily from mid-May to Thanksgiving. A small admission is charged.

All the cottages as well as a completely renovated motel have been constructed from lumber cut from the owners' woodlot, with rustic pine walls and floors and cathedral ceilings in an open-beam country style. With such amenities as hot tubs and two playgrounds for children, owners warn visitors to book as far ahead as January for weeklong stays. Rates are moderate to deluxe. Write to the resort at Route 6, PE C0B 1M0. For information call (902) 886–2882; for reservations, call (800) 361–2882.

In the resort complex you will find **Stanley Bridge Antiques, Gifts & Gallery** a good bet for locally made quilts as well as reproduction tin lighting, pewter, hand-forged iron, and other collectibles that can help to create a country-style decor in a house.

P.E.I.'s Scenic Heritage Drives

So-called **Scenic Heritage Roads** dot the province and are a good opportunity to experience the old Prince Edward Island. The clay roads are generally covered with a canopy of trees casting shade across the unspoiled beauty of farmlands that ramble down to the water. You'll have views of old farmhouses and barns, paint fading and cracking off, and herds of grazing dairy cows. Some fields are carefully laid out in row after row of potato plants. It's like time travel. This is the land that Lucy Maud Montgomery wrote about so lovingly in Anne of Green Gables.

These roads are best traveled after a brief spell of rain, when they're not too wet to turn into mud yet not so dry as to be a dust bowl.

Near Mill River Resort, along Route 136, you will find a scenic drive called the John Joe Road or the Hackney Road. It is bordered by fields of grain and potatoes, alternated with woodland to create a habitat much beloved by the gray partridge and the ruffed grouse.

It runs about 1.5 miles (2.2 km) south from Route 136 until it meets Kelly Road, also known as Route 142. Before 1912 this was a cart track that led to a homestead in the woods. Near its southern end you will find traces of an old stagecoach route.

Other craft shops in the area include ***Granny's Trunk*** on Route 6, west of Cavendish. This store, which features some prize-winning quilts, also sells home-baked goodies. It's located 1½ miles (2 km) from the intersection at Stanley Bridge, in the direction of Cavendish. Call (902) 886–2030. It's open from 9:00 A.M. to 5:00 P.M. daily in the tourist season.

On this end of The Island, the eatery with the reputation for the freshest fish is the ***New London Seafood Restaurant.*** Situated right on the wharf in New London, it gives new meaning to the phrase "catch of the day." It's a huge place, with a seating capacity of one hundred. Two full walls of windows yield a spectacular view of the bay, featuring the comings and goings of the local fishing fleet and pleasure boats. Owners Linda and Roger Cole run this family-style restaurant.

This area is noted for its Island blue cultured mussels as well as Malpeque oysters, which are exported worldwide. The chowders in this end of the country are delicious and reasonably priced. The restaurant also has a traditional lobster dinner. These dinners include potato salad, either seafood chowder or mussels, rolls, and homemade pie. Lobsters also find their way into sandwiches and salad rolls. The restaurant is open from early June until early October. To reserve, phone (902) 886–3000.

Two antiques shops are also in the neighborhood. On Route 238, off Route 6, you will find **Linden Cove Antiques.** The shop specializes in high-quality mahogany, walnut, and oak furniture and tableware.

If you are interested in looking at or buying a painting, the best selection is at **The Dunes Studio Gallery,** overlooking Brackley Beach on Route 15. You cannot miss this building: Virtually all windows, it is a contemporary masterpiece complete with spiral staircase, an excellent view, and a substantial water garden.

The works of many prominent provincial artists are on display here. Their works include The Island's most high-end paintings, pottery, crafts, sculptures, photographs, and prints. The Dunes has a cafe, a roof garden, and a fourth-floor lookout. It opens for the summer in May, closes for the winter in October, and will open at other times of the year by appointment. From June to September, the Dunes is open from 9:00 A.M. to 10:00 P.M. The gallery is open from May to October with modified hours. Phone (902) 672–2586.

The North Shore and Charlottetown

To bypass the most heavily visited end of Prince Edward Island National Park near Cavendish but still sample The Island's best beaches, continue east along the coastal route until you reach **Dalvay by-the-Sea.** This is a small, intimate, and charming establishment at the far eastern end of the park, a short drive from the park's eastern gateway. Dalvay overlooks Tracadie Bay and is reached by a left turn after Grand Tracadie.

At the turn of the century people from other parts of the country discovered Prince Edward Island's unique charms and the opportunity it offered to get away from it all. Some wealthy families built large summer homes here. Dalvay by-the-Sea, built in 1895, is the most notable of these homes. It was originally the home of the U.S. citizen and president of Standard Oil Company, born in Scotland, who found in Dalvay the perfect home-away-from-home. He therefore named it for his birthplace. The home eventually changed hands several times and became a hotel.

Along with the calm atmosphere and lovely vista, Dalvay boasts an excellent restaurant. There are canoes and croquet sets, big old-fashioned bathtubs, and the massive stone hearths of half a dozen fireplaces.

Fans of the television show *The Road to Avonlea* will recognize the Dalvay, on which it is depicted as the "White Sands Hotel." This Victorian hotel is unquestionably one of the most elegant country inns on all the east coast of Canada. Reserve rooms by writing to D. Thompson, Box 8, Little York, PE C0A 1P0 or by calling (902) 672–2048. Rates are deluxe.

From Dalvay you have the choice of cutting across the province to Charlottetown or continuing east to the more remote fishing villages and beaches
of the far eastern end of The Island. Traveling from Dalvay to Charlottetown is
a simple matter. Get onto Route 6 and drive in the direction of Bedford. Just
after Bedford turn right onto Route 2 and continue on into Charlottetown.

Charlottetown may be the provincial capital, but it is a far cry from a big
city. Its streets were so narrow in the early part of this century that when cars
came on the scene, they were banned from the entire province in 1913. This
law was not repealed until 1919.

Charlottetown is a relaxed little place that played a starring role in the
founding of Canada, since it was the site of the first conference on Confederation in 1864. (P.E.I. opted out of joining when Confederation took place in
1867, joining later, in 1873.)

The town is a good starting point for a cycle tour of the province. For
rentals and advice, visit Gordon MacQueen at 430 Queen Street, Charlottetown,
PE C1A 4E8. The proprietor of *MacQueen's Bike Shop* can also arrange for
on-road service. For reservations or a brochure, call (800) WOW-CUBA or (902)
368–2453. The shop and touring company has a detailed Web site that outlines
a variety of bike touring resources on The Island for either the independent
cycle tourist or for groups desiring more support. In the off-season, the shop's
experienced guides offer trips to other exotic locales like Cuba and Sicily. Visit
www.macqueens.com.

While in Charlottetown you can engage in a little time travel by visiting
Beaconsfield Historic House, which is in the city's poshest neighborhood.
This museum overlooks the harbor and the lieutenant governor's residence,

Beaconsfield Historic House

Charlottetown's Historic Homes

Charlottetown's many Georgian, Queen Anne Revival, and Victorian buildings add to the town's charm. Among the more interesting houses are:

Beaconsfield Historic House, at 2 Kent Street (902–366–6603). This three-and-a-half-story house was built in 1877.

Government House, on the grounds of Victoria Park, at the corner of Pond Road and Park Roadway (no phone number available). Built in 1834, Government House is the home of the lieutenant governor, who acts as a representative of the queen. The house is open to the public only during the annual New Year's levee.

Province House, at the corner of Richmond and Saint George Streets (902–566–7626). It is here that you will find the provincial government, when it is in session. The house's Confederation Chamber is where in 1864 the Fathers of Confederation discussed the possibility of the British North American colonies joining together to form the Dominion of Canada. Three years later Nova Scotia, New Brunswick, Ontario, and Quebec did join together, but P.E.I. did not.

Ardgowan National Historic Site, at 2 Palmers Lane (902–566–7050). When the delegates were finished at Province House, they gathered for a grand reception at the home of fellow politician William Henry Pope at what is now known as Ardgowan National Historic Site. The home's Victorian-style grounds have been restored to illustrate the style of the 1860s.

Government House. Beaconsville is located at 2 Kent Street; you may find yourself driving around in circles if you don't hang a right after Richmond Street, thereby avoiding several one-way streets.

The home was built by a shipbuilder in 1877 at a cost of $50,000, at a time when decent annual salaries averaged $300. The three-and-a-half-story home features a double drawing room, nine decorative fireplaces, gaslight, and central heating. Faced with financial ruin after five short years, the original owner moved on.

Some of the original owner's creditors took it over, and when they couldn't sell it, they moved in. The new residents, the Cundalls, were a sober and dour lot. None of them married, and in 1916, when the last of them died, the home was turned into a "home for friendless young women" where they could get training in "useful arts." By 1935 it had become a student nurses' residence.

In the mid-1970s Beaconsfield became the headquarters of the Prince Edward Island Museum and Heritage Foundation. The home is restored to the era when it was a private home, with period furniture and careful renovations. Even the little nursery is laid out as if the children had just been called away to supper.

Take a moment to look over the floor in the main hallway, made of painstakingly hand-laid tiles in an intricate mosaic pattern. The base of the spiral staircase has an original classic Greco-Roman statue lamp, converted from gas to electric. If you climb the stairs to the top, you can enter "the belvedere," an elegant enclosed lookout that offers beautiful views. Admission is by donation.

Every Friday during the summer there is an excellent *ceilidh,* or Gaelic party, at the ***Irish Hall,*** at 582 North River Road, featuring traditional Celtic song and dance by The Island's best traditional performers. This is a bargain at only $8.00 admission for adults, $3.00 for children younger than twelve. Music plays from 8:00 P.M. to 10:30 P.M. For details call (902) 892–2367.

Also in Charlottetown is the much-loved ***Confederation Centre of the Arts.*** In 2005, the production of *Anne of Green Gables* enters its fortieth year of successful performances. It is the must-see show of The Island, quite possibly of the Maritimes.

Here you can also take in a free show of the young performers-in-training, at the outdoor amphitheater at noon in the summer. Other performances take place at 5:00 P.M. The Young Company presents shows attended by more than 1,000 spectators at times. Seating is on steplike benches and on the ground, so bring a pillow, blanket, or chair if you wish. Many of the young people in these shows end up with careers in the performing arts, so it's a good opportunity to see them in their fledgling roles. For details, call (800) 565–0278 within the Maritimes or (902) 566–1267; or write to 145 Richmond Street, Charlottetown, PE C1A 1J1.

The Confederation Centre of the Arts also houses the largest art gallery and museum east of Montreal, with more than 15,000 works in the permanent collection. To find the complex, head to downtown Charlottetown via Queen Street. From there turn left onto Richmond Street, a block before the harbor. It is wheelchair accessible.

If you decided to pass up Charlottetown for more rural delights, or if you wanted to save the capital until you've worked your way fully around the circle, exit Dalvay onto Route 6, but then turn left onto Route 2. (You will still take this route if you head east from Charlottetown.)

Following Route 2, you will steadily drive uphill until you come to ***Mount Stewart.***

Mount Stewart is the perfect spot for sampling a bit of the Confederation Trail, the multiuse railroad bed turned trail stretching from one tip of The Island to the other. The trails are 10 feet (3 m) wide, and are surfaced with stone dust. They accommodate walkers, bicycles, and even wheelchairs. Along this segment of the trail, three bridges span rivers and estuaries and skirt the north shore's pristine St. Peters Bay.

At Mount Stewart you can rent bikes or, to ease bike-touring stress, take advantage of a shuttle service operated by *Trailside Adventures.*

Trailside Adventures also operates an outdoor adventure shop, a small cafe, and overnight accommodations in a Heritage-style inn. Guidebooks and maps are also on sale here. You can find them on Route 22, off Route 2. The street address is 109 Main Street, Mount Stewart. Trailside Adventures is open from June to mid-September and off-season by appointment, according to owner Doug Deacon. He advises that since cycle tours are so weather dependent, summertime cyclists make their arrangements when they arrive. On a recent night every room in Deacon's inn was rented to a cyclist. Deacon can make rental deals for his guests, or shuttles luggage to other inns, and connect you to a canoe rental off-site, so a number of adventures await. For details or reservations call (888) 704–6595 or (902) 676–3130, or visit www.trailside.ca.

The *Trailside Inn and Cafe* has also become a venue for live musical performances by many noted Canadian artists. Check the Trailside Inn's Web site for dates and times.

Still on Route 2, in the midst of Mount Stewart, you will come to St. Peters Road. Take a right turn onto this road and drive another 2 miles (3.2 km) to the small community of *St. Andrews,* where you'll see a sign designating the *Bishop MacEachern National Historic Site.* This is where you will find the "Little Church that's Been to Town and Back," a historic chapel built in 1803.

St. Andrews Chapel was built by the Scottish settlers who had immigrated in 1772. It was the first major church on The Island, but by 1862 it was abandoned in favor of a larger building. Two years later the congregation embarked on a strange undertaking: With the help of 500 men and fifty teams

St. Andrews Chapel

of horses, the old church was placed on runners and hoisted onto a frozen river to be transported down to Charlottetown. As the little church approached the thin ice of the channel, disaster struck. The building crashed through the ice. With considerable effort the church was dragged out of the water and landed on Pownal Street. There it served as a girls' school for more than one hundred years.

The church was returned to the village in 1990, following a fire that destroyed some additions but left much of the original structure intact. To achieve this second move, the building was cut into four pieces and mounted on a flatbed truck. Now back in its former home, the fully restored church is a fine example of eighteenth-century Georgian architecture, which at the time of the church's original construction was much in use by the early settlers from England and Scotland.

The round-headed windows on the building were discovered during the restoration and refurbishing that followed the near-destruction of the little church by fire in 1987.

The church is designated the Bishop MacEachern National Historic Site because it shares its site with the mausoleum of the revered Bishop MacEachern, who oversaw its original construction in 1803. As a young priest Father MacEachern proved his mettle by ministering to a flock that spread as far afield as New Brunswick. To cover his vast territory on the rudimentary roads, he resorted to snowshoes, skates, horseback, and, finally, a vehicle that combined the features of carriage, boat, and sled. This unusual conveyance can still be found at **St. Joseph's Convent** in Charlottetown.

The Friends of St. Andrews is a community group that administers the restored church. Concerts are held here from time to time, so it is a good idea to ask about upcoming events at the reception desk. The Friends of St. Andrews can be reached by calling the home of Mary McInnis at (902) 676–2045 or by writing to The Friends of St. Andrews, P.O. Box 1864, Charlottetown, PE C1A 7N5.

Retrace your steps 2 miles along St. Peters Road and rejoin Route 2 headed east, which will take you along the north shore.

Although the eastern end of the province is not geared up for large numbers of tourists, there are some nice campsites and charming bed-and-breakfast inns. In the area of **Albion Cross** is the **Needles and Haystacks Bed and Breakfast.** This is inland rather than on the shore, but its central location offers some advantages to golfers, outdoors-people, and fans of the fiddle. The B&B is about 15 miles (25 km) from the Links at Crowbush Cove Golf Course and about twenty minutes from Brudenell Golf Course.

To get there drive inland on Route 2 from St. Peters until you get to Ding-well's Mills, then turn right onto Route 4 and continue to Albion Cross. Make a left on Highway 327; a sign will soon direct you to the inn.

The big yellow home with dormers and bay windows dates back to the 1880s and is furnished with antiques. For years, before the passing away of proprietor Fred Foster's wife, Betty, one could witness traditional quiltmaking in the house. The finished quilts are still there.

The hospitality remains. Fred Foster plays an active role in the community and is a good source of information on local events, including outings for Celtic music fans. The annual Rollo Bay Fiddle Festival, held the third weekend in July, is a short drive away. "It's a blast," says Fred. "People just have a great time, and a lot of Cape Breton fiddlers come over, too." Rates for the inn are moderate. Call (902) 583–2928. Golf packages are available.

Along with quiet walks through the fields and woods, you have the oppor-tunity in this area to go on a deep-sea-fishing charter. Just after St. Peters Bay, a few miles up the coast, is a cozy little harbor, *Naufrage,* which is French for "shipwreck." It is a rustic harbor, complete with picturesque cliffs and light-house, a tiny river flowing through the middle of the cove, and a sandy beach.

There are a number of options for fishing in this end of The Island. At **North Lake** are several charter operations: One is **MacNeill's Tuna and Deep-Sea Fishing** at (902) 357–2858.

Some tours charge as little as $25 per person and half price for kids for a simple deep-sea excursion. Paying for a tuna fishing trip can be a bit like buy-ing a lottery ticket. A full eight-hour tuna boat charter can run $500, with a half-day charter at $250. But, if you land a bluefin tuna on MacNeill's boat, you don't pay a cent. Then again, let's see you pack a tuna into your suitcase.

If you decide to use North Lake as your point of departure for a fishing expedition, you may prefer to stay in St. Peters Bay.

Where the Tides Meet

Continuing along the coast on Route 16, turn left at East Point and drive a short distance to the easternmost point of The Island and the 64-foot **East Point Lighthouse.** Energetic visitors who opt to climb to the top will be rewarded with a view of the swirling tides as the waves from the Northumberland Strait meet and crash against the surf of the Gulf of Saint Lawrence. Ask the guides for the lowdown on what to look for before you take the climb.

The building that originally held the fog alarm and radio equipment has now been turned into a small shop featuring an excellent selection of regional books and Island-made crafts, including Island-made woolen garments using wool from local sheep. The small canteen makes a good bird-watching pit stop. You can indulge in a cup of coffee and then stretch out and watch cormorants dive for fish while seals loll about the shore.

The coastline here has been so heavily eroded by the action of the waves that the lighthouse has been moved twice, including after the shipwreck of a British warship. This lighthouse was built in 1867 and is one of the oldest on The Island. Admission is $2.50 for adults, $1.00 for children six and older, and free for those younger. For details call (902) 357–2106.

After viewing the lighthouse head back to East Point. Take a left turn onto Route 16 southbound.

At South Lake is the junction of Route 16A. At this point turn right to drive to *Elmira* to visit the *Elmira Railway Museum.*

The museum is located next to the end point of the *Confederation Trail,* converted from the railroad line when train service was shut down on The Island. The portion in this area was the section chosen for the pilot project. All along this beautiful nature trail are rest stops in converted train stations. The rustic entranceway to the trail is just to your right as you approach the Elmira Railway Museum's reception center. You can rent bicycles at the museum.

The museum is set in the eastern terminus of the railway. Finished in 1912, it was the last station built. It has telegraph equipment that is still in working condition; there are also fare books, schedules, and artifacts from days gone by. The station office looks exactly as it must have looked when the railway was still being run in the British colonial tradition: Gentlemen and ladies had separate waiting rooms, because, the guide explains, "The men would spit into

Touring P.E.I. on Two Wheels

Why is bicycling so popular on Prince Edward Island? Because it is almost impossible to find a more ideal place for this mode of travel. On the Confederation Trail, the original railway builders avoided the high cost of cutting through hills and valleys by winding the track around such annoyances instead. The result is a really smooth trail ride that yields abundant natural beauty and a stunning view around every corner. And all you need are a moderate level of skill and muscle power, unless you are trying to set speed records.

Distances from one community or amenity to the next are short. Every few miles, cyclists will discover a coffee shop, tearoom, antiques shop, bed-and-breakfast, or even a bicycle repair shop. Traffic is nonexistent. The climate is mild, which is ideal for outdoor activity. And, more important than anything for lazy cyclists such as myself, it's not very hilly. When it comes to biking, you can't beat P.E.I.

Railway Fever and the Story of Confederation

As tiny as The Island is, the railway boom of the last century played an important role in P.E.I. history. Remember that although there was a conference on confederation in Prince Edward Island in 1864, Islanders decided not to join the union of Nova Scotia, New Brunswick, Ontario, and Quebec in 1867. They feared that their voice would be overwhelmed by the much greater numbers of voters elsewhere.

By 1870, however, "railway fever" hit The Island in a big way. Islanders were convinced that a railroad would bring new factories, easier access to markets for farmers, and prosperity to every doorstep. Soon all the villages wanted to be connected to the main line, and the rails zigzagged across The Island like topstitching on a crazy quilt.

In short order the railway ran up an unmanageable debt. The Island government was unable to pay its lenders, mostly British banks, and by 1872 a series of railway scandals had toppled it. The Canadian Confederation offered to take over the debt and provide railway service under its administration. In exchange P.E.I. would become part of Canada—hence the name Confederation Trail.

the spittoons and curse and shock the ladies." After Canadian National took over, separate waiting rooms became a thing of the past, and ladies were free to be as shocked as they pleased. Admission is $2.00.

From here turn back onto Route 16A, then right onto Route 16, and continue driving south toward **Basin Head.** This is a great spot for photography buffs and bird-watchers. The area boasts the **Basin Head Fisheries Museum** (902–357–7233), constructed on a headland overlooking one of The Island's finest white-sand beaches. The sand here is so pure that it squeaks when you walk on it. The main beach is popular; however, a five-minute walk south, along the beach, takes you to miles of blissfully secluded sands.

The museum depicts the transition of Prince Edward Island's inshore fishery. By now you will have noticed the large number of "farmed mussels" on The Island; aquaculture has grown into a thriving segment of P.E.I.'s fishery. Here you can also tour a one-time fish cannery that now houses a coastal exhibit.

The museum is open from mid-June to late September. In July and August it is open daily from 9:00 A.M. to 5:00 P.M. In other months, times vary. A small admission fee is charged.

After Basin Head you will head south in the direction of **Souris.** If time allows and you feel like a country walk, you can take in a Heritage Scenic Road—one of The Island's prettiest—by making a small detour. To do this, when you reach Little Harbour, turn right off Route 16 onto Route 303, also known as the New Harmony Road. From there continue to Greenvale.

A small clay road connects Greenvale Road to the Tarantum Road (also known as Route 304) for a distance of about 1 mile (1.6 km). Sunlight peeks through a lush canopy, created by a mixture of hardwoods and softwoods, and falls on the brilliant green of thick vegetation and the hardened clay of the old road. On the eastern side of this road, the Provincial Department of Energy and Forestry operates a demonstration woodlot that is open to the public.

During Prohibition years the isolation of the canopied road made it a favorite haunt of rum runners, who used the area to stash illegal cargo.

Souris is also the ferry terminal for the boat to the Magdalen Islands, so the town always has a flow of visitors passing through during the summer. Incidentally, the name *Souris* comes from the French word for "mouse." In the early to mid-1700s, plagues of field mice overran the settlement, giving the place its unusual name.

A nice place to stay in Souris is **The Matthew House Inn,** which features Victorian art and furniture, and several fireplaces (nice for cozy breakfasts). The spacious Victorian inn was once the home of Uriah Matthew, a partner in Matthew, McLean, and Company, which operated the village's general store, the harbor wharf, and a fleet of thirty fishing boats as well as a lobster company and shipping operation that sent goods as far afield as the West Indies. The charming redecorated Victorian-era inn was acquired in 1995 by the Olivieri family, who blended its nostalgic contents with their own antiques and artwork brought from their home in Rome, Italy. Their street address is 15 Breakwater Street, Souris, PE C0A 2B0.

You can't miss the inn if you look for the Magdalen Islands Ferry, which is a stone's throw away. Call (902) 687–3461 for reservations. Rates are deluxe.

Just outside Souris, on Route 2, is Rollo Bay. Each summer, on the third weekend in July, lovers of traditional fiddle music can have a great time at the **Rollo Bay Fiddle Festival,** which features talent from all over North America. The big attraction is fiddle music, including traditional Celtic violin strathbanes, jigs, and reels played in open-air settings. There are also old-time dances. For a detailed itinerary, call (902) 687–2584 or visit their Web site at www.rollobay fiddlefest.com.

Just south of Rollo Bay, you'll come to a fork in the road that leads to **Bay Fortune.** Turn onto Route 310. Here you will find **The Inn at Bay Fortune,** one of the best restaurants on The Island. It was the location for Canadian Television's Life Network cooking show **The Inn Chef.** At a chef's table each evening, guests are seated in a glassed-in, air-conditioned, and sound-reduced room inside the kitchen to watch the meal take shape. Periodically throughout

Island Blue Mussels and Sweet Potato Chowder

Courtesy of the Inn at Bay Fortune

5 pounds Island blue mussels

4 tablespoons water

4 tablespoons (½ stick) butter

1 large onion, chopped (about 2 cups)

4 cloves garlic, chopped

2 cups milk

1 cup heavy cream

1 teaspoon Bay Fortune seasoning (see recipe next page)

1 teaspoon salt

1 teaspoon Tabasco sauce

2 medium carrots, peeled and grated

2 medium sweet potatoes, peeled and grated

1. Place mussels and water in a pot with a tight-fitting lid. Steam the mussels over high heat for 10 to 12 minutes, until the shells open. Discard any mussels that didn't open. Remove meat from shells and set meat aside. Reserve some shells to use in presentation. Strain and reserve remaining liquid.

2. In a large pot, melt the butter, and sauté onions over high heat for about 10 minutes. Stir frequently, turning the heat down slightly every few minutes to prevent burning. Add garlic and continue cooking until onions are golden brown. Add the remaining ingredients and 1 cup of the reserved mussel broth.

3. Bring mixture to a boil, reduce heat to low, cover pot, and let simmer gently for 30 minutes. Stir frequently to prevent scorching on the bottom of the pot.

4. While the soup is simmering, make the spicy butter (see recipe next page) After 30 minutes, check the soup vegetables for doneness. If soft, remove the pot from the heat. If the vegetables are still slightly al dente, simmer a few minutes longer, or until done.

5. Puree soup thoroughly in a blender, and strain through a fine mesh strainer. If necessary, adjust consistency of the soup with remaining mussel liquid. The soup should be pleasantly thick, but not goopy.

6. Return soup to the pot and heat it, stirring frequently, until it is almost at serving temperature. Add the reserved mussel meat and heat, stirring, for a few minutes until heated through. Serve chowder immediately, with spicy butter swirled around the surface of the soup.

the meal the chef visits the guests to go over details of the menu and meal preparation. The inn is open from Victoria Day weekend in May until Canadian Thanksgiving weekend (U.S. Columbus Day) in October. For details or reservations, call (902) 687–3745 in the summer or (860) 563–6090 in the winter, or write to The Inn at Bay Fortune, Souris, PE C0A 2B0, or visit www.innatBay Fortune.com. Rates are deluxe.

Spicy Butter Swirls

2 tablespoons butter

½ tablespoon Tabasco

2 tablespoons heavy cream

¼ teaspoon ground allspice

2 tablespoons molasses

¼ teaspoon ground cloves

Put all of the ingredients in a small saucepan and bring the mixture to a simmer, stirring frequently. Remove from the heat, and allow the mixture to cool to room temperature.

Bay Fortune Seasoning

To make Bay Fortune Seasoning, simply combine equal parts, by weight, of whole dried bay laurel leaf, coriander seed, and fennel seed. Grind together in a spice grinder and store powder in an airtight, opaque container (light will damage the flavor of this seasoning).

Apart from the class and gourmet delights, the inn is a cozy place with an interesting history. It was the former summer home of playwright Elmer Harris, who wrote the 1940s play Johnny *Belinda*. After this was a huge success on Broadway, it was made into a movie. The playwright's summer home was a writers' colony where many of his friends summered and wrote. Eventually it became the home of actress Colleen Dewhurst, well known in her many film roles and also as Marilla in the television series *Anne of Green Gables*. She was the wife of George C. Scott, whose son was married here.

When the beloved actress died of cancer several years ago, her summer home was made over into an inn. The place has a lovely view of the bay.

Hills and Harbors

After enjoying Bay Fortune, continue south along Route 2 until you reach Dingwells Mills, where you'll turn left onto Route 4 and continue to Pooles Corner. Then turn left onto Route 3 and continue until you reach the ***Brudenell River Provincial Park.***

This park has quite a lot to offer in the way of pleasant diversions: trail rides, canoe and kayaking adventures, a championship-level golf course, a riverside beach, and a marina for water sports. If camping is not your style, there is a collection of chalets along the river, although they seem quite small and boxy and lacking in privacy. Organized activities emphasize the natural setting, with walking trails that will take you along pathways lined with wild-flowers or through marshland. Bike paths lead to Georgetown and Cardigan, at 5 and 7 miles (7 and 11 km) respectively, with the Cardigan path traversing the old rail-line-turned-Confederation Trail. To make campsite or cabin reservations, call (902) 652–8966.

The golf course at **Brudenell** has been host to numerous national and Canadian Professional Golf Association tournaments. Its pristine riverside setting, immaculate greens, and tree-lined fairways offer a challenge to golfers of all levels. Greens fees are $70 to $80.

At Brudenell you can rent horses and go on a romantic, not to mention scenic, trail ride along the beach at sunset and other times, accompanied by an experienced guide. These are available only by reservation. For information call **Brudenell Trail Rides** at (902) 652–2396. There are several other exciting diversions in this area, including an opportunity to go sea kayaking along secluded offshore islands and sandy coves.

The marina comes in handy if you are interested in taking a look at a harbor seal colony. **Cruise Manada,** run by Captain Dan Bears, departs from the Montague Marina at various times throughout the day. Along with the cruise,

Collector's Side Trip!

During the second-to-last weekend in September, antiques and collectible fans will have a field day at this end of the province. A loop of road that follows the coast from Cape Bear to Orwell Corner (more or less), is home to the *70-Mile Coastal Yard Sale,* which features over a hundred yard sale sites along the route. Many of these are multifamily sites with lots of treasures culled from old farmsteads and Grandma's trunk. No need to pack a lunch; lots of food is available en route, everything from home-baked goodies to barbecue, chili, chowder, and sandwiches. Hot coffee and soft drinks are also in abundance.

Many gift and craft shops hold special sales along the route, and there is an art show and sale at the Little Sands United Church. Entry points to the sale will have maps of the route.

This sale happens rain or shine.

When you get tired of collecting, you just have to stop along the shore to visit some of the beautiful lighthouses in the area. Besides Point Prim's lovely redbrick lighthouse, you can visit Cape Bear's lighthouse and the nearby Marconi Station, where the Titanic's distress signal was first received.

Bears takes his passengers to a mussel farm where The Island's famous Atlantic blue mussels are grown. The whole trip takes two hours. If you are lucky, you may see a whale, harbor porpoise, or osprey in addition to the many seabirds in the area. The cruise is $20 for adults, with discounts for seniors and children. For information call (902) 838–3444.

Stay at nearby Montague or try camping at Panmure Island. To get to **Panmure Island Provincial Park,** drive east along Route 17 from Montague. Panmure Island offers two kinds of beaches: one fronting St. Mary's Bay and one open to the gulf. Set in a lovely pastoral area, the view of the ocean and the spaciousness of the hundred-acre campground are a bargain, with camping fees starting at $19 daily. For information on this or other camping areas in the eastern end of The Island, write to P.O. Box 370, Montague, PE C0A 1R0 or call (902) 838–0668.

Where do the buffalo roam these days? This wouldn't seem to be a likely question if you're on Prince Edward Island, but you will find a herd of buffalo at **Buffaloland Provincial Park,** just 3.8 miles (6 km) south of Montague on Highway 4.

In May 1970 fifteen young buffalo arrived on The Island as a gift from Saskatchewan to the government of P.E.I. Culling the herd keeps their number down to about 25.

The park is bisected by a long, fenced-in column that people can walk down to get a feeling of being surrounded by a herd of wild buffalo. A raised platform with steps makes it possible to look out over the herd.

Calves are born in May or June. In the past the herd has reached 60 or 70 head before culling. To thin the herd the animals designated for slaughter are put out to pasture. The day I visited, several carloads of Mi'Kmaqs from Nova Scotia were there to take a look. They had just been to the big annual Abegweit Powwow at Panmure Island.

A herd of buffalo is something to see in the spring, when the animals are in heat. The elder bull buffalo make a circle around the females to protect them at the first sign of humans dropping by to take a look. If you get too close, they'll charge right at you and ram into the fence, which doesn't look like a very sturdy defense.

Interpretive signs explain details of the life of the buffalo. On sunny days it takes a lot to coax them out from under the trees at the back of the park, so if you have time and want to see the buffalo at their best, pick an overcast morning or early evening that's not too hot. Admission to Buffaloland is free.

Next drive southeast to **Murray Harbour,** a nice, out-of-the-way fishing community. When you reach Murray River, cross the bridge and exit left onto Route 18 in the direction of Murray Harbour.

There are several things to see in this area, including the ***Log Cabin Museum.*** It's located on Route 18A, the exit for which is just before you reach the village.

This privately owned museum houses antiques dating back 200 years as well as a collection of still-operable phonographs, including Edison cylinder machines from 1895 and 1905 and a 1905 RCA Victor. Highlights include hearing the old phonographs and playing a cylindrical record of Sir Harry Lauder, an English singer from the turn of the century. The more recent record player was shown off with a record from the 1940s: Patti Page singing "How Much Is That Doggie in the Window?"

The impressive group of antiques was assembled by a private collector named Preston Robertson, who had to keep building additions onto the original log cabin in order to house his ever-growing collection. Another large log structure extends out the back to contain his sleighs and buggies, including a beautiful 140-year-old sleigh. Admission is $2.50 for adults, 50 cents for school-aged children.

Murray Harbour also has a good seal-watching opportunity in the form of ***Marine Adventures Deep-Sea Fishing Cruises.*** During July and August (in Murray Harbour) passengers visit the largest seal colony on The Island, and at Bird Island they can see thousands of cormorants, blue herons, arctic terns, and bald eagles. The cost is $25 for adults, $15 for children. For details call (800) 496–2494.

From Murray Harbour you can drive in either direction on Route 18, but if you take the inland route you will soon reach a fork in the road to Route 4. Turn southwest toward Little Sands. Here you will find the charming little ***Rossignol Estate Winery.*** In addition to its seven acres (three hectares) of hardy Franco-American hybrid wine grapes, the winery has recently experimented with greenhouses to grow the more tender varieties of wine grape, such as Chardonnay, Cabernet Franc, and Pinot Noir. The result is that the postcard-pretty winery has garnered several All-Canadian Wine Championship awards. At the winery retail outlet and art gallery you can sip some of these or select from a variety of fruit-based wines.

While imbibing, take time to enjoy the spectacular view of Northumberland Strait and the shoreline of Nova Scotia. The winery is open May to October, Monday to Saturday from 10:00 A.M. to 5:00 P.M., Sunday from 1:00 to 5:00 P.M.

A quaint bed-and-breakfast establishment is ***Bayberry Cliff Inn,*** only 0.6 mile (1 km) west of the winery on Route 4, Little Sands, a few minutes' drive from the Wood Islands ferry terminal. This place overlooks a cliff, offering a spectacular view of the ocean, with five different levels and a number of sitting areas and balconies.

The inn's front porch and yard are full of chairs made out of tree branches, complete with birdhouses and other bits of over-the-top whimsy.

Room rates are moderate, with weekly rates available. For more information call (902) 962–3395.

At this point you are within minutes of a ferry to Nova Scotia, but if you want to linger another day on The Island, continue for a half hour on TCH Route 1, the same stretch of the TCH that passes in front of the ferry terminal.

You will come to a sign indicating the *Orwell Corner Historic Village,* reached by taking a right turn after the junction of Routes 1 and 23, up a small hill and at the start of a clay road. This site re-creates the life and times of a small crossroads agricultural village from the last century. The village includes a farmhouse from 1864, a smithy, and a shingle mill, which I haven't seen anywhere else in the Maritimes. Timing is a factor here: If you come on a Wednesday, you'll be able to take part in a really good ceilidh, one of the best of these traditional Gaelic parties on The Island. Events during the harvest and Christmas seasons make the village particularly picturesque. Other events at the historic village are scheduled throughout the year. To check the schedule, call (902) 651–8510.

The village operates cooperatively with the nearby restored homestead of one of Prince Edward Island's most noteworthy citizens. Sir Andrew Macphail was a physician and professor at McGill University in Montreal. He was also an author intensely interested in sustainable agricultural and forestry development. At age fifty he volunteered to work with a field ambulance corps in World War I. He was knighted by the King of England on New Year's Day 1918.

His birthplace is now called the *Sir Andrew Macphail Homestead,* a 140-acre (56-hectare) site with a reforestation project, including a tree nursery and wildlife gardens. A nature trail meanders along the side of a stream. Visitors can dine or have tea in the facilities provided in the restored home, which also boasts a large conference room in the former dining room. Dinner is quite reasonably priced, and the restaurant is licensed to serve alcohol. For details of upcoming events at the homestead, call (902) 651–2789 in season, or visit www .islandregister.com/macphailfoundaton.html.

From Orwell Corner you can backtrack in the direction of the Wood Islands ferry. There is just one more thing that you ought to do to make your Prince Edward Island sojourn complete: Turn left off TCH Route 1 onto Route 209 and visit *Point Prim Lighthouse.*

Point Prim is a charming peninsula that seems like a little world unto itself. You can visit the lighthouse here and, just to the west of it, the *Point Prim Chowder House.*

Point Prim Chowder House
Irish Moss Pudding

⅓ cup Irish moss (packed)

4 cups milk

¼ teaspoon salt

1½ teaspoon vanilla

1. Soak moss for 15 minutes in enough water to cover; drain.
2. Pick over the Irish moss, removing the undesirable pieces.
3. Add moss to milk and cook in double boiler for 30 minutes.
4. Add salt and vanilla. Pour through a sieve.
5. Fill molds and chill. Serve with a fruit topping.

Of all the old lighthouses on The Island, the Point Prim dates back the farthest, to 1845. The 60-foot tower is the only round brick lighthouse in the entire country. You can climb inside to the polygonal lantern house and catch a spectacular bird's-eye view of Northumberland Strait while you check your pulse.

Once you've worked up an appetite, drop by the Point Prim Chowder House (902–659–2023, in season) and try the Irish moss pudding. When recipes are made with this ingredient in other parts of P.E.I., they call it seaweed. But the owner of the Chowder House hates that terminology, because it's not really seaweed. (You can also buy some dried Irish moss to take home for your own culinary experiments.)

Places to Stay on Prince Edward Island

ALBION CROSS

Needles and Haystacks Bed and Breakfast
Highway 327
(800) 563–2928
(902) 583–2928

BAY FORTUNE

The Inn at Bay Fortune
off Route 310,
(902) 687–3745
A lovely private setting.
Deluxe.

BRACKLEY BEACH

Shaw's Hotel
Route 15
(902) 672–2644
Canada's oldest continuously operating inn is a step back in time. Charming. Moderate.

CHARLOTTETOWN

The Inns on Great George
58 Great George Street
(800) 361–1118 or
(902) 892–0606
fax (902) 628–2079
e-mail: innsongg@atcon.com
Comprising a cluster of restored heritage buildings, the inns are fitted with antiques, claw-foot tubs or Jacuzzis, and an exercise room.
Deluxe.

GRANDE TRACADIE

Dalvay by-the-Sea Inn
off Route 6
(902) 672–2048
The perfect romantic
getaway.
Deluxe.

LITTLE SANDS

Bayberry Cliff Inn
Route 4
(5 miles/8 km east from the
Wood Islands Ferry dock)
(902) 962–3395
Eclectic inn near Wood
Islands ferry. Great views.
Adults/older children
preferred.
Moderate.

SOURIS

Matthew House Inn
15 Breakwater Street
(902) 687–3461
Deluxe.

STANLEY BRIDGE

**Stanley Bridge
Country Resort**
Junction of Routes 6,
224, and 254
(800) 361–2882
(902) 886–2882
fax (902) 886–2940
Moderate to deluxe.

TIGNISH

Tignish Heritage Inn
Maple Street
(877) 882–2491
(902) 882–2491
Converted convent at
beginning of the
Confederation Trail.
Moderate.

TYNE VALLEY

The Doctor's Inn
Route 167
(902) 831–3057
Standard.

VICTORIA BY-THE-SEA

Orient Hotel
Main Street
(800) 565–6743 or
(902) 658–2503
Historic.
Moderate.

WEST POINT

West Point Lighthouse
Route 14
(800) 764–6854 or
(902) 859–3605
Canada's first inn housed
in an active lighthouse.
Moderate.

Places to Eat on Prince Edward Island

BAY FORTUNE

The Inn at Bay Fortune
off Route 310
(902) 687–3745
Outrageously scrumptious
food. Reserve ahead to
avoid disappointment.

GRAND TRACADIE

Dalvay by-the-Sea
off Route 6
(902) 672–2048
Excellent food and setting.

HOPE RIVER

**St. Anne's Church
Lobster Suppers**
Route 224 (off Route 6)
(902) 621–0635
Over thirty years of
operation, St. Anne's Church
has set the standard for The
Island's church-based
lobster suppers. Open from
4:00 to 9:00 P.M., Monday
through Saturday. Closed
Sunday.

MIMINEGASH

Seaweed Pie Cafe
Irish Moss Interpretive Centre
Route 14
(902) 882–4313

MONT-CARMEL

Étoile de Mer
Acadian Pioneer Village
Route 11
(902) 854–2227
Acadian and seafood
specialties.

NEW GLASGOW

**New Glasgow
Lobster Suppers**
Route 258
(902) 964–2870
Lobster straight from their
own saltwater pond. It
doesn't get any fresher than
this. A big place, reservations
not needed. In operation for
more than forty years.

NEW LONDON

New London Seafood Restaurant
(902) 886–3000
On the wharf.

NORTH CAPE

North Cape Lighthouse Wind and Reef Restaurant
Route 14
(902) 882–3535
Fresh seafood.

ORWELL CORNER

Point Prim Chowder House
Route 209

ORWELL CORNER HISTORIC VILLAGE

Sir Andrew Macphail Homestead
Route 1
(902) 651–2789

OYSTER BED BRIDGE

Cafe St.–Jean
Route 6
(902) 963–3133
Listen to live east coast music and eat scrumptious food in this relaxed, rustic setting overlooking a river. Fifteen minutes from Charlottetown, twelve minutes from Cavendish.

TYNE VALLEY

The Doctor's Inn
Route 167
(902) 831–3057
Organic, yet classic dining.

Nova Scotia's Sunrise Trail and Atlantic Coastline

If you have followed the routing outlined in this book to explore the Maritimes, you will have entered Prince Edward Island from New Brunswick and exited P.E.I. via Nova Scotia.

You will no sooner arrive in Nova Scotia than you will be pointed toward Cape Breton, a route commonly followed by travelers to the area. This often leads to an unfortunate bypass of much of the Northumberland Strait coast of Nova Scotia. There are a number of wonderful beach areas along the Northumberland Strait, and you can take a detour to the shore before heading east on the Sunrise Trail.

Sunrise Trail

Although this book is planned so that visitors can travel in one unbroken, clockwise route, the two highlights of this area warrant a side trip if you are coming in from Prince Edward Island. If you are entering Nova Scotia's Sunrise Trial from the Glooscap Trail, the area is equally accessible. To avoid confusion, I will outline the routing as if you were driving west from Pictou. On Highway 6—the Sunrise Trail—34.5 miles (54 km) west of Pictou, you will come to Tatamagouche, a cozy village overlooking sheltered **Tatamagouche Bay**. The town has a number of

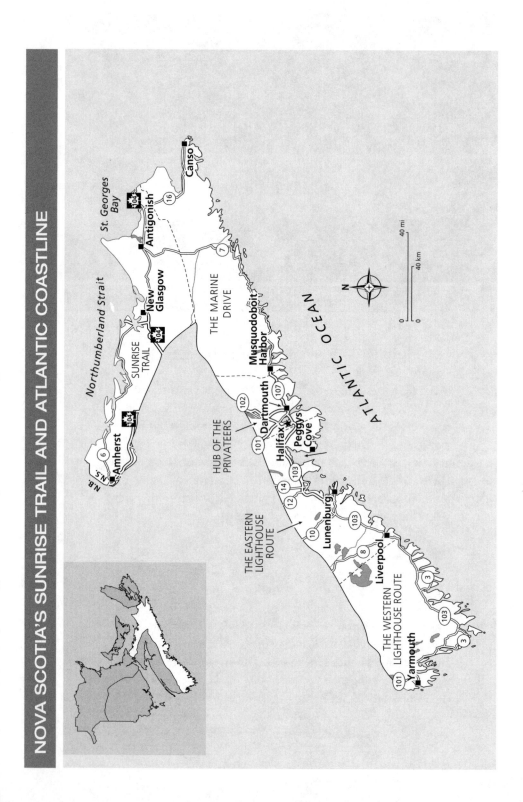

children's summer camps. It's also the location of one of only two inns in North America that feature a train station and railcars for accommodations.

The terminus that now houses the **_Train Station Inn_** was rendered obsolete in 1973 and eventually came into the hands of railway buff Jimmy LeFresne. As a child LeFresne lived next to the station, and the old stationmaster even taught him how to use the telegraph. "Other kids had toy trains to play with!" LeFresne told me.

To keep the defunct station from being torn down, LeFresne leased the building for $50 a month from the time he was eighteen until eventually he was able to buy it outright in 1989, when trains stopped passing through.

Over time, he obtained seven cabooses and a boxcar. The upstairs of the station has three bedrooms. It used to be the stationmaster's quarters.

The cabooses have been converted into bedroom suites full of railway icons: old train posters, toy trains, pillowcases with steam locomotive motifs, and books on old railways. To reserve your very own caboose, call (888) 724–5233 or (902) 657–3222. Rooms in the station and cabooses are moderate. Breakfast at the **_Jitney Cafe_** downstairs in the station house. Eat in their dining car, which features lobster suppers.

trivia

In the late nineteenth century, a giantess from Tatamagouche by the name of Anna Swan (1846–1888) married a giant named Martin Van Burin Bates, making them the world's tallest married couple. She was 7 feet 5.5 inches (227 cm). Her husband was 7 feet 2.5 inches (220 cm).

TRUDY'S FAVORITES

Barrington Woolen Mill,
Barrington

The Chester Playhouse,
Chester

Firefighter's Museum,
Yarmouth

Halifax Public Gardens,
Halifax

Kejimkujik Seaside Adjunct,
Kejimkujik National Park

Maritime Museum of the Atlantic,
Halifax

Oak Island

Ross-Thomson House,
Shelburne

Sherbrooke Village

Tancook Islands

boxcarjimmy

"There's more to buying a railcar than one might expect," says railway buff and *Train Station Inn* owner Jimmy LeFresne. First LeFresne tracks down a caboose that's about to be sold by its railway. With fewer trains in operation, that's no easy task. Sometimes LeFresne even buys a caboose before its retirement date and rents it to the railway for its remaining working years.

Next there's the expense. The cost of hiring a flatbed, a truck, a crane, and an operator to lift the caboose onto LeFresne's stretch of rails often exceeds the cost of the caboose itself—and that's without considering the money needed to transform it into a cozy hotel room!

And complications can arise. LeFresne tells about the time he lost a caboose. "It went missing shortly after I bought it," he says. "It seems some brakeman, tired of hanging out of the back of a boxcar, thought it was an extra caboose and put it on the train." That "loose caboose" was later spotted traveling through Burlington, Kingston, and other points in Southern Ontario.

After a short detour inland along Trunk 311 from Tatamagouche, you will come to the **Balmoral Grist Mill Museum,** in the village of Balmoral Mills. This little museum is open from June to mid-October, Monday to Saturday from 9:30 A.M. to 5:30 P.M. and Sunday afternoon from 2:00 to 4:00 P.M. Even when it isn't open, I love just stopping here to eat my picnic lunch next to the charming mill and its stream. This particular mill has been in operation since 1874. Featuring a 0.6-mile (1-km) nature trail through glorious scenery, including a gorge, the mill itself is pretty enough to paint. There are two daily two-hour-long demonstrations of the mill in operation, at 10:00 A.M. and 2:00 P.M. The result is a surprisingly nutty-tasting whole-wheat flour of oats, barley, rye, and buckwheat. The museum gift shop sells the freshly ground grain. A small admission is charged.

Continuing along that same coastal Highway 6, you will come to a village known as **Malagash.** A series of grape cluster signs will indicate the **Jost Winery,** just outside of town. Pronounced "Yost," this is a vineyard and winery started by a German man who came to Canada in the early 1970s to do other kinds of farming. Descended from a long line of viticulturists in Germany, he couldn't get the vine-growing habit out of his system.

Because the vineyard is located downwind of the sheltered Northumberland Strait, the area is particularly warm and beneficial to wine grapes. The result is that Jost wines have garnered a number of international awards over the last few years, including several gold medals.

The Jost legacy is continued by the founder's son, Hans, who now has a vineyard stretching over forty-five acres (eighteen hectares). Jost Vineyards has a shop and visitor center where you can take a wine tour from mid-June to mid-September daily at noon or 3:00 P.M. Afterward, you can shop for wine-lovers' paraphernalia and even have a picnic under the Jost arbor, with its wine and cured meats and gourmet cheeses made by other local producers.

The afternoon I visited, the temperature was ideal for a picnic. Lunch consisted of a bottle of Marechal Foch, cardamon-spiced Gouda cheese from Buttercup Farms in Bridgewater, and salami from a nearby smokehouse.

Jost also makes barbecue grilling facilities available to visitors on its licensed deck. And there is a local artisans' co-op, so you can get an early start on Christmas shopping.

The vineyard also has added a selection of festivals to its summer visitors schedule. These include a wine fest near the end of June and a "grape stomp festival" toward the end of September. At this festival competing teams squish grapes for charity, while spectators cheer them on. Exact dates for these festivals change from year to year, but if you can gather a team that has a yen to stomp on the fruit of the vine, check out www.jostwine.com for specific dates. Call (800) 565–4567 or (902) 257–2636, or fax (902) 257–2248.

After Malagash, return to Highway 6 and retrace your steps to Pictou. **Pictou Lodge** was originally built by the Bungalow Camps Company in 1922. The original dining room is in a huge log house that still retains all of its rustic appeal. It features luxurious dining in a room made cozy by a huge stone fireplace. Guest accommodations consist of large, three-bedroom log cabins decorated with many of the original furnishings. They also feature big, old-fashioned claw-foot tubs like the one Grandma luxuriated in. Prices for Pictou Lodge run from moderate to deluxe. For advance reservations, call (888) 662–7484 or (902) 485–4322.

A small beach running along one side of the lodge is good for beach-combing and walking. You may prefer to swim in the heated pool that is near the cabins. A small man-made lake is used for water sports. You can also hike on nearby **Munro's Island.** This small wilderness is unspoiled by motorized vehicles. You will be able to see deer, ducks, osprey, eagles, geese, and possibly even a fox on this island, now owned by the Nature Conservancy of Canada.

trivia

More than 600 men have died in mine disasters in Pictou County's underground coal seam. Many deaths were due to methane gas explosions.

The town of **Pictou** is just 3 miles (4.8 km) west of Pictou Lodge. Braeshore Road will take you right into town. Visiting Pictou is a good way to connect with the origins of Nova Scotia, since this was the point of entry of many of the province's original Scottish settlers. Of course, this was the reason for renaming Acadia "Nova Scotia" in the first place, to encourage would-be Scottish settlers to think of it as their new homeland. Nova Scotia means "New Scotland" in Latin.

The settlers first arrived in 1773 on the ship *Hector,* which carried more than 200 passengers, including thirty-three families and twenty-five single men. The province's first Highland Scots came too late in the season to plant crops, having been blown off course by a fierce gale near Newfoundland. People onboard the ship also suffered from smallpox and dysentery outbreaks that claimed the lives of eighteen children before the ship reached land. Immigration to "New Scotland" reached a peak in the early 1800s. Between 1802 and 1807, historians recorded the arrival of more than 25,000 Scots in Cape Breton alone.

The original *Hector,* which brought the first Scottish families, was a fully rigged Dutch ship known as a flute, characterized by its flat bottom with full pear-shaped ends. Captained by John Speirs, the ship was reputed to have a smuggling past. Provisions were rationed: a daily pint of water and three pounds of salt beef, four pounds of bread, and four pounds of oatmeal a week. Because the storm that had blown them off course delayed their arrival by two weeks, provisions started running out at the end of the voyage. Vinegar was added to green, scummy water to make it drinkable. Moldy oatcakes that had earlier been discarded were now retrieved and shared to stave off starvation.

You can explore all this history at the **Hector Heritage Quay** and visit a full-size replica of the *Hector,* which was built right here on a dry dock outside the interpretive center. In the center are a number of wax models and displays depicting the passengers aboard ship. A small admission is charged.

You can watch a blacksmith turn out iron tools and candlesticks, which are for sale. Gift shops on the quay feature excellent local crafts, pewter, and music CDs by noted east coast artists.

If you are in the mood for some pub crawling, be sure to check out **The Old Stone Pub,** 300 feet (90 m) or so past the quay on Depot Street. This favorite local hot spot occupies the bottom floor of a brick and sandstone building that dates back to 1870. This former customs house (until the 1950s) offers visitors a chance to enjoy live music Wednesday and weekend nights.

Upstairs, but through a separate entrance on the opposite side of the building, you will find the **Customs House Inn,** run by twin brothers Dave and Doug DesBarres. I should add that due to the solid construction of the building, sound from the downstairs pub does not carry, so you can sleep soundly in their king-size beds.

The building is a registered Heritage property and is charmingly furnished and decorated to reflect its history. It also has first-class modern fixtures, like

TOP ANNUAL EVENTS

The Greek Festival,
Halifax (first weekend in June);
(902) 479–1271
Sponsored by the local Greek Church, this event has mushroomed into one of the city's favorite parties.

The Multicultural Festival,
Dartmouth waterfront
(third weekend in June);
(902) 455–1619
Lots of exotic food, dance, and crafts. A great chance to graze rather than eat a sit-down meal.

The Antigonish Highland Games,
(early July);
(902) 863–3330
Lots of burly guys in kilts throwing objects the size of trees. Ale, a parade, and highland dancers galore.

Maritime Old-Time Fiddling Contest,
Dartmouth (Wednesday, the second week in July, through Sunday);
(800) 565–0000
Excellent acoustics, the region's top fiddlers and intense competition make this a mecca for any fiddle fan.

The Wooden Boat Festival,
Mahone Bay (first week of August);
(902) 624–8443
The bay's biggest party of the year. Explore the boatbuilding heritage of an area noted for its rumrunners and privateers.

Lunenburg Folk Harbour Festival,
(second Wednesday in August through Sunday);
(902) 634–3180
The picturesque waterfront and assorted venues are filled with the best folk musicians and fans from across the region. The daytime concerts are free.

Halifax International Busker Festival,
(mid-August);
(902) 429–3910
A good event if you like crowds. Sample an act or two, then visit Halifax's charming waterfront and downtown areas.

The International Woodsman's Competition,
Greenfield (second weekend in August);
(800) 565–0000
Unusual and fun. Local lumberjacks try their luck at logrolling, tree climbing, and many other lumberjack job skills.

Atlantic Fringe Festival,
Halifax (early September);
(800) 565–0000
"Out there" theatrical events and related activities for the artsy crowd.

whirlpool baths and large-screen televisions. Breakfast is included in the price. Prices are moderate. For reservations, call (902) 485–4546.

Another delightful place to stay, and quite possibly the best bargain in town, is the 1865 *Auberge Walker Inn.* The inn is in a pre-Confederation building that has been decorated with many period pieces. A large-screen television draws guests to the living room, where they can socialize with other visitors. The continental breakfast (included in the price) is served in a sunny, elegant dining room. Rates are standard to moderate.

The friendly owners, Laurent and Jacqueline LaFlèche, are bilingual, which encourages a number of French-speaking visitors to stay here. Jackie has studied the history of the inn's owners and many of the town's dignitaries of the past century and has unearthed old photographs and the original architectural plans of this historic home. To reserve a room, call (800) 370–5553 or locally at (902) 485–1433. The inn is on Coleraine Street, 1 block from the Hector Quay.

As you leave Pictou, you will reach a fork in the road and signs indicating the turnoff for Highway 104, which leads to Stellarton and New Glasgow (8 miles, or 13 km). Take this road, also known as the Old Haliburton Road, until you find the *Hector Exhibit and Research Centre* and *McCulloch House Museum.* The home of the founder of Pictou Academy, McCulloch House dates back to 1806 and overlooks a charming beaver pond. Much-needed restoration work has recently been undertaken to bring the brick home back into shape.

Thomas McCulloch was an avid naturalist, and his collection was studied in 1833 by the visiting John Audubon, who personally presented him with his prints of wildlife. On the same property is the Hector Exhibit and Research Centre, which houses the records of the Pictou County Genealogy and Heritage Society. This is an excellent resource for people of Scottish descent who wish to trace their roots. The day I visited there were notices posted from clans as far away as Australia. The center also has a rotation of exhibits put on by local societies and craft guilds, and items are sometimes for sale. For information call (902) 485–4563.

New Glasgow and Stellarton are two closely linked communities; you can easily travel from one to the other without using the main highway. Your first stop to the area should include a visit to the *Nova Scotia Museum of Industry* in *Stellarton,* just off Highway 104 at exit 24, which brings you to the museum's doorstep.

This is a great museum to visit with children, who seem to be endlessly fascinated with old machinery and interactive displays. Visitors will be handed a time card and asked to punch a time clock, as if they were showing up for work. Kids will continue to get their card punched as they proceed through the exhibit, which advances in time, keeping apace with the improvements in technology.

The museum is the size of seven hockey rinks, making it the province's largest museum. It has to be big, because of the heavy machinery, steam locomotives, and cars that it houses. One of the most noteworthy items is the Samson steam locomotive, the oldest surviving steam locomotive in Canada. (The steam chamber is encased in wood, making it resemble an oblong whisky barrel.) The Samson arrived in 1839, twelve years after the General Mining Company obtained a lease to mine coal in the province. This marked the beginning of industrialization in Nova Scotia.

Early automobiles are also featured in the museum—from the Victorian horseless carriage, a one-of-a-kind, two-horsepower vehicle made in Hopewell in 1899, to the 1912 McKay Touring Car. The McKay was the product of a local enterprise that was in operation only from 1912 to 1914, during which time only 175 were produced. These posh automobiles sold for $2,300, a lot of money at the time. Admission is $7.00 for adults, $15.00 for a family.

When you exit the museum, follow Route 374, also known as the Stellarton Road, to **New Glasgow.** Just as you cross the small bridge that traverses the East River, you will come to the most historic section of town and New Glasgow's oldest building, which houses one of the town's liveliest pubs. Built in 1841, the Squire Frasier Building was made from stone ballast used in the ships that brought the town's British settlers. You will find it just a block from the waterfront.

Abandoned for three years, the ground floor of the building has been turned into a pub by an Irish couple, the Margesons. Now called **The Dock, Food, Spirits and Ales,** it stands as one of the biggest drawing cards to date in the town's revitalized riverside. (They've recently added an outdoor patio.)

"It's certainly given people an opportunity to come into the oldest building and to see it as it used to be," said owner Carmel Margeson, a native of Cork, Ireland, whose family owns a pub in Ireland. Since a river runs through New Glasglow, customers sometimes arrive by boat, docking at the nearby marina. The Dock has a variety of imported ales on tap, and Irish, Nova Scotian, and Canadian flags decorate the front of the pub, just so you know where their hearts are.

At the beginning of the railway era, some locomotives ran on all-wooden tracks and covered only short distances, because they were used for hauling goods from a mine or factory to a pier. Later technological improvements involved substituting iron and steel in the construction of railroad tracks. In downtown New Glasgow you'll find the **Sampson Trail,** a pleasant promenade approximately a half mile long between downtown New Glasgow and downtown Stellarton. This trail is on the railroad bed of the first iron and steel railway in Canada and is named for the first locomotive to run on it, the Sampson, which was used to haul coal from the mine to the dock.

The **Thorburn Rail Spur** yields another trail and access to a marshland area with bald eagles and rare species of flora and fauna.

Before you leave New Glasgow be sure to visit the ***Carmichael Stewart House Museum,*** on Temperance Street. This is designated in downtown New Glasgow by a series of signs and arrows indicating, simply, museum. A sign outside the building is labeled PICTOU COUNTY HISTORICAL MUSEUM. Despite the multiple designations, it's all the same place.

The Carmichaels were wealthy shipbuilders who produced a missionary sailing ship that went to the South Seas in search of Christian converts. The ship itself was paid for with donations from schoolchildren in Canada, Scotland, and England. Apart from shipbuilding artifacts, what I found most noteworthy about this museum collection was the variety of antique clothing, including a century-old wedding dress and several handmade christening gowns.

Because there are a limited number of mannequins, the museum guide tries to change the costumes often, so repeat visits will still yield fresh surprises.

The museum is open June to August, Monday to Saturday from 9:30 A.M. to 4:30 P.M., Sunday from 1:00 to 4:30 P.M. Admission is free, but donations are welcome.

Just outside New Glasgow is one of the area's best-kept secrets. ***Melmerby Beach*** has my vote for the warmest saltwater beach in Nova Scotia. To get there, take Route 289 north on Little Harbour Road in downtown New Glasgow until you reach the junction with Route 348. Take a right turn from here to get to Melmerby Beach Provincial Park. The beach came by its name because a French ship, the Melmerby, ran aground here. It's not surprising, since the water is shallow for a considerable distance. Lifeguards are on duty all summer long, and there are changing facilities.

Backtrack on Route 289 to New Glasgow to reconnect with Highway 104. Continue east until you reach the community of ***Barneys River Station.*** Turn right off the main highway and follow Barneys River Station Road a few hundred feet until you see a sign indicating the ***School House Museum.*** This tiny one-room schoolhouse, built in 1865, accommodated forty-two pupils at its peak. It closed in 1971.

More than two decades later, the last person to teach at the school, Nova Bannerman, spearheaded an initiative to have the community-owned building reopened during the summer months as a museum. A number of artifacts related to the old school were resurrected in the community, and the effect is a convincing step back in time. Having been a Nova Scotian schoolgirl in the early 1960s, I can attest to the authenticity of the classroom setting, right back to the double desks and inkwells, the mint-condition schoolbooks, and even the strap used to administer punishment for naughty behavior. The old schoolhouse is open July and August, Tuesday to Saturday from 11:00 A.M.to 5:00 P.M., Sunday from noon to 5:00 P.M. Admission is free, but donations are welcome.

From Barneys River Station you can continue on Highway 104 to ***Antigonish*** and then Cape Breton. You can continue on Highway 104 only until exit 32, the Antigonish turnoff, and get on Highway 7, heading toward Sherbrooke and the Marine Drive.

If you happen to be in the vicinity of Antigonish at the end of the first week in July, you can enjoy the ***Antigonish Highland Games.*** Plan to stay for a few days, but expect to find hotel rooms in short supply. This may mean staying outside of town so that you can take part in the biggest and longest-running highland games outside of Scotland.

The core of the games are musical performances from pipe-and-drum bands, highland dancing, and, of course, the ancient heavyweight events such as the caber toss. A caber looks like a spruce telephone pole and is tossed in a two-handed motion by hunky men in kilts. Competitors come from Scotland, Australia, and the United States.

Celtic music is featured under the big top at Columbus Field. Expect to hear some of the finest fiddling in eastern Canada. Along with the highland games, Antigonish has other delights you can sample. The long-standing summer theater, called Festival Antigonish, has professional actors presenting plays written by local authors. It's possible to check out the program of events by visiting www.festivalantigonish.com.You can also obtain a dinner-theater package to dine at award-winning ***Gabrieau's Bistro*** and attend a main-stage show. For details or reservations, call (902) 863–1925. Located at 350 Main Street, Gabrieau's is famous for cedar-roasted salmon, raspberry coulis, crab cakes with lemon aioli, and scrumptious squid.

The Gloomy Bard of Barneys River Station

In the early days of Barneys River, many Highland Scots came to live in the neighborhood. Among them was a poet, or bard, who was highly esteemed in his native Scotland. **John McLean,** the "Bard of Coll," settled here, and became disillusioned with the hard life of a settler. Many of his finest works were composed here, but the one that really left his mark had a title that translates from Gaelic as "The Gloomy Forest."

Following his presentation of this homesick lament in Iona, Cape Breton, 500 of his fellow countrymen decided to abandon their hope of making a life in "New Scotland" and left for the presumed greener pastures of New Zealand.

The bard John McLean didn't leave Nova Scotia, but he did move to James River, in Antigonish, where he and his poison pen remained until his death.

The Marine Drive

One Guysborough highlight must be a visit to the town of **Sherbrooke Village,** which, starting in the 1860s, was the site of a massive gold rush that went on for twenty years until it suddenly collapsed. The remains of those days are a collection of thirty perfectly preserved buildings fronting the beautiful St. Marys River. These include a school, drugstore, courthouse, blacksmith shop, and barn (complete with horses). House after house is filled with artifacts from the town's "golden era."

Costumed guides explain the history of Nova Scotia's gold rush. The economic activity of Nova Scotia gold rushes of the last century produced an income higher than that of the Klondike gold rush. Several old mines are still around in the province, and a few are reopening thanks to modern technology.

Sherbrooke Village has its own costume department, where staff members create outfits authentic during the village's heyday. I recommend that you visit their workshop to get a sneak peek at the behind-the-scenes work of historic re-creation. It's worth mentioning that needlework is very high quality in this

Chair-Making at Sherbrooke Village

At the **Woodturner and Chairmaker's Shop** in Sherbrooke Village, you can get an excellent feel for the art of making reproductions of 1860s-style furniture. The carpenter, named Dennis, showed us a long wooden trough, which attached to a kettle. Strips of white ash, "the poor man's oak," are heated in the trough, which becomes a steam chamber when the water in the kettle boils. The strips are heated for an hour for every inch of thickness, then removed and bent into shapes dictated by wooden forms.

Chair seats are carved out of wood with hand tools. For finishing, the carpenter uses modern sandpaper, a compromise solution. Dennis told us that in olden days, sandpaper was made by locals from animal-hide glue and various grades of sand. The finest grade of sandpaper was made from fish skin. "Sandpaper didn't come in all the grades we have today," Dennis said. "A carpenter just had to go by the feel of it and be his own judge."

No two chairs made in this traditional way are ever exactly alike. In fact, not even the spindles are absolutely consistent. It's the slight irregularities that distinguish a handmade reproduction from modern machine-made chairs. Chairs made throughout the summer in this small shop are sold for prices ranging from $100 to $300.

Sherbrooke Village is open daily from June 1 until mid-October. Some of the village's houses are still privately owned and occupied by families year-round, so it is never totally deserted, but you will not be able to go inside the buildings in the winter.

area, and if you're in the mood to buy a quilt to take home, you'll find many good examples in craft stores in the area. The Sherbrooke Village museum staff organizes a variety of special events throughout the year, including a Courthouse Concert Series and parties revolving around themes such as harvesttime or cider-making. See museum.gov.ns.ca/sv/ for details. Sherbrooke Village is open daily from June 1 to October 15, from 9:30 A.M. to 5:30 P.M. Admission is $9.00 for adults, $3.75 for children, $7.25 for seniors (65-plus), $25.00 for families. Season passes range from $15.00 to $32.00. For details, call (888) 743–7845 or (902) 522–2400.

If you are eager to spend more time in this area, you can find cabins, some overlooking the rapids of St. Marys River, at **Liscomb Lodge.** The lodge offers the opportunity to get completely away from it all. You can enjoy a closeness with nature on a par with wilderness camping, while still benefitting from the luxuries of a cozy lodge. In the dining room I had a feast of plank salmon and was able to watch an assortment of colorful songbirds at a feeder just a few feet away. There was also a very people-friendly groundhog on the premises, who seemed to be as interested in the guests as we were in him. The lodge offers an indoor pool and a fitness center, as well as access to a wide range of outdoor sporting equipment and guides. For reservations, call (800) 665–6343. Rates are moderate to deluxe.

If you're just passing through, you might want to drop by the restaurant to enjoy a bite or to check out the dozens of locally handmade quilts and other crafts that adorn the post-and-beam ceiling of the main lodge's second floor. These items are for sale.

There are several good excursions that you can take at Liscomb Lodge. Guests can take a harbor cruise on the lodge's flat-bottom boat with skipper Chester Rudolph. He often visits an island, to which he brings the discarded bones and heads of salmon from the lodge's kitchen. By leaving these scraps for the eagles to eat, Rudolph boosts the chances of getting a good view of the feeding birds on a return trip. The day we visited we saw several pairs of eagles.

There are also good walking trails, including one that leads to a salmon ladder, a man-made series of rapids that were constructed to aid the fish in their annual migration (and to improve the salmon count). After the salmon ladder was constructed, the river's course was partially rerouted so that half of it would flow through the ladder.

You can take a footbridge that traverses the river just down from this ladder. Maps of this 5-mile (8-km) trail are available at the lodge desk. If you are driving a vehicle with a high undercarriage and good shock absorbers, you can travel the rough road right up to the footbridge or salmon ladder. Otherwise, it's a four-hour hike, round-trip. Bring plenty of water, bug repellent, a hat, and

Woodstock Grows Up

The wonderful three-day *Stan Rogers Folk Festival* is held in Canso usually in late June. It has grown to include more than 50 musical acts from around the world, performing on six stages. Stan Rogers was a local folksinger/songwriter who penned many popular ballads that can best be described as "working man's anthems." After he died tragically in a plane crash, his hometown became host to this festival, which runs at the beginning of the summer. You can check festival times and book your tickets in advance by calling (888) 554–7826. The Stan Rogers Folk Festival is clean, well organized, and family friendly, with a wide range of people in attendance. It has a hint of the Woodstock generation aspect—now that they've grown up and found jobs—that is reflected in the event's congenial yet wholesome atmosphere.

To get to Canso from Antigonish, continue on Highway 104 toward Cape Breton until you reach the Route 16 exit at Junction 37. Take Route 16 east to Canso. After the festival you can rejoin the Marine Drive by taking Route 316 south, all along the Atlantic coast.

an effective sunscreen. Maps for the hike are available at the front desk of Liscomb Lodge.

After Liscomb, continue west along Highway 7. You will see a Nova Scotia Provincial Government campground marker indicating *Taylor Head Beach,* one of the unspoiled wonders of the province. Turn left and drive a short way to the shore along a small peninsula. Taylor Head Beach has a wonderful white-sand beach that looks striking against a backdrop of dense fir trees. The area includes a 3.6-mile (6-km) hiking trail. Along this coastline you stand a good chance of seeing not only eagles, but also great blue herons in flight, with their exceedingly long legs dangling behind them. The best thing about Taylor Head is that it is truly undiscovered, so don't tell anyone.

After you exit Taylor Head, you will come almost immediately to the community of Tangier. This stop involves some advance planning. So, assuming that you've been reading ahead a little bit, here goes. Tangier is the headquarters of Dr. Scott Cunningham, biologist, writer, and, most important for our purposes, sea kayaking expert. He takes groups on a number of sea kayaking expeditions along these shores, through his company *Coastal Adventures,* the longest-running sea kayaking operation in Atlantic Canada.

Cunningham has published a book, *Sea Kayaking in Nova Scotia,* and in addition to circumnavigating the province in 1980, he has extensively explored other regional wilderness areas. His tours take from three to eight days and cover the biology, geology, and history of the shorelines explored. All gear is supplied, apart from tents, sleeping bags, and personal items. Coastal Adventures also offers daylong trips for $100. For details, you can visit www.coastal adventures.com, or e-mail coastal@dunmac.com, or call (877) 404–2774, or fax (902) 772–2774.

The first thing that comes to mind when you mention Tangier to gourmets throughout the region is *Willy Krauch and Sons Ltd.,* home of the ultimate wood-smoked Atlantic salmon, which is also endorsed by Her Majesty the Queen. It is truly incredible melt-in-your-mouth salmon. You can visit and shop at the Krauch smokehouse, located right on Highway 7. While there, be sure to try the hot smoked lemon-pepper salmon. Chances are you'll find you've devoured your entire souvenir before you even get home. Thankfully, they'll ship salmon anywhere. For details call (800) 758–4412 or (902) 772–2188.

Continue south along the Marine Drive until you reach the little communities of Jeddore and Oyster Pond. All along this highway you will pass through centuries-old fishing communities. Some of these date back to the era of the Acadians.

You can get a glimpse into the lives of these hardworking fishing folk at the *Fisherman's Life Museum,* in Jeddore. This was the homestead of Ervin and Ethelda Myers, parents of thirteen daughters. Ervin was an inshore fisherman who also worked in the woods each winter.

Costumed guides use the home's woodstove to do their morning baking, and on the day I visited, they offered me tea and traditional ginger snaps right out of the oven. The ladies were also busy making hooked rugs from scraps. The residents of this home enriched the poor coastal soil with seaweed mulch, manure, and compost. Sheep still graze in the yard of the one-and-a-half-story house. To make their own yeast and cold medicines, the Myers grew hops near the orchard.

Century-old dishes still grace the kitchen cupboards. A lady's coquettishly embroidered bloomers lay on the master bed, as if waiting for their owner. "Wouldn't Ethelda be mortified if she saw her bloomers on display?" chuckled one of the guides.

The museum is open from June until mid-October from 9:30 A.M. until 5:30 P.M. Monday to Saturday, Sundays 1:00 to 5:30 P.M. Admission for adults is $3.00, $5.00 for families.

If you are looking for some countryside peace and quiet that's only three-quarters of an hour from Halifax or the airport, try the *Salmon River House Country Inn,* just a mile from the museum in Head Jeddore. A Heritage inn located along the Salmon River, it includes several cottages as well (two are off-site and oceanside). The owners also operate the Lobster Shack. They offer outdoor activity and weekend packages, including a lobster supper package. The three-and-a-half-star inn won the provincial tourism association's top food and beverage award for 2001. Prices are standard to moderate. For reservations, call (800) 565–3353 or locally at (902) 889–3353. You can also take a peek at www.salmonriverhouse.com.

Hub of the Privateers

They don't teach this in local history lessons, but the truth is, piracy was big business in Nova Scotia once the British got hold of the territory. After hostilities broke out with the renegade colonies to the south, Britain took full advantage of the colony's strategic position and commissioned all sorts of ships for "privateering," which was piracy by all intents and purposes. Young men signed on with privateers as a way of avoiding being "press-ganged" into service with the notoriously brutal Royal Navy. Add to this the fact that Britain was almost constantly at war with somebody or other, and you can see that the high seas represented a tremendous career opportunity for the adventurous sort with a strong stomach. Captured booty was taken to Halifax, where it was "libelled off" in public auctions and the proceeds split between the shipowners, the court, and government officials.

It was this piracy and war that really gave Halifax a leg up. Even the cobblestones of the city's first streets were quarried from the shattered ruins of Fortress Louisbourg, which fell to the British shortly before Halifax's founding. Some areas of downtown **Halifax** still contain these stones, such as the Granville Street entrance to the art college. But after the War of 1812 drew to a close, piracy was no longer government endorsed.

trivia

The population of the Halifax Regional Municipality in 2004 was 39.5 percent of Nova Scotia's total population. That's 370,000 inhabitants.

Halifax's waterfront is still a fun place to hang out, pirates or no, because the city boasts a lively music scene, excellent shopping for local arts and crafts, and gourmet seafood.

Driven by the demands of six universities full of students, the nightlife can be relaxed, fun, and easy on the wallet. For both visitors and locals, the focus of interest stretches from Argyle Street, a few blocks from the harbor, to Historic Properties, with its restored waterfront buildings from the nineteenth century. Early each August the **Halifax International Busker Festival** draws street entertainers from around the world.

Overlooking the city, the fortress to which the city owes its birth, **The Citadel**, provides a stunning lookout. **Point Pleasant Park** is an extensive

About That Hurricane

In the early fall of 2003, following what has to have been the most glorious September in any Nova Scotian's living memory, Halifax and the surrounding Atlantic coastline was directly hit by *Hurricane Juan,* the most powerful hurricane to reach our shores in over one hundred years. It left over 90 percent of the province's most populous metropolitan area without power (some for up to 10 days), and wiped out an estimated 700,000 trees in the metropolitan area alone. While much of the damage to houses and businesses has been cleared up, some of the damage to parks and wilderness will have a long-term impact.

The famous *Halifax Public Gardens* lost roughly eighty of their most majestic trees, some as old as 160 years. The site reopened on Canada Day, 2004. A $3-million restoration project is ongoing. One highlight is the refurbished nineteenth-century wrought-iron fence, complete with a magnificent set of ornamental gates, that are now restored to full function. Since many of the shade trees are gone, the gently restored park has been remodeled on the original Victorian plan. It shows no visible signs of destruction and is reputedly as sunny as it was roughly sixty years ago.

Not so fortunate was *Point Pleasant Park,* which had huge stands of trees completely flattened by the storm, as it literally barreled up the harbor mouth. History buffs point out that the park was originally used to garrison troops in tents, and that meant open fields. They also point to the park's round Martello tower commissioned by Prince Edward, Queen Victoria's father, in 1796. It was originally intended as a lookout over the harbor, but with all the dense tree growth of the last century, its original purpose was forgotten. Now, with the trees gone, the tower can once again offer a harbor view. Many creative ideas for the use of the park have been put forward, but at press time, nothing has been decided. In the meantime, when you visit the park, enjoy the wide-open spaces and the unobstructed view of the harbor, courtesy of Hurricane Juan.

rustic park at the tip of Halifax's posh south end. The city also boasts large, traditional English-style gardens.

Opinions about Halifax are as varied as the people who live here. Unself-conscious, or perhaps totally lacking in pretense, is the best way to describe it. When an article in *Harper's Bazaar* cited the place as the next cool city in North America after Seattle's grunge thing, everyone in Halifax had a good laugh. Halifax cool? Can't be. And yet, the city is an eclectic mix that somehow manages to be avant-garde.

The downtown is full of funky little cafes decorated with original paintings and folk art, the epitome of which must be the Soho Kitchen on Granville Street. The cafe culture is no doubt a by-product of the Nova Scotia College of Art and Design. Called NSCAD by locals, the school was founded by the one-time governess of the King of Siam's children, Anna Leonowens, whose day job was immortalized in the movie *The King and I*. For many years NSCAD was the only degree-granting art college in Canada.

NSCAD has left an indelible stamp on the funky downtown core of Halifax, as has the city's seafaring past. The Privateer's Wharf and the shops down by the waterfront are converted old-time warehouses from the Age of Sail. You are as likely to hear an avant-garde band perform original music that has won fans from all over Canada as you are to watch a crowd of Maritimers pouring onto the dance floor to the tune of "What Shall We Do with the Drunken Sailor?" a traditional Halifax jig if ever there was one.

trivia

The official name of Halifax's harbor is Chebucto Harbour, which in Mi'Kmaq means a "great long harbor." The Mi'Kmaq weren't exaggerating. It is the world's second-largest natural harbor.

Where to go when in Halifax? Lately, a lot of visitors have been stopping at three of the city's cemeteries. Their interest has been piqued by the city's connection to the *Titanic* disaster, which is considerable. Halifax was the port where the bodies of the victims were brought for identification and, sometimes, burial. The bodies were scooped from the freezing North Atlantic by a steamship, the Mackay-Bennett, which normally laid and repaired telegraph cables on the ocean floor.

The steamship, which was crewed with Nova Scotians from across the province, retrieved 306 bodies. When its supply of ice and embalming fluid was exhausted, it was joined by another local ship, the Minia. In all, 328 bodies were recovered from the water. Burial at sea followed for 119 victims, whose bodies were too damaged to preserve. Each victim was identified by a small canvas tag, numbered to indicate the order in which he or she was taken out of the water. These numbers are to be found on the victims' headstones. In many cases they are the only identification marks given, apart from the date of death shared by all the headstones: April 15, 1912.

A total of 150 casualties of the *Titanic* disaster are buried in three of Halifax's graveyards. At the ***Fairview Cemetery,*** 121 are buried in a curved arrangement resembling a ship's hull. You will find the gravesites near the intersection of Windsor Street and Kempt Road, overlooking Bedford Basin. The entrance is on Windsor Street, across from a Ford dealership. This is where James Dawson's remains lie buried. Dawson (victim number 227) was a third-class seaman, an Irish coal trimmer—not an artist as the *Titanic* movie portrays him.

Most Halifax residents know that the numerous bouquets of flowers and weeping preteen girls at the James Dawson grave are there because of a case of mistaken identity and the charms of a Hollywood idol. What is generally not known is the story of another case of mistaken identity involving a victim buried at the **Baron de Hirsch Jewish Cemetery,** final resting place of ten *Titanic* victims. This graveyard is just south of the adjacent Fairview Cemetery but is not generally open to the public.

Here is buried the fugitive Michel Navratil, a man who assumed a false identity and name, Louis M. Hoffman, in order to make off with his two children, whom he had kidnapped from his estranged wife in France. When the great oceanliner was sinking, Navratil handed his two sons over to the lifeboat crew, never revealing that the two boys were also traveling under false identities. The children survived the sinking, and were called the "Orphans of the *Titanic*" by newspaper headlines around the world until their mother recognized their pictures and traveled to America to reclaim them. Although by this time Navratil's true identity was known, his body was not exhumed; it remains buried in the Jewish cemetery, under marker number 15.

The third *Titanic* graveyard, **Mount Olivet Cemetery,** is on Mumford Road, near Dutch Village Road. Many of its nineteen victims are unidentified. It does hold the grave of a *Titanic* band member, John Clarke, a native of Liverpool, England.

worthmentioning

The **Nova Scotia International Tattoo** (which incidentally, has nothing to do with what one gets permanently drawn on a body part) is a huge pageant of military and civilian bands. More than 2,000 performers from more than a half-dozen countries come each year to perform at the Tattoo, which takes place at the Halifax Metro Centre the first week of July. To order your tickets in advance, call at (800) 563–1114 or (902) 420–1114. You can also check out www.nstattoo.ca for information on the upcoming show. If you are not sure whether it's your cup of tea, you can check out the free performances usually held around noon just prior to the show in the popular downtown park called the Grand Parade. The Tattoo is definitely not off the beaten path, but it is considered by many to be the highlight of their vacations.

He and his other band members are reported to have continued to play on deck until the last of the lifeboats were filled and the waves began to claim their first victims.

Halifax is no stranger to marine disasters. Decades before the sinking of the *Titanic,* came the disaster of the SS *Atlantic* (also launched by the White Star Line). The *Atlantic* ran aground in Terence Bay, just outside Halifax Harbour. Less than half the ship's approximately 1,000 passengers escaped with their lives. Divers like to explore the wreck of the *Atlantic* where it lies off-shore in only 80 feet (24 m) of water.

The most famous of the city's disaster connections is the Halifax Explosion, depicted along with the story of the *Titanic* and the SS *Atlantic* at the **Maritime Museum of the Atlantic,** located on Halifax's waterfront.

The 1917 Halifax Explosion was the largest nonnuclear man-made explosion in history. Caused by the collision of two ships, the munitions ship *Mont Blanc* and the *Imo,* formerly a White Star ship, the explosion killed 1,635 people.

The museum also displays Canada's first hydrographic vessel, the CSS *Acadia,* which makes for a fascinating afternoon of ship exploration. Hydrographic vessels are used to map the ocean floor. If you look closely at coastal maps, for example, you will note that the shallow areas are indicated, as well as particularly deep fault lines. These measurements are important for navigation and resource exploration. Included in this complex is a restored ship's chandlery (supply store), William Robertson and Son, with lots of authentic marine curios. The museum is open year-round. Summertime admission is $8.00 for adults, $4.00 for children ages six to eighteen. Summer hours extend from May 1 to October 30, Monday to Saturday from 9:30 A.M. to 5:30 P.M., Tuesday until 8:00 P.M., and Sunday from 1:00 to 5:30 P.M. Winter admission is half price. After October 30, the museum is closed on Monday, and doors are locked every day but Tuesday at 5:00 P.M. The CSS *Acadia* is not open off-season. For details, call (902) 424–7490.

giftofthanks

As a thank-you for the food, shelter, and clothing Bostonians gave to the people of Halifax in the aftermath of the explosion, Nova Scotia gives the city of Boston an annual Christmas gift. It is a large evergreen tree, illuminated with great ceremony in that city's downtown.

One positive offshoot of the Halifax Explosion was the reconstruction of the north end of the peninsula afterward, the area most devastated by the blast. Known as **The Hydrostones,** the now-quaint neighborhood of Tudor-revival houses boasts European-style markets, several cozy dining establishments, and upscale shops along Young Street. Bubbling over with the atmosphere of an English garden suburb, the area takes its name from the building material used to create the 86 buildings of Canada's first public housing project. (Hydrostone is a mixture of crushed stone, sand, gravel, and portland cement molded under intense pressure.)

If disasters and ships are not your thing, gravitate toward the beautiful **Halifax Public Gardens,** and from there meander along Spring Garden Road toward the harbor.

Between these two points, you will find countless coffee shops; all manner of restaurants, pubs, and fish and chips wagons; and grunge-clad teens, bohemian types, college students, and out-of-towners.

The seventeen-acre (seven-hectare) Public Gardens were originally created as a private garden in 1753, only four years after the founding of Halifax. In 1836 they were taken over by the Nova Scotia Horticultural Society. Since 1889 the park has been enclosed by a wrought-iron fence, punctuated by an ornate pair of ornamental gates imported from Glasgow, Scotland.

The gardens are now recognized as the finest original formal Victorian gardens in North America. They have rhododendrons so massive that you can walk under a huge canopy of leaves, hidden from the passersby on the other side. The duck pond in the middle of the garden leads into a stream, lined with irises and day lilies, that passes under a small arching stone bridge. Swans share the pond with the ducks, and if you arrive at a propitious time of year, you may catch glimpses of baby swans and little ducklings dutifully swimming after their mothers.

Along with the carefully tended roses, there are floating-style flower beds in French Formal and English Romantic styles. The Victorian bandstand in the center of the park is the site of free concerts on Sunday afternoons.

Across Sackville Street, which borders the gardens on the north side, you will see greenhouses. Next to them a charming stone house, Public Gardens Cottage, dates back to the life and times of Richard Power, one-time gardener to the duke of Devonshire in Ireland. His descendants tended the gardens until the 1960s.

trivia

Canada's first newspaper was the *Halifax Gazette*, published in 1752.

It is possible to find a low-key, elegant, secluded-feeling place to stay, right in the city. My choice for a relaxing stay is the *Halliburton House Inn,* located at 5184 Morris Street, a few blocks south of the corner of Barrington Street and Spring Garden Road, which informally marks the end point of most of downtown's clubs (just far enough that the noise of the clubs won't keep you up at night, but close enough that it's a five-minute walk to hopping nightlife).

The Halliburton House Inn now comprises its original Heritage house and two adjacent buildings. It has all the feel of a Victorian-era country inn, with all the polish and four-star conveniences as well. At the back of the inn is a series of garden courtyards, some ultraprivate and attached directly to the suites. It has an excellent restaurant with a menu showcasing seafood and wild game, and several dining rooms from which to choose, including a private dining room suitable to small meetings or intimate tête-à-têtes. Among the twenty-nine guest rooms, several have their own working fireplace. My favorite, complete with Jacuzzi and king-size bed, has its own veranda.

The main building, dating from 1809, is the former home of Sir Brenton Halliburton, chief justice of the Nova Scotia Supreme Court. The home briefly served as the Dalhousie Law School from 1885 to 1887. To reserve a room at the antiques-filled inn, call (902) 420–0658, or write an e-mail to innkeeper @halliburton.ns.ca, or check out the Web site at www.halliburton.ns.ca. Rates are moderate to deluxe.

For a small city, ethnic food abounds, with lots of Lebanese, Italian, Greek, Vietnamese, Thai, East Indian, and vegetarian places awaiting your discovery. Later in the evening embark on a pub crawl, a sport heavily favored by the city's many university students.

The Eastern Lighthouse Route

Take a Canadian 10-cent piece in your hand and examine the sailing ship that enjoys equal billing with Her Majesty the Queen. That is the famous Nova Scotia sailing ship, the **Bluenose,** as photographed by W. R. MacAskill. For two decades during the early part of the last century, this schooner won one international race after another. Eventually, it came to symbolize the pride of Canada's seagoing easterners. A replica of the *Bluenose* (the *Bluenose II*) graces the Halifax harbor today.

MacAskill, whose famous photograph found its way onto the Canadian dime, also made famous another Nova Scotian landmark: **Peggys Cove.** This once-isolated fishing cove has become so synonymous with "quaint fishing villages" that it has become anything *but* off the beaten path. Now busloads of tourists come to soak up the "unspoiled beauty" of this village.

Those who consider a pilgrimage to Peggys Cove mandatory do themselves a disservice if they do not continue farther down the **South Shore** to the historic villages and other unspoiled and largely untouched coastal communities along Highway 3, which is provincially designated the "Lighthouse Route."

During the Colonial era the British Crown supplied Nova Scotian privateers with letters of marque, entitling them to loot and plunder enemy ships. This freewheeling approach to the seafaring tradition was revived during the era of Prohibition, when rumrunners smuggled contraband booze into the United States from the tiny fishing communities that dot the South Shore. From the south end of Halifax to the southernmost tip of the province, some of the grandest old homes had their beginnings as the houses of sea captains who owed their wealth to their success on the high seas and hidden coves.

The *Bluenose II* in Halifax Harbor

To reach the South Shore from Halifax, follow the "shore road," also known as Route 333, which will give you a glimpse of the many unspoiled coastal communities, such as Seabright, French Village, and Indian Harbour, that line **St. Margarets Bay.** You can also drop by Peggy's Cove if you really have to take a look. If you want to bypass this area and get into the South Shore more directly, take Provincial Highway 103, which you can also access from Route 333 at exit 5. At this point you will have reached the head of St. Margarets Bay.

City dwellers looking for a good beach often head to this bay because it is shallow and runs sufficiently far back that the water is reasonably warm in late summer. Several beaches that offer excellent swimming are in Hubbards and Queensland.

There is a charming little Heritage inn and restaurant located in Hubbards, which makes the local beach communities even more enticing during a short jaunt from the city. The **Dauphinee Inn,** at 167 Shore Club Road, is the second-oldest inn in the province, having operated since 1920. It overlooks a small inlet, just off the main road, so you can spot it easily. The little restaurant is also very cozy, with a panoramic view of the shore, and it features assorted "packages," in which all the details are worked out for rooms, a candlelight lobster dinner with wine, for example, and the use of a canoe or bicycle. Rates are moderate. For information, call (800) 567–1790 or (902) 857–1790, or visit www .dauphineeinn.com. The inn is open only during the summer.

If you follow along Route 329, you'll reach the point of the peninsula that separates St. Margarets Bay from **Mahone Bay.** Here you will also find a provincial picnic park and Bayswater Beach, with its broad stretch of white sand. From time to time seals can be seen sunning themselves nearby.

The name Mahone actually is derived from the French word *mahonne,* which was the kind of vessel favored by French pirates. Foremost among the bay's islands are ***Big*** and ***Little Tancook Islands,*** with populations of permanent residents numbering 218 and 32 respectively. The islands can be reached by a small pedestrian-only ferry that runs two to six times daily, depending on the day of the week. For details on the ferry, call Tancook Island Transportation at (902) 228–2340. Avoid taking the last ferry of the day to Tancook if you want to return the same day, because it docks on the island for the night.

In earlier days the combined population of the two Tancook Islands exceeded 1,100. Isolation, a downturn in the fishing industry, and the need to move off the islands for junior and senior high schooling all contributed to the population shrinkage. Islanders must rely on the ferry to transport their groceries, which are loaded in a large metal crate and then hoisted onto the ferry with a crane. Locals get around mostly with all-terrain vehicles or dirt bikes, but some other vehicles have been brought to the island, although the ferry carries only passengers.

The shallow, pebbly swimming beach at Southeast Cove on Big Tancook Island is quite warm and accessed by a pleasant hike through the island. It's near the tiny, locally run Island Museum which presents an interesting portrait of the two islands' early inhabitants. Next door you can purchase snacks and treats at Ferrar's General Store. The island also has a basic, wilderness campsite near Southeast Cove's beach.

The first Europeans on the islands were German farmers who settled here because they could let their cattle range freely. They soon discovered that the soil was perfect for growing oversize cabbages; even today Tancook is noted for its superb sauerkraut. You can't miss it in local grocery stores. It is imaginatively labeled "Tancook Sauerkraut" and comes packaged in something resembling a red-and-white-striped milk carton.

The permanent residents are now most commonly involved in the fishing industry; historically, they engaged in schooner-building. In addition to the company of seagulls, the thrill of isolation in a completely out-of-the-way seaside setting, and nature trails, Big Tancook Island offers a bed-and-breakfast, a canteen, a grocery store, and a gift shop.

Two colorful villages overlook Mahone Bay. On three fingers of one peninsula you will find ***Chester,*** which was, from its beginning, a hub of privateer raids. Its first residents were transplanted Bostonians, in 1759. These were followed by United Empire Loyalists, along with the French, Germans, and Swiss.

Its early links to New England did not spare Chester from being the focus of raids by American privateers. In 1782, while the village's men were off gathering firewood, three such ships threatened to sack the defenseless village. The broomstick-carrying women of the village marched back and forth along the hill above the community, the red linings of their cloaks worn outward.

The privateers, thinking that the village was guarded by British redcoats, decided to sail farther south and sack neighboring Lunenburg instead.

Check out one of the colorful platters or bowls made by folk artist Jim Smith, who operates ***Nova Scotia Folk Pottery*** on Front Harbour during the summer months. Also in Chester you can shop for quality woven crafts, such as quilts and linens, at the ***Warp and Woof*** on Water Street.

For the past hundred years or so, Chester has been the summer retreat of sailing enthusiasts, from the descendants of U.S. president Grover Cleveland to the presidents of universities, along with a smattering of cabinet ministers, former prime ministers, and famous authors.

The affluent summer crowd swells the village's permanent population of 1,000 by as much as 30 percent, giving it both a touch of cultural vibrancy and the lotus-eater quality of exotic haunts. There are gleaming yachts, Jaguars and Mercedes, seaside eateries with trendy menus, and Cape Cod architecture without the New York crowd. Yet few people even in neighboring Halifax give Chester a second thought except in mid-August during ***Race Week,*** which since 1904 has been the culmination of the social season.

The race draws sailors from Boston and beyond, filling the bay with sleek yachts. Parties spring up everywhere, and people flock to ***The Chester Playhouse.*** The playhouse was purchased and then donated to the village by financier and author Christopher Ondaatje, who spends his summers on his hundred-acre (forty-hectare) island in Mahone Bay. He summed up the reason for his generosity: "None of the people who come here want to make a buck out of Chester."

Some time back the playhouse was enjoying enormous success presenting opera with puppets. Every summer something new and fresh keeps the regulars coming back. To get a brochure outlining the program write to The Chester Playhouse, P.O. Box 293, Chester, NS B0J 1J0, or call (800) 363–7529.

Perhaps owing to the affluence of its summer visitors, the tiny village has a surprising number of eating establishments serving excellent seafood. You can also find a decidedly civilized breakfast or snack at ***Julien's Bakery,*** which specializes in croissants, cappuccino, and sandwiches. Add to this the village's watering holes (the oldest and most popular of these is the Fo'c'sle), and you get the impression of an uncluttered corner of the Hamptons.

Farther along Provincial Highway 103 or closer to the shoreline on Highway 3, you will pass ***Oak Island,*** reputed to be the site where Captain William Kidd hid his treasure. For two centuries people have risked their lives (and sometimes lost them) trying to get at the treasure supposedly hidden under an elaborate network of underground tunnels. Visitors can tour the site, where excavation is ongoing.

Continuing along Highway 103, you'll come to the community of Mahone Bay, which has several star attractions tucked in among this sailor's paradise and its bay with 360-odd islands.

As soon as you enter the community, you'll see the village's star attraction: The pretty shoreline, dotted with churches, is a postcard waiting to happen. Pull into the **Innlet Cafe,** situated at the perfect bend in the road for photographing Mahone Bay. Set up your tripod or prop your camera on the stone retaining wall at the front of the cafe, and you will get a picture of one of the most photogenic spots in the province.

This village gives the impression of being a bit busier than Chester, since a number of craftspeople have set up shop here.

This is a good place for antiques hunting, and visitors can also visit pottery, pewter, and rug-hooking studios and photo and art galleries. It seems that few can resist buying a quilt when visiting this part of Nova Scotia, and this area of the province is a great place to look for these. Foremost among the shops offering stunning patchwork apparel and quilts is **Suttles & Seawinds,** on Mahone Bay's Main Street. Nearby is a pottery shop of note: **Birdsall-Worthington Pottery Ltd.** has eathernware pottery and handmade earrings. Another shop worth a visit is the upscale **Teazer,** on Edgewater Drive, which is noted for fine local crafts and quality clothing.

Privateers figured prominently in the community's history. During the War of 1812, an American ship, *The Young Teazer* was chased into Mahone Bay by a British warship. One of the crewmen aboard the privateer was a British deserter who set fire to the ship's powder magazine rather than be captured by the British. The resulting explosion killed twenty-eight on board.

The flourishing shipbuilding trade of old-time Mahone Bay brought with it considerable wealth, as shown by the many stately old Victorian, Georgian, and Cape Cod homes here. Many Main Street businesses occupy buildings formerly used by shipbuilders. A "walking tour" brochure gives a closer look at the local architecture. It's available at the **Mahone Bay Settler's Museum,** at 578 Main Street. The village hosts a wooden-boat festival at the beginning of August. It includes workshops, demonstrations of maritime skills for all ages, schooner races, and boatyard tours. Admission is free. For details, call (902) 624–6263.

The stretch along the coast from Chester to Mahone Bay is also a favorite area for cycle touring, since it offers picture-perfect coastline and frequent rest stops—in the way of seafood restaurants.

After Mahone Bay continue along Trunk Highway 3 until you reach **Lunenburg,** the birthplace of many famous ships. It was here that the *Bluenose* and its replica were built, as well as the full-scale replica of HMS *Bounty* used in the Marlon Brando version of *Mutiny on the Bounty.*

As far as picturesque fishing villages go, they don't get any prettier than Lunenburg and its harbor, proof of which you will find on the back of a Canadian $100 bill. The scene hasn't changed a whit since that photograph was taken.

Most prominent of all the waterfront buildings is a large red one beside a wharf. This is the **Fisheries Museum of the Atlantic.** Along with the aquarium and working dory shop, the museum has several fishing vessels, including the schooner *Theresa E. Connor.* This sailing ship, built in the 1930s, was used in the fisheries for twenty-five years. Here you get the opportunity to practice traditional fishermen's skills, such as net repair and rope-making, that have been Lunenburg's lifeblood from its founding. These traditions go way back and have stamped the area permanently with the lore and spirit of the people who make their living from the sea. Admission is $9.00 for adults. It is open daily from 9:30 A.M. to 5:30 P.M.

One of the big outcroppings of this is a strong tradition of folk music and art, as evidenced by the **Lunenburg Folk Harbour Festival,** held the second weekend of August every year from Thursday through Sunday. This is a really great party well worth attending, so keep it in mind when you time your visit.

There is also an annual craft festival, in which many local artisans display their wares. It is timed to take place the second weekend in July. Since the town is so pleasant and picturesque, many craftspeople and artists live in the vicinity, making this a good bet for people interested in buying or looking at some folk art or crafts.

In Lunenburg you can stay at the historic **Boscawen Inn,** built in 1888. It is located at 150 Cumberland Street, overlooking the harbor. Its twenty guest rooms are furnished with antiques. Rates are standard to moderate. The inn has a three-and-a-half-star rating. The restaurant is also highly rated and participates in the "Taste of Nova Scotia" program. For reservations, call (800) 354–5009 or (902) 634–3325, or write to Boscawen Inn, 150 Cumberland Street, Box 1343, Lunenburg, NS B0J 2C0.

What really gave Lunenburg its color was the influx of large numbers of German Protestants by boat from Halifax at its founding in 1753. *Deutsch* (German) soon became "Dutch" in everyone's parlance, so everyone began calling them the Lunenburg Dutch. Their descendants have put an indelible stamp on the local lingo. The accent is strong and verbs sometimes find their way to the end of the sentence. If you meet a Nova Scotian nicknamed "Dutchy," you can bet he's from Lunenburg.

The German connection continues today. Many German nationals have recently purchased homes along this coast for use as summer homes, which they fly to annually, thanks to cheap and convenient air connections and a strong Euro currency.

Before leaving the town, plan to stroll around and look at some of its lovely architecture, which dates back to its founding, just four years after Halifax.

Of all the buildings, by far the most imposing structure is **Lunenburg Academy,** built in 1894 high atop Gallows Hill, where it can be seen for many miles around. This is the province's only surviving academy building dating from the nineteenth century. It is full of all sorts of Victorian bits of fancy: oval-shaped portholes, towers, decorative shingles, and intricate bracketry. And when you reach the hill where this municipal, provincial, and federal Heritage building stands, you are presented with a panoramic view of the town's many beautiful old homes.

Traveling south from Lunenburg, take a fifteen-minute detour off Highway 3 and travel on Route 332 in the direction of East LaHave. Just before you reach this point you will come to the head of Rose Bay and a small sign indicating the exit to **The Ovens.** This is a sight you must not miss, for here was the scene of a major gold strike in 1861.

It still holds some gold deposits to this day. For an admission fee of $6.00, you can enter the park and pan for gold along the beach. On the day that I visited, I spoke with some men who went at least once a week, always coming away with some grains of gold. It's easy to get on-the-spot prospecting lessons, because the beach is the regular haunt of helpful amateur prospectors. The management also gives periodic demonstrations of proper technique.

After an afternoon of panning I must confess that my family came away with six grains of gold. Not much, but the experience was greatly enhanced by the kids' "get-rich-quick" fantasies and by the occasion to hang out with some real gold diggers.

At The Ovens you can descend a series of concrete steps set into the side of sea caves. These are so massive that they are legendary to the Mi'Kmaq, who believe that a brave once traveled from one of these caves to a similar one on the Bay of Fundy, on the other side of Nova Scotia. Once you get to the bottom of the steps of some of the bigger caves, you will be treated to the earthshaking boom of the waves as they crash against the rocks. You can also take a boat with a guide, who will lead you right into the biggest caves.

The Ovens has campsites and some log cabins for rent, a pool, and a restaurant with a surprisingly good menu, considering its secluded location. Rates are standard to moderate. For reservations call (902) 766–4621.

After visiting The Ovens, take Highway 332 back to Route 3 outside Lunenburg and then turn south at exit 12, onto Provincial Highway 103. After a half hour's drive, you will come to **Liverpool,** once favored by the privateers.

From 1750 until the War of 1812 ended, Nova Scotia's and, in particular, Liverpool's ships were commissioned to roam the high seas in search of vessels to plunder. Liverpudlian Enos Collins, owner of a privateer ship called *The Packet,* was rumored to be Canada's richest man; he died with a fortune of $10 million.

The wealth brought in is evidenced by the historic buildings and museums here, recalling the wild days of the town's youth. Liverpool is the site of the oldest house in the entire collection of Nova Scotia museums, of which there are now twenty-four. To find it, exit Provincial Highway 103 on Main Street and proceed in the direction of Moose Harbour. Just after Bristol Avenue you'll see the museum at 105 Main Street, set far back on a lawn that it shares with the county museum.

Called the ***Perkins House,*** after its original owner, this one-and-a-half-story building was the home of a twenty-seven-year-old Connecticut widower who came to Nova Scotia in 1762. Here he successfully established himself as, among other things, a justice of the court of common pleas, a judge of probate, and a member of the legislative assembly.

In this simple home, Simeon Perkins entertained privateer captains, governors, and traveling men of the cloth. He wrote about his life in a diary that he kept faithfully from 1766 until his death in 1812. It now serves as a valuable historical record on the early life of this province's settlers. A copy is on site for your perusal, and every day museum staff members turn to that date's corresponding entry in his diary so that visitors can take in the history of the area's early settlers.

The entries tell of both mundane and profound concerns, from outbreaks of smallpox, to raids by American privateers, to the stuff that made up his day-to-day life with his first and second wives and his six daughters and two sons. A small admission is charged. It is open June 1 to October 15 from 9:30 A.M. until 5:30 P.M. Monday to Saturday and Sunday from 1:00 to 5:30 P.M.

Liverpool wasn't the most tranquil place to raise children. In 1783 Americans landed at nearby Fort Point and overran the town. Through the efforts of Perkins, they were repulsed.

Perkins House, Liverpool

In the 1930s, when the museum was being established, the problem arose of how to furnish the home in period furnishings that matched the inventory of its original occupant. Pieces had to be purchased at an auction in Massachusetts.

All parts of the diary that were written in Nova Scotia have been published by the Champlain Society. The original is on display at the **Queens County Museum,** which is adjacent to Perkins House. This museum represents the warehouse of Perkins's business.

Another highlight of this museum is a diorama and model railroad, built by seniors, that demonstrate how in the 1940s the railway connected all the little communities along these shores. The shoreline has been meticulously reproduced. The attendant will set the train in motion for you, then playfully blow into a wooden whistle that makes the characteristic train sound.

If you have any ancestral roots from this end of Nova Scotia, this is a good place to trace them. The building, which is operated by the historical society, houses the Thomas Raddall Research Room, which features a library and genealogical records for Queens County. Thomas Raddall, one of the province's most noteworthy writers, published many novels set in Nova Scotia. Admission to the museum is $1.00. It has the same hours as Perkins House next door.

Explore your artistic side at the **Gallery of Roger Savage,** at 611 Mersey Point Road in a bedroom community called **Mersey Point.** To get there take the next right turn after Perkins House and drive down School Street toward the Western Head Lighthouse. The drive takes about 15 minutes.

Savage is one of the region's most highly esteemed artists. He not only does paintings of coastal landscapes, but also creates watercolors, portraits, and lithographs. For information or to register for a workshop, call (902) 354–5431. To reserve one of the two bedrooms in his home or for details, visit www.bbcanada.com/galleryguesthouse.

There are a number of cozy places to stay in the area, two of which are located near wonderfully unspoiled beaches. One, **White Point Beach Lodge,** is rated three and one-half stars and is quite popular. It occupies the shoreline of White Point Beach.

This well-known resort can be reached via exit 20A or 21, off Highway 103. The restaurant here has nightly bonfires and features the local specialty: plank salmon—salmon that is barbecued over an open fire after it's been laid out on boards. There is a play area for children in the dining room, which owner Doug Fawthrop assures me keeps the little critters out of the adults' hair quite effectively. Mussels are cooked in fire pits with hot rocks. The older kids of guests can go on a supervised overnight camping trip to a small neighboring island, accessed by a rowboat. You can reach the lodge by calling (800) 565–5068. Rates are moderate to deluxe.

A much smaller-scale set of beachside villas can be found at neighboring Summerville Beach, at a place called *The Quarterdeck Beachside Villas and Grill.* It provides intimate, two-story condo-style accommodations over-looking the tranquil, spotless white sands of Summerville Beach, on a site that was occupied by much older rustic cottages for fifty years. The new villas are so close to the shoreline that you are lulled to sleep by the steady lapping of the waves.

If you are in the mood for an early morning hike, walk to the far southern end of the beach and then cross over a small arm of water via a one-time rail crossing. This leads to another tranquil little cove, where you can watch shore-birds do their thing. The beach is home to piping plovers and sandpipers.

Each villa has lots of pleasant little extras: propane-powered fireplace, two bathrooms, one featuring a Jacuzzi complete with rubber ducky, well-equipped kitchen facilities, a patio overlooking the ocean, and a second-floor deck, also facing the sea. The walls are decorated with original artwork, all for sale.

The restaurant here overlooks the ocean and serves plank salmon, among other delicious fare. The Quarterdeck is off Highway 103; turn at exit 20 and head for Summerville Beach. For information and reservations, call (800) 565–1119 or (902) 683–2998. For details, visit www.quarterdeck.ns.ca or e-mail qdvilla@auracom.com. Rates are moderate to deluxe.

From Liverpool you have the option of turning inland onto Route 8 to experience the wilderness of *Kejimkujik National Park,* or you can continue heading south on either Route 3 or Highway 103 (which briefly overlaps Route 3) around the tip of Nova Scotia, and reserve Kejimkujik for later. In the next section we will continue to follow the route southward, toward Yarmouth, the southern gateway to the province.

The Western Lighthouse Route

Just past the town of Liverpool, on Highway 103, is a wonderful but little-known wilderness area. It is the nesting ground of endangered species, an unspoiled stretch of shoreline completely lacking in "development." During the piping plovers' mating season, parts of this area are closed to the public.

In 1985 the province handed over 5,400 acres (2,160 hectares) of this land to the National Park Service, which now administers it as part of Kejimkujik National Park. Called the *Seaside Adjunct,* it offers two pristine beaches, both 2 miles (3 km) long, completely unspoiled wilderness, and rocky headlands. (There are no facilities for human visitors, so plan accordingly.) It is very easy

The Endangered Piping Plover

The *Seaside Adjunct* is a nesting ground of the ill-fated piping plover, which has become increasingly rare due to its unfortunate habit of laying eggs in piles of rock near the shoreline. The spotted eggs look decidedly like rocks, which would be a nice form of camouflage if only they didn't get stepped on by human passersby.

Bear this in mind if you decide to walk along the pristine beaches of this coast: What may look like a rock may actually be the egg of an endangered baby bird. So crucial is this area to the survival of piping plovers that parts of the annex are closed from late April to late July so that the birds can hatch safely.

to miss the road for the Seaside Adjunct, so as you drive south down the one and only stretch of highway (Route 3/Highway 103), be on the lookout for the Port Joli Community Centre. Take a left here and follow a gravel road to the Seaside Adjunct. It is well signed.

Along with birds, you may get a look at some coastal seals as they frolic in the waves off this blissfully solitary shore.

Just south of the Seaside Adjunct, off Highway 103 and about 25 miles (40 km) from Liverpool, you will come to the ***Port l'Hebert Pocket Wilderness,*** a piece of woodland set aside by a pulp and paper company that has extensive land holdings in western Nova Scotia. Look for a sign on the road 6 miles (10 km) after Port Joli and just before you reach the Shelburne County line.

At Port l'Hebert you will find about 2 miles (3 km) of graveled walking trails that cut through 150 acres (60 hectares) of woodlands and salt marshes. These paths stretch from the small parking lot on the side of the highway where you turned off, to the shores of a tiny bay called Port L'Hebert Harbour, which draws its name from an apothecary who sailed with Samuel de Champlain in 1604. Louis l'Hebert's name lives on at Louis Head as well.

These lands are the wintering grounds of a flock of Canada geese. They need eel grass, open water, and as little disturbance as possible to get through the winter; few places suit them as well as this site. Due to its importance, the Canadian Wildlife Service has designated the marshy shoreline a waterfowl sanctuary.

You may also spot the common yellowthroat warbler and red-eyed vireo here. The trail is quite an easy walk, with some boardwalk aiding your travel, but if you stray from the path you may discover your feet sinking into the bog. The water looks quite uninviting here, stained as it is a murky tea-brown. In fact, however, it is nutrient-rich, and the saltmarshes that border this bay are nurseries for all manner of sea life. Before white settlers arrived, inland Mi'K-maq families came here to gather shellfish and to fish.

Once you have finished stretching your legs, return to your vehicle at the end of the trail loop and head, camera-ready, 12 miles (20 km) south on Route 3 to the scenic village of **Lockeport.** This is the site of the province's first officially designated Heritage streetscape, which slates it for historic preservation. **Crescent Beach,** which runs along the entrance to the town, was once on the back of the Canadian $50 bill.

A visitor's information bureau overlooks the beach. Here you can change into a bathing suit or arrange for the rental of a nearby cottage. Be sure to check out the tile mural by local artist Rebecca Tudor, whose studio is in Sable River. (Her work also appears on the floor of the Shelburne Visitor's Center.) Natural elements such as tulips, wildflowers, and fish blend in her pieces to create a harmony reminiscent of Tiffany's elegant stained-glass windows.

The road to Lockeport runs the length of the beach, giving the impression that you are driving along a sandbar to an island. Its location off the main highway adds to the impression that you are visiting a separate island. The beach is spectacular—hence its appearance on the $50 bill.

Apart from strolling around the tiny village taking pictures, there is not a lot to do here. When your interest is sated, get back in your car and head farther south on Route 3 to a string of villages peopled by the descendants of Loyalists from Nantucket and Cape Cod who came to this area after 1760.

From Lockeport it is only a half-hour's drive to **Shelburne** along Provincial Trunk Highway 3 until you reach exit 25. Following the road will lead you into the town's historic waterfront **Dock Street.**

Try to park near the visitor's center, which is built right at the water's edge. If you stop in, be sure to take a good look at the floor tile mosaic by Rebecca Tudor. From here all of the historic area is to your left as you face the water.

trivia

The Nova Scotia Loyalists had a banner on which was inscribed the Latin word: RESURGAM. It means: "I shall rise again."

In Shelburne you can visit the **Ross-Thomson House,** a remnant from the era of the United Empire Loyalists. It is located on Charlotte Lane, which intersects Dock Street, quite near the harbor. As you walk inside, the most striking thing is the rich patina of the building. Goods from the era of the former store are laid out as if the company were still in business, right down to birch brooms and wooden toys.

In early 1783 the shores around here were the landing site of some 5,000 settlers from New York and the Middle Colonies of America. Acting on the promise of free land, tools, and provisions, many had chosen to leave the new republic and head north to live under British rule. This first wave of settlers was followed by another wave in the fall, many of them entrepreneurs.

By the following year the population of Shelburne was double that of Halifax, and larger than Montreal or Quebec at the time. In fact, at its peak it was the third-largest town in North America. Because of the huge influx of colonists, it has become one of the continent's genealogical treasures.

The Ross-Thomson House is the last original store building from that era. It was the site of intense trading. The owners, a pair of brothers originally from Scotland, sold local wood; fish and salt from Turk's Island; tobacco, rum, sugar, and molasses from the West Indies; fine goods from Britain; Portuguese wine; and many other local and imported items.

trivia

The first solo circumnavigation of the world was made by Nova Scotian–born sailor Joshua Slocum, aboard the *Spray*. He started his journey in April 1895 and finished over three years later in July 1898.

Little by little, however, the town's population began to dwindle. The lack of arable land meant that when the government withdrew from distributing food, living here became increasingly difficult. By the 1820s the town had shrunk to a mere 300 souls.

The building is typical of the type favored by the Loyalists. The house shows a strong New England influence, with its gambrel roof and gables. Finished with heavy plank doors, the house had the added security of studs, bars, and a double lock. For a time the house served as the town post office; the shutter on the north window has a slot into which late mail could be slipped.

The house also features a "Loyalist Garden" out back, which demonstrates how day-to-day provisions were grown by people like the Ross brothers and the Thomson family 200 years ago.

Upstairs in the house, you will find an exhibit on the Shelburne Militia. The Ross-Thomson House is open daily June to mid-October from 9:30 A.M. to 5:30 P.M. A small admission is charged. For details on the museum, call (902) 875–3141.

Much of Shelburne's Loyalist past is still in evidence in the town, as shown by the number of buildings still standing that date from the time of the American War of Independence. Among these, one has been turned into a small inn, overlooking the harbor. Called **Cooper's Inn,** it dates from 1785 and has been sufficiently preserved and restored that it has received an award from Heritage Trust Nova Scotia. Like all the other buildings on Dock Street, it is finished in deep-brown shingles. Located near Ross-Thomson House, this building was constructed under the direction of a blind Loyalist merchant named George Gracie.

Through the centuries it has housed mariners, shipbuilders, gentlemen esquires, merchants, and coopers. Apart from the cozy Colonial atmosphere, the highlight of this place is the dining room, which features superb meals during the season. It is open from April to October. For reservations call (800) 688–2011 or (902) 875–4656. Rates are standard to moderate, with breakfast included.

Cooper's Inn, along with several other places on Dock Street, was part of extensive restorations undertaken prior to a visit by the newly married Prince and Princess of Wales in 1983.

Because of the facelift, the harbor area is quite a pleasant place to roam aimlessly and soak up atmosphere. Think of it as time travel. It is sufficiently authentic that it was used as the location for the 1995 movie *The Scarlet Letter.*

More information on the Loyalist era can be found at another Dock Street locale, the **Shelburne County Museum.** For those of you who have families dating back to Revolutionary days and a link to Loyalists who settled in Nova Scotia, this is the place to track down some family history. The museum has extensive genealogical records. There are even eighteenth- to twentieth-century newspapers on microfilm so that you can peruse the old news at your leisure. The museum is open year-round, with summer hours daily from 9:30 A.M. to 5:30 P.M. For information call (902) 875–3219. Admission is $3.00, or for the village's four museums, pay $8.00 as a flat fee.

Another source for genealogical information is next door to the museum, at the **Shelburne County Genealogical Research Centre.** Eleanor Smith is a certified genealogist on staff who assists people in tracing their Nova Scotian roots.

moviemaking magic

You will no doubt wonder how the asphalt was hidden from the camera during the filming of *The Scarlet Letter.* The solution was to truck in loads of dirt and cover the paving. No detail was too small to ignore during the making of the movie. To ensure that the white houses of a distant point were not in the background, for example, the set designers had bushes strategically planted to obscure the distant shore.

Members of the Shelburne County Genealogical Society can search records for free, but a mere $5.00 fee gives you access to considerable research.

The center has indexed church records and vital statistics, an in-depth census, and the international genealogical index, as well as records for the whole county. It also keeps newspaper statistics on various people and information on Heritage homes in the area. Smith points out that not all the families in this area were Loyalists: A number of Welsh, Icelandic, and Scottish people settled here. Blacks from the United States also settled in nearby Birchtown at the time of the Revolution.

Of those settlers who were Loyalists, some returned to the United States after a few years, leaving relatives behind here. Other Shelburne-area people moved to American cities in the early 1900s. Their descendants now often come in search of distant relatives still living in this area.

Of particular interest is the history of **Birchtown,** named for General John Birch, the New York commander who gave protection to Loyalist blacks, whose direct descendants still live here. At the time of the Revolution, many black American slaves chose to take sides with the British, who promised them their freedom. Expecting equal treatment with other Loyalists, they came to live under British rule. But few of them received the land that the white Loyalists received as a matter of course, and those who did get land received substandard lots.

Most ended up working as wage laborers, but the pay was so low that a group of disbanded soldiers rioted against the unfair competition that the blacks' low wages created. The result was that twenty black Loyalist homes were destroyed in ten days of rioting.

In 1783, when the village was settled by 1,500 freed slaves, it was the largest free black settlement in North America. But by 1792 the settlers in Birchtown were fed up, and they joined other black Loyalists in the province who had decided that a return to Africa was in order. That year 1,200 of them left the colony and founded Freetown in Sierra Leone.

Recent archaeological digs in the neighborhood of Birchtown have revealed remnants of the early days of these settlers. Eleanor Smith points out that some of them had homes that were little more than holes dug into the ground and then covered with a roof.

The museum is open year-round Monday to Saturday, from 9:00 A.M. to 5:00 P.M. There are reduced hours in winter. For information, call (902) 875–4299.

One other Dock Street site is worth a special mention: **The Dory Shop.** You may have visited a dory shop along the Lighthouse Route (Route 3), but if you haven't, this one is operated by the Nova Scotia museum system and comprises three stories of dory-making memorabilia. A factory from 1880 to 1970, it is all that is left in the town of seven dory shops. It opened as a museum in 1983 and featured as its star attraction master builder Sidney Mahaney, who made dories according to the traditional methods he learned in his youth. Mahaney began building dories at age seventeen and continued until his death at age ninety-six in 1993. One of his miniature dories was given to Prince William as a present.

A large photograph of Mahaney, decked out in a Nova Scotia tartan shirt, acts as a backdrop for his last hand-built dory, which is displayed here. In the early days, this particular shop produced two dories a day, and sold them for

$18.00 apiece. When Mahaney started in 1914, his wages were 45 cents a day. (They reached their peak back then at $2.00 a day, after a man had received a raise every three years.)

Anyone who has lived along Canada's Atlantic coast has at one time or another placed personal safety in the hands of one of these reliable little boats. The story of their construction and the role they have played in inshore fishery is fascinating.

On the premises you will find an information booth that can fill you in on local events. Admission is $3.00 for adults or you can buy a general ticket for all four sites. The shop is open daily mid-June to mid-September from 9:30 A.M. to 5:30 P.M. Call (902) 875–3219.

After you've visited the town of Shelburne, you can resume your drive down the Lighthouse Route (Highway 3), or Highway 103 until twenty minutes later, when the roads converge at the head of Barrington Bay in a village called Barrington Passage.

If you ever had the urge to get onto a Cape Islander boat, here is your chance. The Barrington Passage Tourist Bureau has one you can visit. (It's also on Highway 3.) *The Seal Island Light Museum* is open to the public, and you can climb the five stories to the top, which offers a panoramic view of the bay.

Continue along Highway 3 in Barrington until you cross the Barrington River, indicated by a road sign. Here you'll find the *Barrington Woolen Mill,* where you can get a good look at an old-time water turbine–powered woolen mill. This had its beginnings in 1882 as a community enterprise, to provide fishermen with wool clothing. Inside the mill is a magnificent wall hanging woven by Bessie Murray. In addition to its depiction of Nova Scotia's history, the wall hanging features a piper wearing the Nova Scotia tartan, which was designed by Murray. This was the origin of the tartan, and the wall hanging you see here was its unveiling, as it were. Outside is a pleasant picture: The mill overlooks a rushing stream and is quite lovely.

trivia

The world's second-most abundant seal species is the harp seal, seen every winter off the Atlantic coast.

For several decades the mill was an important supplier of specialized woolen goods for the people of this region. It is now part of the Nova Scotia Museum system and features jennies, looms, a dye house, and equipment for scouring wool. It is open June 1 to September 30 Monday to Saturday from 9:30 A.M. to 5:30 P.M., Sunday from 1:00 to 5:30 P.M. For information call (902) 637–2185. Admission is $1.00 for adults, $4.00 for families, 50 cents for children five to twelve years of age.

A change of pace from the dory shops and elegant old homes is the **Old Meeting House in Barrington,** located at the head of Barrington Bay. The barnlike meetinghouse was built in 1765 by Loyalist pilgrims who used it as a place of worship and for public meetings. It is the oldest New England–style meetinghouse in the province. Barrington Township itself was founded in 1761 by fifty families of Cape Cod planters, who brought their religion, customs, and building style north with them.

To meet the religious needs of all denominations, they built the meeting-house for " . . . all preachers of the Gospel. . . ." Eventually, the different denominations built their own places of worship. The old meetinghouse almost fell prey to the wrecking ball until a community group saved it. It is now part of the Nova Scotia Museum system.

Be sure to stroll through the graveyard adjacent to the building, where you will see the markers of many of the area's early settlers. One fine day, in the mid-dle of a funeral on the morning of May 4, 1783, the mourners noticed a great cloud of white sails crowding the harbor mouth. There they saw the singular event that was to transform Shelburne into one of the most important towns on the continent. That morning a convoy of transports carried into the harbor thou-sands of United Empire Loyalists, newly exiled from their New England homes.

The meetinghouse is open June 1 to September 30 Monday to Saturday from 9:30 A.M. to 5:30 P.M., Sunday from 1:00 to 5:30 P.M. For details call (902) 637–2185.

You can live in Nova Scotia for decades and never visit the remote fishing villages of the southernmost tip of the province unless you are headed for one of the ferries to Portland or Bar Harbor, Maine. This is decidedly off-trail and well worth some lazy puttering.

As for archetypical fishing villages, they don't get more authentic than **Clark's Harbour,** Cape Sable Island, the southernmost part of Nova Scotia. Once the British won their final battle with the French, this whole area opened up for settlement, in large part encouraged by the expulsion of the Acadians and supplemented by the American Revolution, which followed a few years later.

One of the first places to be settled by exiles from the other colonies was **Cape Sable Island.** In 1761 the island was settled by forty families from outer Cape Cod. The following year a number of whalers and their families from Nantucket moved into neighboring areas. Even Halifax Harbour's eastern waterfront was a site of a Cape Cod whaler settlement, as evidenced by some of the houses near the Old Dartmouth waterfront.

On Cape Sable Island especially, traces of the Cape Cod housing style and even the accents linger. Fishing and related industries have always been its main-stay. It was here in 1907 that the Cape Island boat was first built for fishing off the coast. To this day it is the standard for small fishing boats to withstand the cruel seas of the North Atlantic.

They are not as elegant as the schooners of yore, but the Cape Islander, like the dory, is outstandingly seaworthy, sitting high in the water. The standard Cape Islander is 38 feet (11 m) long, with a 12-foot (3.6-m) beam. The old ones had a pulpit on the bow for harpooning.

Stay on Highway 3 as you proceed around the southern tip of the province and you will see a string of small fishing and farming communities peopled by the descendants of Loyalist planters and returned Acadians, among others: Ste.-Anne du Ruisseau and **West, Middle West,** and **Lower West Pubnico** are a few of these villages, partially peopled by the descendants of the Acadians who originally settled here in 1653. If you look carefully, you will see traces of these early days, from an old stone bridge to the **Musée Acadien,** or Acadian Museum, in West Pubnico.

This Acadian Museum is a homestead dating back to 1864. Today it contains artifacts from Acadian pioneer days along with land grant documents from the 1700s. To visit turn off Highway 3 onto Highway 335 and drive east for 3 miles (5 km) until you reach West Pubnico. Admission is $3.00. It is open from early June to September 15, Monday to Saturday from 9:00 A.M. to 5:00 P.M., Sunday from 12:30 to 4:30 P.M. For details call (902) 762–3380.

> ## trivia
>
> The first shipwreck in Canada was the *Delight,* which ran aground on Nova Scotia's Sable Island in 1583. Since then, more than 500 ships have met their end on this island, known as the "Graveyard of the Atlantic."

The name Pubnico is derived from the Mi'Kmaq word for "cleared land." The actual village of Pubnico (not Middle, West or Lower West) was settled by transplanted New Englanders who came in 1761, filling the void created by the expulsion of Acadians from the region.

After you check out the local history, hop into your car and drive to the end of the line, about 2.5 miles (4 km), to Charlesville. There is nothing much going on here, though the shoreline was the landing site of well over one hundred Sikh refugees a few years back. Stop anywhere to buy a bottle of soda pop. Naively ask, "Say, wasn't this where all those guys landed?" and you'll be treated to the full story. It's a great icebreaker.

Just before you reach Yarmouth proper, turn off Highway 3 at Arcadia and follow the sign for Kelly Cove and Chebogue Point. Soon after joining the lupine-edged shore road, you will come to the tiny **Town Point Cemetery.**

Apart from the many old settlers who found their final resting place here, a sad and beautiful love story is linked to the place. Among the weathered headstones you will find a life-size carving of a woman reclining, as if asleep, on sheaves of wheat, sickle in hand. This is the grave of one Margaret Webster, who died in 1861. Several years before this date, her Yarmouth-born husband was a young medical student in Scotland.

One day he was walking through the fields when he came upon just such a sleeping figure. He paused for a long time to watch the beautiful woman, exhausted by her work, catching forty winks. When the woman awoke, he introduced himself, and soon a relationship developed. The two were married, and that would have been the end of the story had Margaret Webster not died suddenly.

The bereaved young man returned to Yarmouth, where he searched until he found a talented artist to make a marble effigy of his young wife, who reclines to this day, seemingly asleep, on the sheaves of wheat where her husband first fell in love with her.

It's just a statue and a sentimental side trip, but the detour is worthwhile. The roadside is strewn with lupines, and if you look out over the water, you will get a sweeping view of the Tusket Islands.

Westbound from Yarmouth, the Lighthouse Route takes on a new name, the Evangeline Trail, in honor of Longfellow's epic poem about the banished Acadians. Therefore, you will enter **Yarmouth** on the very last leg of the Lighthouse Route and meet the beginning of the Evangeline Trail where Highway 1 meets Highway 3.

The junction is also the corner of Starr's Road and Main Street, down by the waterfront in beautiful downtown Yarmouth, population 7,781. From this corner take a left, continue half a block, and keep your eyes open for the **Firefighter's Museum** on your left at 451 Main Street.

If you are arriving from Maine on a ferry, you'll be departing the boat just slightly farther down that same waterfront road. In this case, as you drive off the Marine Atlantic Ferry, turn left onto Main Street. Continue past the Parade Street intersection to 451 Main Street on your right. The Firefighter's Museum is the only provincial firefighter's museum in Canada. It has every type of fire engine ever in use in Nova Scotia, as well as all kinds of other vintage fire-fighting gear.

There is an 1880 Silsby Steamer that looks like a madman's boiler on wheels. A bright-red hand pumper dates back to 1819; it is so dinky that one expects a monkey and organ grinder to be next to it and a hot roasted-chestnut concession to be operating out of it. The shiny metal doodad-covered Holloway Chemical Engine from 1892 is so ornate that it could donate parts for Cinderella's carriage. Apart from the three horse-drawn steamers, the museum has some antique toy fire engines and other nostalgia for anybody who ever wanted to grow up to be a firefighter.

Firemen swear this is the best collection they've ever seen anywhere. In addition to possessing a fleet of mint-condition firetrucks, the Firefighter's Museum takes the bait for unusual stories. Check out the photo display on the Circus Ship Fire of 1963, where the local firefighters were called upon to save the lives of cheetahs, a Brahma bull, a zebra, and a llama. It may not have been the most dangerous fire they ever tackled, but it presented its own set of hazards. All were saved but the zebra.

The **National Exhibit Centre,** in the same complex, features traveling exhibits. For more information write to 451 Main Street, Yarmouth, NS B5A 1G9, or call (902) 742–5525. Admission is $3.00 per person, $6.00 per family. Hours are 9:00 A.M. to 9:00 P.M. Monday to Saturday in July and August. The rest of the year it is open Monday to Friday from 9:00 A.M. to 4:00 P.M. but closes daily from noon until 2:00 P.M.

Yarmouth's shoreline is a working waterfront, including a ferry dock, fish processing plants, and a fishing fleet. In addition, it is a major point of tourist entry for Nova Scotia. For easy exploring, the 3-mile (5-km) stretch of shoreline includes walkways, marina berths for pleasure craft, and a refurbished railway station dating back to the 1800s. The restored **Parker Eakins Building** houses a microbrewery and bakery with an informal dining room on the second floor.

Before leaving Yarmouth, you may want to explore local history at the **Yarmouth County Museum,** 22 Collins Street. Among other artifacts here, you will find a 400-pound (182-kg) stone inscribed by a group of Vikings including, it is believed, Leif Eriksson, in the year A.D. 1007. The inscription is nothing outstanding, being a Norseman's version of "Kilroy was here," but it is offered as proof that Christopher Columbus was not the first European to reach the New World and that Jacques Cartier and John Cabot were mere Johnny-come-latelies as well. The runic symbols are drawn from one of approximately a dozen distinct Norse alphabets, so the translation, although doubtful, is roughly believed to read: "Leif to Eric raises this monument."

The museum is a great place for would-be sailors, Viking or otherwise. The collection of Age of Sail artifacts, including ship portraits and models, is drawn from a seafaring past that saw Yarmouth as the home of the third-largest merchant navy in the world. When sailing ships ruled the day, this little town boasted the world's highest per capita ship tonnage. The remnants of this legacy are found at this museum, including one of the largest collections of marine paintings in the country as well as a lighthouse lens, a stagecoach, historic costumes, furniture, tools, and glass. For more information, call (902) 742–5539.

To get to the Yarmouth County Museum from the Firefighter's Museum, turn left when you exit the building and go south down Main Street toward the ferry terminal, until you get to the Collins Street intersection. Turn left again and you will be at the door of the museum. Admission is $3.00 for adults, less for children, students, seniors, and groups.

The museum is open June 1 to October 15 Monday to Saturday from 9:00 A.M. to 5:00 P.M., Sunday from 2:00 to 5:00 P.M., and October 16 to May 31, Tuesday to Saturday from 2:00 to 5:00 P.M.

After leaving the museum, get back onto Main Street and continue past Starrs Road. Turn left on Vancouver Street, then take a left again onto Route 304. Follow this route to Overton and *Cape Fourchu.* In a matter of minutes after leaving the town of Yarmouth, you'll be deep in the heart of photographer's heaven: Cape Fourchu is one of the most photogenic lighthouses in the province, set at the tip of a rugged granite coastline. (At one point a high wall en route to Cape Fourchu protects cars from the waves on rough days, and the road seems precariously close to the water.) The original lighthouse, built in 1840, was replaced by a more up-to-date facility in the 1960s.

Just past the lighthouse is the *Leif Eriksson Picnic Park,* the landing site of the famous Viking explorer. Apart from its historical significance, the park overlooks spectacular coastline and offers visitors a good spot to picnic, tables and all.

After this stop head back to town until you reach the end of the little peninsula.

This is the end of the Lighthouse Route and the Atlantic coastline. From here the communities change from descendants of the Germans and Loyalists, whalers and privateers, to communities with a strong Acadian heritage. To explore this next region turn right onto Route 1.

Places to Stay on Nova Scotia's Sunrise Trail and Atlantic Coastline

HALIFAX

Halliburton House Inn
5184 Morris Street
(902) 420–0658
Converted Heritage brick homes. Four-star dining. Moderate to deluxe.

Lord Nelson Hotel
1515 South Park Street
(800) 565–2020 or
(902) 423–6331
Luxuriously refurbished landmark hotel. Overlooks Halifax Public Gardens. Moderate.

HEAD JEDDORE

Salmon River House Country Inn
Route 7
(800) 565–3353 or
(902) 889–3353
The right balance between the great outdoors and proximity to the city, with excellent on-site food. Standard to moderate.

HUBBARDS

Dauphinee Inn
167 Shore Club Road
(800) 567–1790
(902) 857–1790
Heritage inn full of charm in a seaside setting, featuring lobster and the great outdoors. Moderate.

LISCOMB MILLS

Liscomb Lodge
Marine Drive (Route 7)
(800) 665–6343 or
(902) 779–2307
Beautiful rustic setting. Moderate to deluxe.

LIVERPOOL

White Point Beach Lodge
Highway 103 exit 20A or 21 to Route 3
(800) 565–5068 or
(902) 354–2711
Large resort overlooking White Point Beach. Try the plank salmon and other seafood specialties. Offers children's programs. Moderate to deluxe.

LUNENBURG

The Ovens Oceanview Cottages
Route 332
(902) 766–4621
Cabins set high above the coastal cliffs. Sea-cave boat tours available. Standard to moderate.

Boscawen Inn
150 Cumberland Street
(800) 354–5009 or
(902) 634–3325
Standard to moderate.

PICTOU

Auberge Walker Inn
34 Coleraine Street
(800) 370–5553 or
(902) 485–1433
Restored Heritage inn. Standard to moderate. Includes breakfast.

Customs House Inn
38 Depot Street
(902) 485–4546
Historic building with first-class modern fixtures. Moderate. Includes breakfast.

Pictou Lodge
Braeshore Road
(east of Pictou)
(888) 662–7484 or
(902) 485–4322
A rustic hideaway. Moderate to deluxe.

SALMON RIVER BRIDGE/ HEAD JEDDORE

Salmon River House Country Inn and Lobster Shack
Route 7
(800) 565–3353 or
(902) 889–3353
Standard to moderate.

SHELBURNE

Coopers Inn
Dock Street
(800) 688–2011
(902) 875–4656
Standard to moderate.

SUMMERVILLE BEACH

Quarterdeck Beachside Villas and Grill
Highway 103 exit 20 to Route 3
(800) 565–1119 or
(902) 683–2998
Moderate to deluxe.

TATAMAGOUCHE

Train Station Inn
21 Station Road
(888) 724–5233 or
(902) 657–3222
A must for railway buffs.
Choose from rooms in the
station or rent your very
own caboose.
Moderate.

Places to Eat on Nova Scotia's Sunrise Trail and Atlantic Coastline

ANTIGONISH

Gabrieau's Bistro
350 Main Street
(902) 863–1925
Dinner theater and
fantastic menu.

Lobster Treat
Post Road, off Highway 104
(902) 863–5465

LISCOMBE MILLS

Liscombe Lodge
Marine Drive (Route 7)
(800) 665–6343 or
(902) 779–2307
Great natural setting.

LOURNEVILLE

Amherst Shore Country Inn
Route 366
(between Amherst and
Pugwash)
(902) 661–4800
By reservation only.

PICTOU

Braeside Inn
126 Front Street
(902) 485–5046
Overlooking harbor.

Pictou Lodge
Braeshore Road
(east of Pictou, and 2.5
miles/4 km from P.E.I. ferry)
(888) 662–7484 or
(902) 485–4322
Extensive midday buffet.

SALMON RIVER BRIDGE

**Jeddore Lodge
Dining Room**
Marine Drive (Route 7)
(902) 889–3030

SALMON RIVER BRIDGE/ HEAD JEDDORE

**Salmon River House
Country Inn and
Lobster Shack**
Route 7
(800) 565–3353 or
(902) 889–3353

STELLARTON

The Heather Hotel
TCH 104, off exit 24
(902) 752–8401
Intimate dining room,
excellent service.

TANGIER

Willy Krauch and Sons Ltd.
Route 7
(800) 758–4412 or
(902) 772–2188

TATAMAGOUCHE

**Balmoral Motel and
Dining Room**
Main Street
(902) 657–2000
German and Canadian
cuisine.

**Jitney Cafe at the Train
Station Inn**
21 Station Road
(888) 724–5233 or
(902) 657–3222

Western Nova Scotia

Along the Nova Scotian shoreline of the Bay of Fundy is a culture that has withstood massive deportation and centuries of isolation. As visitors ramble along Route 1, the little communities of this Acadian heartland stretch one into the other, giving the impression of a massive, church-dotted "Main Street" that extends right through the villages where the French first set up shop on their Canadian adventure.

This region boasts the first-ever European settlement on Canadian soil. It was from here that the governments of France and, later, England ruled the whole region of Acadia, which included Nova Scotia and New Brunswick.

Possession of the area fluctuated between the English and French armies. In the end, when France lost control for good, the settlers' neutrality came into question. Finally the new military commanders made a decision that was to echo as far south as Louisiana.

The Land of Evangeline

It was from the shores of Northwestern Nova Scotia that thousands of Acadians were forced to board ships that would disperse them along the eastern seaboard and as far south as

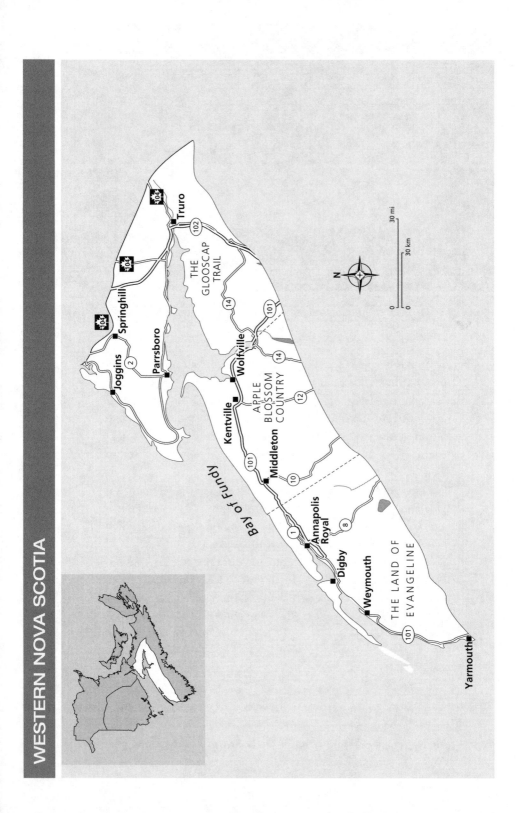

WESTERN NOVA SCOTIA

Bay of Fundy

Truro
Springhill
Parrsboro
Joggins
Wolfville
Kentville
Middleton
Annapolis Royal
Digby
Weymouth
Yarmouth

THE GLOOSCAP TRAIL

APPLE BLOSSOM COUNTRY

THE LAND OF EVANGELINE

N

30 mi
30 km
0
0

Louisiana, where they eventually became known as Cajuns. Among the exiles dispersed was a couple separated on their wedding day. Years later the bride, who had become a nun, finally found her husband—on his deathbed. This was the true story that inspired the epic poem Evangeline, for which this region is now named.

The Acadians, once exiled from Nova Scotia and now returned, can boast of a thriving francophone culture and lively community life.

The Evangeline Trail, which is actually Route 1, begins in Yarmouth (end point of the Lighthouse Route), at the intersection of Main and Vancouver Streets.

Traveling east along this historic route, you will shortly come to *Sandford,* a scenic harbor and home of what is claimed to be the *world's smallest wooden lift bridge.* To see this bridge, turn left at the Sandford breakwater and drive right down to the wharf. The wharf is strewn with mountains of seashells, which in photographs look like abstract art. From here you will see what initially appears to be an upside down V. This is the bridge. A winch operates it, with the help of whoever is standing by, but the bridge is never flat, allowing small boats to pass under easily. It's like walking up a steep ramp.

Just after this wonder of engineering, you will come to Darling Lake and, high up on a hill just off the coastal highway, the one-time home of a hero and industrialist who is reputed to still haunt the place. *Churchill Mansion* is now an inn, but for six decades prior, its sole occupants were a pair of ghosts, according to owner and innkeeper Bob Benson. Many of its original light fixtures, furnishings, and features remain intact, since a caretaker maintained the place for many years after Aaron Churchill's passing in 1920. (For thirty-three

TRUDY'S FAVORITES

Annapolis Royal Historic Gardens,
Annapolis Royal

Apple Blossom Festival,
Annapolis Valley

Balancing Rock,
Digby Neck

Brier Island,
Digby Neck

Churchill Mansion/Psychic Fair,
Sandford

Fundy Geological Museum,
Parrsboro

Habitation at Port Royal

Oaklawn Farm Zoo,
Aylesford

River rafting,
Maitland

World's smallest wooden lift bridge,
Sandford

World's Smallest Wooden Lift Bridge

of these years, there was $3 million in jewelry locked in a safe that no one bothered opening.)

The Churchill Mansion is host to a *Psychic Fair* every May, "during the full moon," Benson intones gleefully. The rest of the year, there are murder-mystery weekends and visits from fans of the paranormal, some of whom swear they have been visited by Churchill, the original owner of the mansion. The innkeeper refers to him as Aaron, in tones that imply an old acquaintance.

Aaron Churchill became famous in 1866 as a sixteen-year-old crewman aboard an ocean-bound ship off the coast of Labrador. When the ship's rudder broke, Aaron went over the side six times attempting to fix the damage. In frigid water temperatures and life-threatening conditions, the young man per-severed. His eventual success saved the ship's crew and cargo. His reward was a check for $1,500 from Lloyd's of London.

Churchill was descended from the same line as Britain's wartime prime minister. If a streak of greatness ran through the Churchills, so also did the supernatural. Bob Benson has been in contact with owners of other "Churchill mansions" built by close relatives of Aaron Churchill. Several of them have rep-utations as haunted houses. One of them, in Savannah, Georgia, is the starting point for a walking tour of haunted houses.

After Churchill died, it became the home of his "niece" Lottie (perhaps his daughter, a result from a liaison between Churchill and his brother's wife), who had been put away in an asylum for many years following the mysterious death of her illegitimate infant. (A staff of thirteen servants saw to her every need while she did "soft time.") Following her death she was buried alongside Churchill in the neighboring cemetery, where she remains to this day except for the occasional late-night sightings of her wandering apparition.

There are eight guest rooms in the inn, which is open from May 1 to mid-November. For reservations call (888) 453–5565 or (902) 649–2818. Rates are standard to moderate.

Along Highway 1 you'll drift through Beaver River, Salmon River, and then the gorgeous **Mavilette Beach,** which winds for about 1 mile (1.6 km) along the shoreline to Cape St. Marys.

This is undoubtedly one of the prettiest beaches in this end of the country, although the water temperature is low enough to chill champagne. There are a provincial picnic park and walking trails along the grassy dunes.

Boardwalks protect the sea grasses, which are all that holds the sand back from the relentless forces of Mother Nature. Stay on the boardwalks and heed the signs at this beach—the day I visited there was a sudden drop of 10 feet (3 m) or so at the end of the boardwalk, marked only by a tiny sign and barrier.

Beachcombing on the fine white sand can yield a wide choice of shells and driftwood. Be aware that the extensive sand flats of low tide are a temporary thing; here you will be reminded that the Bay of Fundy has the highest tides in the world. What people often don't realize is how fast the water level can change. But as the water rises, the sand heats it up to a less brutal temperature for swimming.

There is excellent seafood at the **Cape View Diner,** in particular whole fresh lobster and Acadian specialties. Alongside are the Cape View Motel and

The Great Expulsion

The Acadians of Southwestern Nova Scotia are descendants of French deportees from the Great Expulsion of 1755.

When Nova Scotia's governor lifted the ban against Acadians in 1765, almost 800 of the deportees gathered in Boston and, over the next four months, walked more than 1,000 miles (1,600 km) back to Nova Scotia. Some ran out of steam by the time they got to the Saint John River Valley and decided to settle there. Fifty remaining families continued on until they reached their old homesteads—only to discover that their homesteads had been given to new British settlers. These displaced Acadians wandered the Annapolis Valley until 1767, when the district of Clare was established for them. Joseph Dugas Sr. and his family were the first to settle there, followed the next year by thirteen more families.

The last survivor of the Acadian deportees who returned to Nova Scotia, Marie Babin Surette, died in 1862 at age 110. She is buried on Surette's Island, near Tusket.

TOP ANNUAL EVENT

The Apple Blossom Festival,
Windsor to Digby (last weekend in May).
Just a drive through the valley at this time
is worthwhile for the scenic beauty.
Call (800) 565–0000.

Cottages. For reservations, call (902) 645–2258, or write to P.O. Box 9, Salmon River, Digby County, NS B0W 2Y0. Rates are standard.

Farther along on the route is **Smuggler's Cove,** a rocky stretch of shoreline with massive sea caves that are well known in the area because of the area's historic link to smuggling and rumrunning. The contraband was hidden in the "caves" that the waves carved out of the rock and that are hidden during high tide.

I visited this place years ago and had to climb down the cliffs with ropes. Now you can go down a set of steps, and the headland above the cove has been made into a provincial picnic park.

These days smugglers have been replaced by people in sea kayaks entering the caves. Indian legend says that a brave once traveled between the largest of these sea caves and one at The Ovens in Lunenburg County; most kayakers don't go in much farther than the rumrunners did.

Drop in on artist Denise Comeau, whose **Comeau Studio Gallery** is located in Comeauville. She draws her inspirations from nature as well as from the Acadian community and culture and works in various media. Her paintings are shown widely in the region. The gallery is open by chance or appointment. Call (902) 769–2896.

In **Church Point** (by its French name, Pointe de l'Église), a short way up the road, is **Université Ste.-Anne,** which is the province's French-language university. Especially because of the university's existence, this is a culturally rich area. The school acts as a magnet for Acadian artisans in Nova Scotia. The university archives also offer visitors with Acadian French ancestors a chance to trace their roots.

The campus lines the shore and is stretched out alongside the road. Just beyond it is **Église Ste.-Marie** (Church of St. Mary), the tallest wooden church in North America, which you can see from far off. This church was actually designed in France. The 185-foot (56-m) steeple had to be secured against hurricane-force winds with 40 tons (36 metric tons) of stone ballast. To make "stone" pillars to support the roof, the builders used tree trunks covered with plaster. The "marble" arches are wooden also. Small booklets covering the history of the village and its church are sold here, and a bilingual guide is available for tours. The door of the church is always open in the daytime; no phone number is given.

If you continue along Highway 1 after Church Point, you will come to **Grosses Coques** (translation: "Big Clams"). Keep on your toes, though, because in a flash it turns into **Belliveau Cove.** Belliveau Cove Wharf is one of the prettiest little wharves in this part of the province, with its boats stranded at low tide and a tiny lighthouse to the left.

This place is a good spot to explore shore ecology, particularly periwinkles. There are several different species of periwinkles (the gastropod, not the ground cover), and they are abundant in the Bay of Fundy area because of the tides. If you go down to the shore to look for them, be sure you know when the tide is due to come in, because the beach—and your route out—might end up underwater in an astoundingly short period of time.

The water can rise more than 50 feet (15 m) in some areas of the Bay of Fundy, to the highest levels anywhere in the world. This once caused Joe Howe, Nova Scotian patriot, journalist, and eventually provincial politician, to exclaim in response to a parliamentary put-down, "How high do *your* tides rise?"

His nineteenth-century rebuke still gets a chuckle in some places these days, perhaps making it a record for old jokes. Just keep it in mind if you decide to leave your shoes on a rock somewhere and go strolling out on a large expanse of shoreline.

If you go gastropod hunting in Grosses Coques, you may see artist **Claude Chaloux,** who does his primitive firings at the beach. He works in stone and clay, which he paints and waxes. He creates primitive human and animal forms. Claude Chaloux's studio, Art and Mineraux, on the harbor at 3271 Belliveau Cove, is open mid-May to December 24 from 11:00 A.M. to 6:00 P.M. His work is also displayed at several other provincial galleries: Le Motif in Chéticamp in Cape Breton, and the Other Art Gallery and the Atlantic Arts Alliances in Halifax. Chaloux gives workshops at his studio. For details, call (902) 837–7145.

Just before Grosses Coques ends and Belliveau Cove begins, the road crosses a small river. Immediately after this point a small sign will direct you to the old **Acadian Cemetery.** You'll drive down a road that stretches to the shore, where boardwalks offer the possibility of a walk along windswept **Major Point Beach.**

Nature lovers will appreciate the rugged scenery at this end of the province and the opportunity to watch migratory birds, see wildflowers, and spy whales and dolphins offshore. Artists find the area inspiring, too; you'll find a number of them here.

A tiny, almost closetlike chapel has been erected at the site of the Acadian Cemetery. At the time of the Expulsion of the Acadians, many of them hid in the woods, aided and abetted by their Mi'Kmaq allies. Some made their way to Cape Breton, which was then still in French hands. But others quietly resumed life here after a time, and their earthly remains eventually came to join those of their ancestors, the first white settlers in Canada, in the Grosses Coques Cemetery. The original rough wooden crosses have been replaced by new ones, which are arranged in exactly the same way as the former markers. The handful of souls put to rest here were buried as far back as the 1770s.

Following Route 1 in the direction of Halifax, you'll come next to the tiny village of St. Bernard, population 305. From far off you will see arising out of the countryside *L'Église St.-Bernard* ("Church of St. Bernard"), a massive granite Gothic church, built entirely by the congregation. Construction, which began in 1910, was not completed for thirty-two years. The church is enormous; it can easily accommodate a thousand people, a congregation comprised of several villages. Building materials were supplied by the local population, making the creation of the church a small industry in itself. The stone was quarried in Shelburne and then hauled by train for 120 miles (193.5 km).

Note that L'Église St.-Bernard is at a crossroads in the highway called Junction 28, after which Route 1 is essentially swallowed up by TCH Route 101.

Another interesting side trip presents itself in the area of *Weymouth,* which you can reach in only a few minutes if you turn inland from Gilbert Cove, at junction 28, and follow the old trunk highway. The provincial highway seems to be mysteriously swallowed up by the TCH at this junction anyway, so remember when you return to the route that you will be following Highway 101.

In the meantime you can make the short detour to *Sissiboo Falls* to explore an area that was once a logging boomtown. Weymouth was originally called Sissiboo, a Mi'Kmaq name, when it was founded by Loyalists in 1783. Compared with other Loyalist towns, settlement here was not a huge success. It was named for Weymouth, Massachusetts, after a number of people from that place settled in and things were looking up.

Over the years the town and the surrounding area became a lumbering center. In 1895 a family moved in from Alsace-Lorraine, along the French/German border. The Stehlin family included famous engineers, and one of the Stehlins operated the first steam engine in France. When they came to Weymouth, the family, which had nine sons, purchased 10,000 acres (4,000 hectares) of timberland about 17 miles (27 km) inland from Weymouth in the vicinity of Sissiboo Falls.

They gave the place the ambitious name of New France, and there they established huge sawmills, cleared the land, and hired local workers until the number of residents in New France swelled to fifty. Wooden rails were built to deliver the lumber to town, using a locomotive made in Yarmouth. A passenger car was attached at the back to taxi people to town and back, and all year the private railway hauled lumber into Weymouth.

Soon a store and then a small school were built to accommodate the community. Although a large dam supplied water power to run the mills, the Stehlin family soon installed a General Electric generator, at a cost of $1,850. The tiny community was the first village in the province to use electricity and soon the whole place was lit up—the store, the school, and every home.

For ten years the place was a boomtown, a wonder of modern living! Then decay set in, no doubt aided and abetted by unfortunate forestry practices. All the nearest lumber had been cut, and the railway, since it was made of wood, began to rot. There are still traces of the old settlement, some ruins of the old buildings, rotted wooden carcasses where once a private rail line hauled fresh-felled cargo. A public road will still take you as far as Riverdale, into the land the Stehlins once proudly settled, then abandoned. Pack a lunch and putter around on your own, because you won't find any tour guides or concession stands here.

In recent years the old foundations were cleared of undergrowth, and timber has been placed to outline the foundations where houses existed. The site also features some interpretive signs and walking trails. Admission is free. The area is open the third week of May to early October. An interpretive center beside the tourist information center in Weymouth is open mid-June to mid-September.

Returning to the coastal route, you'll come to **Gilbert Cove,** which has a pretty little lighthouse that has been restored. The lighthouse and grounds are worth visiting, and there is a spot for picnicking here.

About 10 miles (16 km) past Gilbert Cove on Highway 101, you will reach Digby. From Digby follow Route 217 down a long narrow peninsula ending in a ferry ride to **Long Island,** which is followed by another short ferry ride to **Brier Island.** The whole narrow strip of land is referred to as **Digby Neck**—part of the Bay of Fundy's "trail of lava" that runs along the coastline. Boats run hourly twenty-four hours a day, leaving the mainland on the half hour.

Along with Digby Neck's offer of dolphins and five species of whales, the site is crisscrossed in the spring and fall by three flyways of migratory birds from the Arctic, Europe, and Canada. Bird-watchers have a chance to spot specimens from 130 species, including grebes, kittiwakes, and razorbills. The island is also home to fifteen different varieties of wild orchid and is dotted with the yellow-and-white blossoms of the mountain avens, a flower found only in northern Canada, the White Mountains of New Hampshire, and Eurasia.

Where the Whales Are

There are a number of companies that take people to see whales. I went out with **Brier Island Whale and Seabird Cruises** (902–839–2995 or fax 902–839–2075). This is a large, ex-fishing boat, and the captain maintains constant radio contact with other ships in the area to track down the whales. It took about an hour to locate one.

Once we did, the captain repeatedly circled around, bronco-fashion. We circled ever closer and closer to the whale. It would breech (that is, dive into the air) at regular intervals, then shoot forward and lunge neatly back into the sea, with its tail fins skyward. Getting anything other than a snapshot of tail fins is a challenge, demanding foresight, an eye on the whale's trajectory, and quick reflexes. Seasickness tablets came in very handy.

Over the course of the year, five different species of whales come here in search of food. They are finback, minke, humpback, sperm, and North Atlantic right whales. We saw a group of minke whales, one of the smaller species. I got lots of pictures of a whale's tail as he or she went back under.

On top of all this, Digby Neck is one of the best places to get a look at the bizarre igneous (lava-based) rock formations that you will no doubt see photographs of in many local tourist publications. The best place to see the rocky cliffs is a spot on Long Island marked quite inconspicuously by a hand-painted sign announcing **Balancing Rock.** It's easy to zoom past this small sign just beyond Tiverton as you race to meet the ferry to Brier Island. The ferry departures are timed so that there is no waiting if you drive immediately from one boat to the next.

Despite the lack of fanfare, this a fascinating side trip. Follow along the wooded path's well-marked trail past ferns and mature trees. After twenty minutes, you will reach a boardwalk that rapidly turns into a series of wooden steps that wind their way down the steep rock cliff. At this point you will see the most dramatic example of ancient volcanic fury. At the bottom, huge basalt boulders form a coastline that looks like the Viking god Thor had thrown handfuls of lightning bolts at the shore.

The biggest bolt is at the last step: Jutting out improbably from the cliff, it exceeds the height of three grown men. It seems as precariously balanced as a bowling pin in a juggling act, as if the slightest breeze could send it crashing to the jagged volcanic rocks below. At this point, it is easy to imagine oneself at the end of the world, in a land before time.

There are only a few choices for accommodation if you want to enjoy some nature walks and explore Long Island further. In **Sandy Cove,** a pretty community flanked on both sides by beaches, you can stay at the **Olde Village Inn** on Route 217 west. This inn is in a structure that dates back to the nineteenth century. Sandy Cove is a promising spot for rockhounding. For reservations call (800) 834–2206. Rates are moderate.

On Brier Island you can stay at the **Brier Island Lodge,** which also has a good restaurant. You can't miss the lodge; you can actually see it from Long Island as you approach Brier Island by boat. Its main building is a huge log structure built on a headland to the far right end of the island. The hoteliers can book whale-watching tours for you and provide maps of the island. Rooms are standard to moderate. For further information call (800) 662–8355 or (902) 839–2300. They have a three-star Canada Select rating. For more details on the lodge, visit www.brierisland.com.

Due to the depth of its tides, the waters of the Bay of Fundy have a high salt content. Consequently, they are teeming with zooplankton, which in turn attract herring and mackerel, the favorite snacking foods of whales. The result is that the tiny 3-mile-long (5-km) Brier Island is renowned for whale and dolphin watching. Sightings are guaranteed on the daily **whale-watching cruises,** with different species making their appearance at varying times of the year.

A number of naturalists have assured me over the years that the best time to witness the coy display of whales in love and its attendant splashing is in the early weeks of August. Since many people seem to be in the know about this, rooms at local inns are more likely to fill up early at that time, so plan to book ahead.

Along with enjoying the wildflowers and the animals, you can take a long walk along the shore to see the massive, spectacular basalt rocks. Many of the best hikes are detailed on the map supplied by the Brier Island Lodge. One trail starts virtually at the backdoor of the lodge. The innkeeper, Virginia Tudor, lends out her dogs as four-legged trail guides. Luke will take you for an hour across the width of the island until you reach **Seal Cove,** a favored locale for watching seals frolicking on the shore—before leading you back.

At the southwest tip of the island, a narrow footpath at Green Head cuts across a grassy bog, moss-covered rocks, and eventually into an area of basalt cliffs. Across the water, you will see the towering cliffs of Peters Island, a bird sanctuary that plays host to thousands of arctic terns. They stop here briefly on the way to Antarctica, following the longest migratory path in the world.

Late in the day, as the sun turns red, you can still distinguish Peters Island's rocks, like a jagged basalt layer cake, which the sun tints to a sparkling, salmon-pink hue.

Virginia Tudor told me that most of their visitors over the years have been naturalists, who come to study the wildlife. She pointed out that two-thirds of the island are held by the Nature Conservancy. Another interesting fact about Brier Island is that most of the residents have relatives on Grand Manan Island. Years ago, Tudor explained, before roads came in, the people in this area got around only by boat, so the closest communities included Grand Manan, which even by today's standards would seem to be quite a drive.

Although small, Brier Island has three lighthouses. More than sixty shipwrecks have occurred around the island. The salvage has formed part of its enduring legacy. The **Oddfellows Hall,** for example, is a fraternal lodge built completely of salvage from the 1908 shipwreck of the *Aurora*. You'll see bits and pieces of old boats all over Brier Island.

When you want to leave Digby Neck, you will be returning by the same two ferries, the *Spray* and the *Joshua Slocum,* this time for free, since you have to pay only to get on the islands, not off them. (Note that both ferries are named in honor of famous Digby-area sailor Joshua Slocum, who was the first to sail single-handedly around the world in his ship, the *Spray.*)

Once off the islands, drive right off the boat onto Route 217 and continue until you get to the point where this long peninsula was connected to Nova Scotia in the first place. Take Junction 26 and turn onto Route 303, which will take you into **Digby.**

This is the docking site of the ferry from New Brunswick. The wharf in Digby also is home to the world's largest scallop fleet, hence the presence throughout the province's menus of Digby scallops.

The area offers excellent photographic opportunities, as well as golfing. One spot favored by golfers is the **Pines Resort Hotel,** which includes a Norman-style mansion and cottages scattered upon landscaped lawns. For reservations call (800) 667–4637 or (902) 245–2511. Rates are deluxe.

A cozy, conveniently located place to stay, with a two-and-a-half-star rating, is the **Mountain Gap Resort.** It is just a short drive farther north of Digby, in **Smiths Cove,** making it a good staging point for either a trip to Digby Neck or day trips to Annapolis and neighboring areas. To get to Smiths Cove, take either exit 24 or 25 off Highway 101.

Mountain Gap Resort has all the amenities, including a pool and tennis court, and a calming atmosphere, with its many perennial flower gardens trimming the cabins and pathways. Nightly bonfires here are a good excuse to hang out on warm summer nights. The inn is built on a grassy headland overlooking a tidal beach, accessible by wooden steps.

You may notice that in this area of Nova Scotia in particular, the fog comes in with the tide, and quite often goes out with it as well. Days can start off in a quite unpromising way, only to recover, becoming sunny after the tide recedes. It's always a good idea to have a windbreaker handy in this kind of climate.

If the salt sea air is making you too tired to want to roam the nearby town in search of nightlife, the nice thing about the inn is that you can find nightlife of a kind right on the spot. Slocum's Pub is a friendly little bar, with outdoor seating as well in the middle of the complex. It has live entertainment most evenings, but not of the overwhelmingly noisy variety that would spoil the tranquility of the place.

There is also a lovely knotty-pine restaurant, featuring everything from prime rib of western beef to the local specialty, râpure pie. Seafood options are also in abundance.

Mountain Gap Inn arranges a number of different holiday packages, in particular those built around golf and whale-watching. To reserve a room or package, call (800) 565–5020. Rates are moderate. Note that the Mountain Gap reception has a display with a treasure trove of information on local points of interest. The staff can also help you select from a variety of charter boats for a Bay of Fundy excursion. Among the options are sportfishing of the big bluefin tuna to historical sunset tours, and, of course, whale-watching.

Continue along Route 1 for a few miles after the Mountain Gap Inn to *Upper Clements Park,* the largest amusement park in Atlantic Canada. Admission only is $8.00. An unlimited ride and attraction bracelet is $22.00 more.

Upper Clements Park has, among other things, a rattly wooden roller coaster that covers a large, hilly section of what was once an apple orchard. If the roller coaster is your reason for visiting the park, be sure to ask if it is in operation on that particular day, before you plunk down your cash for a ride pass.

As you exit this park, you'll notice the sign for the *Upper Clements Wildlife Park* about a mile-and-a-half (2 km) along on the same road. If you didn't stop by here before visiting the amusement park, you may want to now. Admission is included in your fee to get into Upper Clements Park. You can stretch your legs while you take a look at some native Nova Scotian species such as cougar, porcupines, fox, groundhogs, deer, and moose. You may also see the queen's royal red deer as you stroll along the walking trails.

Past Upper Clements you'll have the opportunity to visit the village of *Annapolis Royal,* which recalls the times of eastern Canada's first European settlements.

The community, which boasts the oldest thoroughfare in the country, is one of the prettiest little villages in this end of the province. It is small, but its historical significance ensures that a considerable number of people visit in the summer. The village has retained its well-mannered charm and historical character, however. There are lots of beautiful, big old homes, many of which have been turned into bed-and-breakfast establishments or inns.

A walking tour, mapped out in a brochure called "Footprints and Footnotes," is available at most village businesses. Following the tour at a leisurely pace should take you about an hour.

The "Footprints and Footnotes" walk begins with a monument erected on the site of a Mohawk fort built in 1712. You can see this cairn down on the waterfront, on Lower Saint George Street. At a time when the British and French were constantly wrangling for supremacy on mainland Nova Scotia, the Mi'Kmaq sided with the French, with whom they had been trading for many years. As a countermeasure, the English brought in one hundred Mohawk braves from New York State in 1712.

Farther along Lower Saint George Street is a one-time inn and tavern, now the *O'Dell Museum.* The founder of this establishment was once a dispatch rider for a pony express that in 1849 became the Associated Press in New York. Today in this restored inn, you'll find a collection of Victorian costumes, furnishings, and shipbuilding artifacts. Back in the days when it catered to cosmopolitan travelers, the best rooms in the house could be had for $1.50 a night. For information, call (902) 532–7754. The museum is open daily June 1 to September 30 from 9:30 A.M. to 5:00 P.M., Sunday from 1:00 to 5:00 P.M.

A short way farther into town on this same thoroughfare is the *Bailey House,* built in 1780 by an artificer at Fort Anne. It was once the home of wealthy United Empire Loyalists whose social standing was so lofty that they could host a grand ball for the Duke of Kent.

A few blocks farther down the street is the *King's Theatre,* built in 1922. This was the home of Henry Goldsmith, a lawyer and great-grandnephew of playwright Oliver Goldsmith, who wrote *She Stoops to Conquer.* The building is now used as the venue for the Annapolis Royal Arts Festival, held every September, and plays and films are shown here year-round.

Just across the street from the theater is the *Old Post Office,* the site of which was home to Colonel Samual Vetch, the captor of Port Royal in 1710. Following Confederation, the newly formed government built a chateau-style post office and customs warehouse on the site.

If you happen to be standing at this corner at lunch- or dinnertime, you may want to break up your tour with a stop at *Newman's,* also close by. This highly acclaimed gourmet establishment is housed in a pink one-time warehouse on Lower Saint George Street. Its obscure location belies its renown—it has been written up in many prominent Canadian publications.

The owner/chef, John Gartland, who received his training at the Culinary Institute of America, has worked in France, Germany, and Israel. At Newman's you can get everything from Cajun-style scrumptious blackened fish to lobster, but if you are really feeling adventurous, try a "ragout of black bear with winter vegetables."

Gartland explained that there have been a lot of black bears around these past few years, and some of them have been particularly bothersome. When the Department of Lands and Forests is brought in to put down a bear that is threatening its human neighbors, he buys the bear and uses it for his restaurant. "So it's ecologically responsible," he noted. The surprisingly tender bear dish has the taste of an Oriental or Mongolian dish, since its rather beefy-tasting broth includes Chinese mushrooms.

The restaurant has a lot of artwork on the walls (not for sale) and eclectic decor. There is a terrace out back where you can dine amid the kitchen's pretty, well-tended herb garden. Call (902) 532–5502.

Two other houses are worthy of mention: the *Adams-Ritchie House,* dating from 1712, and the *Sinclair Inn,* dating from around 1710 and including elements from three early buildings that served as a hostelry. A silversmith from Quebec, Jean-Baptiste Soulard, kept his shop here.

The Adams-Ritchie House, right next to Newman's, used to be the site of government meetings when Annapolis Royal was the provincial capital (before Halifax was founded). One of the Fathers of Confederation, Sir Thomas Ritchie, was born here. *Leo's* has expanded and now occupies the entire house. On the right-hand side they sell deli items and giftware. Downstairs (to the left end of the building), the attraction is a selection of homemade pasta dishes and your choice of sauces in varying degrees of spiciness. For reservations call (902) 532–7424.

Now that you've been well fed, resume your walk by continuing along the same thoroughfare until you reach *Fort Anne.* This national historic site represents the fourth and last French fortress built at this site. Only three buildings remain out of sixty that once stood on this spot.

Fort Anne comprises pieces of several different forts, dating from different eras and under different countries. From the fort's hilly defenses you will get a nice view of the harbor and a stretch of lowland originally reclaimed by a dike constructed by the Acadians.

The original fort was constructed by the French here in 1643. The powder magazine, which dates from 1708, is the last remnant of the French fortifications. The earthworks, which look like empty moats, have been left in the state in which they were found. They are among the oldest historic features in the entire National Historic Parks System.

If you visit the museum housed in the field officers' quarters, which the Duke of Kent had constructed in 1797, you can get the whole story of the

English-French conflict that raged for many years in this region. One room is dedicated to the story of the Acadian settlers. Other rooms feature collections of old military badges and buttons and lots of antique weaponry.

You will be strolling through Fort Anne's star-shaped fortifications, its beautifully tended lawns, and its earthworks dating from 1702. They offer a magnificent view of the basin.

After visiting the fort complex, return to Upper Saint George Street (Lower Saint George Street becomes Upper about halfway through the village) and continue walking past the Military Cemetery and onward past Prince Albert Road until you come to the *Annapolis Royal Historic Gardens* on your right.

Annapolis Royal has many great things going for it. One of its top attractions has to be without a doubt the Annapolis Royal Historic Gardens. They have been growing in brilliance for years now. The ten-acre (four-hectare) gardens are abutted by reclaimed marshland and a wildfowl sanctuary. The gardens contain more than 200 varieties of roses, with a total of 2,000 bushes. Some varieties of these roses were grown by the early Acadian settlers. At their peak, in midsummer, some roses cascade over a huge, rough-hewn log pergola. There is a small replica of an Acadian cottage, complete with a kitchen garden, or *potager,* containing the ingredients for traditional Acadian soups, or *potages.*

Traditional English gardening is represented in the form of the Governor's Garden, carefully tended in eighteenth century style. There is also a Victorian garden, accented by a 300-year-old elm tree. If you compare this garden with Halifax Public Gardens, the most striking difference is that much of this garden is built along an incline, which gradually descends to a marshy area bordering the shore. Make sure you descend to this point in the gardens, the site of the

Acadian Cottage at Annapolis Royal Historic Gardens

early Acadian dikes. My last visit there was in early September, when the reclaimed marshes are full of Norfolk grass, which is taller than most men. This bushy, reedy grass was used for centuries as thatch on cottage rooftops in Europe and in Acadia's early settlements.

This is the end point of the Annapolis Royal walking tour's route. Once you return to your car, if you cross a small bridge to the village of **Granville Ferry,** you will be entering yet another narrow peninsula similar to Digby Neck. Pause for a moment after crossing the bridge and look back across the water at Annapolis Royal. On a clear day this has to be one of the prettiest vistas the province has to offer.

Drive southwest on Route 1 for about 6 miles (10 km) and you will come across an old wooden fortress.

This is the **Habitation at Port Royal,** a re-creation of the oldest European settlement on the continent north of Florida. This reconstruction, built in the 1930s, was based on the records of the inhabitants of a fur-trading post here that dated back to 1605. Historians have never been able to ascertain the exact site of the original Port Royal, but this is definitely in the ballpark if not right at home plate. It was here that the Order of Good Cheer was formed to boost morale during the long winter nights.

Several of the post's inhabitants had literary inclinations, in particular a lawyer named Marc Lescarbot, who wrote copious notes about his year at the site. To amuse the bored pioneers, he created theatrical pieces that were performed for the inhabitants in what he named the Theatre of Neptune. This eventually was honored in the selection of a name for Canada's first professional repertory theater, Neptune Theatre, located in Halifax.

It is because of Lescarbot's notes, and those of Samuel de Champlain and Père Pierre Biard, a Jesuit priest, that historians were able to learn so much about the early days of the Acadians in Nova Scotia. One of the things that strikes the visitor most at this carefully re-created fortress is the size of the beds. The original inhabitants of Port Royal were a stocky lot, with beds that could hardly accommodate Snow White's pals, by modern standards. They were also quite elevated and canopied to retain warmth.

The little charcoal-colored rectangular fortress, with its stone-covered central courtyard and rugged furnishings recalling farm settlements from seventeenth-century Normandy, is so startling in its authenticity that it feels like you have time-traveled. It is hardly a stretch of the imagination to picture the original traders going about their business in the 1600s. This illusion is helped along by the many costumed interpreters, French-accented Acadians from the local area. Wearing *sabots*—wooden shoes—the interpreters do everything from cutting wood into shingles to maintaining a lookout for enemy attacks. Their clothing is made from handwoven material carefully sewn in the manner of the original inhabitants.

Be sure to see the fur-trading room, where the wealth of hides and commercial paraphernalia really re-create the feeling of this old fur-trading post.

Leaving Port Royal, backtrack roughly a mile (1.6 km) in the direction of Granville Ferry and then turn left along the Hollow Mountain Road, an unpaved byway that is nevertheless quite passable in dry weather. When you reach the end of this secondary road, you'll be facing the Bay of Fundy. If you turn left again, you will soon be in **Delaps Cove** (population 65), which has some of the most noteworthy hikes in the province.

It is along this stretch of Fundy coast that the province's unusual prehistoric past is most evident. Basaltic lava flows have hardened into crystals, which have been worn and shaped by the relentless forces of the tide. Anyone who has visited the coast of a volcanic island—for example, the Canary Islands—will instantly recognize the rock formations as the result of hardened lava flows. The only thing that has shaped the lava somewhat differently here is the relentless crashing of the world's highest tides.

Whereas on Digby Neck you will see basalt cliffs leaning precariously like primeval towers of Pisa, here the rocks are sometimes softened into hard, round beach boulders or natural basalt pools that fill up at high tide, allowing the brave and hardy to take a chilly dip in the tidal waters.

Delaps Cove is the one-time settlement of freed black slaves from the United States, who lived here on land granted to them by the Crown. Their old farms have now returned to the wilderness, cleft in two by old logging roads.

If you wish to go on a wilderness trek here, plan on at least two hours for the journey. Finding the area's two trails is easy: Simply follow the signs marked delaps cove wilderness trail. The trails are a little farther up the road than the wharf; if you actually descend to the cove itself, you've gone too far. You can leave your car at the parking lot at the designated trail entrance just before the descent to the cove.

You have a choice between the **Bohaker Trail,** a 2-mile (3.2-km) oval that begins on an escarpment of rocks overlooking the bay, and **Charlie's Trail,** a more challenging 2.5-mile (3.8-km) loop that starts a mile (1.6 km) or so farther down the rock-strewn logging road. Charlie's Trail requires better hiking boots that offer more stability, since the trail consists of harsh granite terrain. The payoff of taking the easier Bohaker Trail is a 43-foot (13 m) waterfall at its end. The Bohaker also allows you the delicate pleasure of salt sea mist mingled with the scent of black spruce.

An alternative walk is simply to follow the coast by walking along the huge basalt boulders that stretch past the government wharf. From here all up along the coast is a daisy chain of fishing wharves and tiny lighthouses that serve the small communities of Delaps Cove, Parkers Cove, Hampton, and Halls Harbour.

Boats along the coast are tied up flush alongside the wharves at high tide and are left immobilized 20 feet (6 m) or so below on the sea bottom when the tide goes out. Depending on when the tides are coming in, you may chance upon lobster boats being unloaded. The fishermen will gladly sell you lobsters from right off the boat, if you are interested in boiling your own, Maritime style.

You can also follow this coast along the unnumbered shore road, turning inland at Hampton or Port Lorne to rejoin Highway 101. Or if you don't want to go that far on an old shore road, you can turn down at Parkers Cove, proceed to Granville ferry, and cross the small bridge that separates it from Annapolis Royal.

From here you can follow the Evangeline Trail into the Annapolis Valley's rich farmlands, or take a side trip into wilderness at a national park in the center of the province. To do this get onto Route 8 in Annapolis Royal and proceed inland toward *Kejimkujik National Park.*

If you do opt for the national park, plan to return to the Evangeline Trail, even though it means backtracking. Otherwise you will miss some of the prettiest countryside in this end of the country and some of the finest country inns and restaurants in the area.

There is a relaxing bit of wilderness just outside Annapolis Royal at the *Milford House Resort* complex. I discovered this gem of a resort just as my last edition went to press, so alas, I didn't get to tell you about it until now. Drive south 14 miles, (or 21 kilometres) from Annapolis Royal to Kejimkujik, then turn off Route 8 into the community of South Milford, and from there turn onto Rural Route 4.

This is a wilderness getaway that dates back to early settlement of the area, in the 1860s, when it was a stopping place for travelers. Following a fire in 2000, Milford House completely rebuilt its main lodge and now offers rooms there or in one of a series of twenty-seven rustic cottages (with fireplaces) nestled along the shores of two wooded lakes. The resort provides the perfect mix of roughing it and being pampered: a dining room offering excellent food prepared by a noted gourmet chef, a well-stocked library, a games room, rental canoes, trails dotted with picnic areas, and pristine lakes suitable for swimming. (There's even a separate play area for children).

Talk about soft-option wilderness: You can have the chef pack you a picnic lunch to take along on your daily explorations, or hold off until dinnertime and feast on local roast duck or rainbow trout. The complete menu changes twice weekly. A screened-in porch off the main dining room ensures that you can enjoy the nighttime call of the wild without these pesky bugs feeding on your exposed flesh. Pure delight. Rates are moderate to deluxe. To reserve, call toll-free, (877) 532–5751, or locally, (902) 532–2617.

Kejimkujik (or Keji, as it is generally called by locals) comprises 147 square miles (381 sq. km) of land, in the center of which is a large lake fed by several rivers. Canoes can be rented by the day or week through **Wildcat River Outfitters,** at Jakes Landing inside the national park. Canoe rentals are $30 for twenty-four hours or $24 for a business day. Weekly rates are $100. The outfitter also rents bicycles, kayaks, and paddleboats and provides shuttle service to other points in the park, which is particularly useful for river trips. **Loon Lake Outfitters,** along Route 2 outside the park, can outfit you with most of the equipment you'll need for wilderness camping and can even provide premade meals ready for cooking at your campsite.

Rates for campers are quite reasonable, but spots are in short supply. If you want to explore the park in the daytime but not camp, consider staying at the **Whitman Inn,** which has been operating nearby for eons. It is a pretty yellow country inn on the right-hand side of the road, just a five-minute drive farther down Route 8 past the park entrance. The Whitman Inn is a restored turn-of-the-century homestead, still with its original furnishings, and boasting a library and parlor with books dating back to the 1800s. The Whitman Inn has its own restaurant, where you can enjoy a nice hearty breakfast of bacon, pancakes, juice, and coffee before going to the national park. Innkeeper Bruce Gurnham told me that increasingly, people who are not guests of the inn have been stopping by for their suppers as well, which is always a good sign. For details on this Heritage inn, call (800) 830–3855 or (902) 682–2226.

Take note that you have to pick your season well for a visit to Keji. At the tail end of August until the second week in September, it is lovely; but from late spring to early summer, you will be an "all-you-can-eat buffet" on two legs for the ticks and blackflies.

There is a standard campsite at the beginning of the park, in an area called Jeremys Bay, where people rent sites by the night and prepare for or recover from their forays into the wilderness. For wilderness camping you will be expected to do some planning for your trip when you reserve your designated campsite in the park. Sites are spaced generously apart allowing for exceptional privacy. Due to the extremely small number of sites and their enormous popularity, park attendants recommend booking these spots up to sixty days in advance during the summer. In the early fall, my favorite time for Keji, these are far more available, but try to plan ahead anyway.

It is well worth your while to purchase a $5.00 map of the campsites, rather than work only with the complimentary map. The better map (available at the park's reception center) has each wilderness site clearly marked; and another, smaller map on the back shows the navigational buoys that you will need to find your way around if you are canoeing to your site. The park guides will also, if requested, show you a more detailed listing of all the wilderness sites, which describes their unique features. It is invaluable in choosing a site that suits your style. They also told me that the biggest problem campers face is getting disoriented while paddling in the lake and not being able to find their site. Frustrated campers sometimes give up and just put their tent anywhere, which is forbidden. Remember that you are allowed to spend only two days at each site, so plan your sites so that they follow a sequential pattern.

Be wary of leaving scraps of food lying around, and be sure to carefully dispose of any of the debris of human consumption. The numerous beaver and muskrat that you will see are not the only nonhuman inhabitants of the park. Bear, cougar, and lynx, not to mention other native Nova Scotian species, also inhabit this park. The last time I camped at Keji, I took the absolutely worst book for my vacation reading: *The Cure for Death by Lightning,* which obsesses about bear attacks for at least the first hundred pages. While I admit that it compelled me to take scrupulous care of my pots and pans, it didn't prove to be good bedtime reading. There are bears in Keji, but sightings are rare. You're much more likely to have your site trashed by marauding raccoons.

Mi'Kmaq people camped in these lands many centuries before the white man. Petroglyphs that are visible when water washes over them are testimony to their early presence. To see these ancient markings, visitors are advised to check them out with an experienced Mi'Kmaq guide. Otherwise visitors may inadvertently destroy some of the markings. When I visited, park guides showed me places where people had unknowingly pulled their canoes on shore and scraped and damaged the markings. In other places contemporary visitors carved their names right over petroglyphs, without noticing what they were defacing. If you want to explore Mi'Kmaq iconography in more depth, you can visit the provincial museum's Web site dedicated to portraits and petroglyphs at http://museum.gov.ns.ca/mikmaq.

The area where they are found is in a small inlet called **Fairy Bay,** which is unnamed on the maps displayed at the information center but can be easily picked out by tracing a line from Jakes Landing, where canoes can be rented, to Merrymakedge, where there are picnic tables. A lookout is indicated midway between these two points, at a spot denoted by the number 12.

This is easily found on the road. A stairway leads to the lookout at Fairy Bay. A trail next to this lookout will lead you to the spot, so getting there is not difficult. Knowing what to look for is another matter; that is where the guides come in.

Historians now know that people lived in Nova Scotia as early as 10,500 years ago, but they have not been able to ascertain whether these early inhabitants were the ancestors of the Mi'Kmaq who greeted and traded with the white men of the 1600s. The land may have witnessed the visits and passings of many peoples after the Ice Age slowly retreated and the trees and forests returned.

The pictographs that the ancient Mi'Kmaq left show elements from their nomadic life as hunters and gatherers. Moose are quite clearly depicted, as well as a snakelike creature, possibly Kipika'm, the Horned Serpent Person, a monstrous snake who lives in the Mi'Kmaq underworld. This character appears in all native legends in Canada, and even in Siberia. Anthropologists theorize that the serpent-creature elements of native oral history go back as far as 11,000 years, back to the original migration from Siberia across the Bering Strait land bridge.

An apt summary of Keji is that the park could easily serve as a destination in itself, for those interested in taking an extended canoe trip into the Nova Scotia of the ancient Mi'Kmaq.

I first visited Keji more than twenty years ago, and each time I return I am amazed at how the place has managed to retain not just its beauty, but also its magic. Every season has its own delights, from the rebirth of spring fauna and flora to the sensuous fullness of summer, the early morning mist rising off the lake, and the haunting call of the loon that echoes for miles. The key to Keji's continued brilliance lies in the tiny number of wilderness sites, giving a feeling of complete isolation. But don't let that fool you. We were still able to call Loon Lake Outfitters via cell phone from a site six hours' paddling away from Jakes Landing.

If you don't feel up to a wilderness camping experience in the cooler months, you could extend the season by staying at the Whitman Inn or the nearby *Mersey River Chalets,* on Route 8, just 3 miles (5 km) before the park as you drive from Annapolis Royal. Their number is (877) 667–2583 or (902) 682–2443. Open year-round, Mersey River Chalets features two-bedroom wooden chalets with full kitchen and woodstove. Rates range from moderate to deluxe. It also has a licensed restaurant, a boardwalk along the Mersey River, tennis, and other complimentary sporting options. You can check it out at www.merseyriverchalets.com. Another accommodation option is Sioux-style tepees, for $70 a night.

Both the Whitman Inn and Mersey River Chalets recently organized workshops in photography, among other activities, so it's a good idea to contact them ahead of time to see if something piques your interest. Early fall, with its spectacular foliage, is ideal for camera buffs.

After Kejimkujik, backtrack to the Evangeline Trail, which you can rejoin at Junction 22, roughly 3 miles (5 km) before you return to Annapolis Royal.

Apple Blossom Country

Provincial Highway 101 and its parallel trunk road, Route 1, from Annapolis Royal to Wolfville, run through some of the prettiest countryside you will ever see: rolling hills dotted with apple trees. These days even an occasional vineyard can be seen, as grape growing becomes more and more popular.

Sheltered on both its western and eastern sides and lying along the fertile Annapolis River, the **Annapolis Valley** enjoys a miniclimate all its own. Spring comes earlier here than elsewhere in the province, summers seem warmer and sunnier, and fall holds out the tantalizing possibility of a profusion of gold, red, and fiery orange trees set amid the soft ochre glow of drying grass in the fields, all with warm Indian summer days thrown in. Winter along the coast is often unpredictable, with first a damp snowstorm followed by freezing rain and then a thaw. But here in the valley, the effect is often pure Currier and Ives, with snow-topped steeples, gorgeous winter scenery, and cross-country ski trails popping up here and there.

As you wind your way through this beautiful country, be sure to turn off at exit 16 in Aylesford to visit the **Oaklawn Farm Zoo.**

"We had no intentions of ever being a zoo," says Gail Rogerson. She and husband, Ron, who own and run the Oaklawn Farm Zoo, had always just liked animals. They collected exotic pets on their Aylesford-area farm. For years Gail was a schoolteacher, and in 1975, her son's class visited the farm. The visits snowballed, and by the end of the 1970s, dozens of teachers were taking groups of students out to visit the farm.

About The Zoo's Zonkey

No, those aren't stockings on the donkey. A few years ago, Oaklawn Farm zoo owners Ron and Gail Rogerson had to deal with the problem of a lovesick zebra, for whom no suitable mate could be found. Eventually, a donkey was willing to make her a happy zebra, but the resulting offspring is a "terminal cross"—a sterile, mule-like progeny with no identifiable gender. This little "zonkey" looks just like a donkey except for the fetching pair of striped stockings that it appears to be wearing, and the war-paint stripes that run down its nose. Ron assures me that there is no reason for wildlife enthusiasts to be upset about the hybrid animal, since its mixed-up genetics will go no further than this particular zonkey.

It reached the point that people would drive up to the farm, insisting that it was a public place. Privacy became a thing of the past. "On a nice weekend our drive would be filled with strangers."

Forced to choose between moving away or opening their doors to the public, the Rogersons became the owners of the only zoo east of Montreal that features exotic animals such as lemurs, Japanese macaques, a gibbon (which you can hear from a long way off), camels, and a yak. You could spend hours watching the monkeys. Kids like the llamas. Several lions live here in spacious quarters, among them, Rutherford, who recently weighed in at a whopping 809 pounds. He is easily three times the weight of a lion in the wild, who would be kept trim by the struggle for survival, as Ron Rogerson explains. Rutherford greets visitors with the same self-satisfied nonchalance as Garfield, that other famous fat cat. Rutherford, however, has gone one better, with his name now entered in the *Guinness Book of World Records.*

The zoo has a canteen where you can take a break from the hot midday sun, coin-operated vending machines that dispense snacks for feeding sheep and other small animals, and a gift shop in the two-story, log-cabin reception building that features wild-animal sweatshirts and local crafts.

Be sure to check out the reception building's animal-head carvings on its second floor. Ten of the carvings are on the rounded ends of the joists. A cougar comes out of the end of two wall logs, while an owl stands out in bas-relief. Every carving represents an animal at the zoo, including resident and pet, Badness the Pug.

The carvings are so subtly crafted that they trick the eye so that you have to search for them. Make a point of looking closely at the log ends and you will see a gibbon, an alligator, a llama, and a host of other critters. The carvings are the work of artist John Murray, who used a Haida Indian knife, traditionally used to make totem poles. Along with other artful pieces, the building has an-almost-life-size papier-mâché zebra crafted by another local artist.

The Rogersons remind visitors that the principal concern of the farm is not to exhibit the animals but to provide a home for them where they can be at ease and breed. The zoo breeds registered dogs as well as exotic animals for sale to other zoos. Many of these animals are endangered in the wild, so their only hope of survival is through zoos and wildlife refuges. Oaklawn Farm Zoo is open April to November, with May and June weekdays the favorite times for school visits. Admission is $5.50 for adults; seniors and students, $3.50; and ages twelve and under $2.50. For information call (902) 847–9790.

If you decide to pick a few mussels and drift along the shore for a bit, take a side road out of Aylesford back toward the Bay of Fundy shore. Head toward **Morden** or Victoria Harbour on the secondary road out of Aylesford. Along the shore, in Morden, you will come to a stone cross, a monument erected to honor the Acadians who once hid out here during the winter of 1755, away from the British who were busily expelling their compatriots. Their food consisted of meat and mussels provided by their Mi'Kmaq allies. In 1790 their descendants erected a church and plastered its walls with powdered mussel shells.

All along this road between the valley and the Fundy coast you have been zigzagging the **North Mountain Range.** This was formed 200 million years ago at a time when the supercontinent began splitting into smaller continents. At that time rifts opened between the sandy plain around the Cobequid Hills of Truro, and basaltic lava was spewed out from the Earth's belly, spilling out into the area. As it cooled, the North Mountain ridge was formed from the fractures and tilting, along with the rock formations of Digby Neck. The most spectacular result to come from this era of upheaval, apart from the Bay of Fundy itself, is the headland that overlooks the Minas Channel. It is known as **Cape Split.** This is the legendary home of the great Mi'Kmaq god, Glooscap.

To get into the rugged-nature spirit of things, the vigorous among you may want to make the trek to the end of Cape Split. This is the must-do trek for Nova Scotia's committed hikers, since the spectacular panorama offered by the end of this excursion is unmatched anywhere else in the province. Count on a day's recovery from this trek, so plan to stay either at Blomidon Park, where you can camp, or at a nearby bed-and-breakfast. To get to Cape Split, stay on Highway 101 until you reach exit 11 just outside Wolfville. Turn onto Route 358 and drive north in the direction of Scots Bay and Cape Blomidon.

Just past Port Williams on Route 358, you'll come to Starrs Point and the historic **Prescott House,** which was built from 1814 to 1816 by Charles Prescott. He was a successful merchant who served as a member of the legislature for Cornwallis Township in the early 1800s. His true claim to fame, however, is apples.

Prescott was the man who introduced the Gravenstein apple and other superior apple varieties to Nova Scotia, forever changing the landscape of the Annapolis Valley. In his day all ornamentals, fruits, and vegetable and fodder crops came from European stock or were adapted to the eastern United States. Because of the harsh winters and proximity to the ocean, some did not succeed here until Prescott established strains that thrived in the Nova Scotian climate.

The honorary member of the horticultural societies of New York, Boston, and London offered grafting stock, in the way of " . . . scions and buds of any kind to every person who may apply in the proper season . . . ," according to a notice posted by Prescott himself.

The impressive Georgian architecture of Prescott House is complemented by the period furnishings that Prescott's great-granddaughter collected when she restored the house in the 1930s. Surrounding the house are beautiful trees, gardens, and lawns. The vista includes the diked lands of the Cornwallis River. For more information, call (902) 542–3984.

Prescott House is open from the beginning of June to mid-October, Monday to Saturday from 9:30 A.M. to 5:30 P.M., Sunday from 1:00 to 5:30 P.M.

The Prescott House also has a fascinating collection of old Prescott family photos. At various times of the year there are presentations on the family history and the role the Prescotts played in medicine and in World War I. A small admission is charged.

One fine spring day I took a notion to roam out into one of the local apple orchards in full bloom, looking for something gorgeous to paint. The experience was something out of television's X-Files: From the road you just can't imagine the terror caused by the ceaseless humming of billions of honeybees. My advice: Go the third week of May, take lots of film, but use a camera with a zoom lens.

Summer comes earlier in this part of the province, and there are many cozy places to stay where you can enjoy the great outdoors early in the season. One nice place is the *Farmhouse Inn* in nearby Canning. The bed-and-breakfast offers standard rates and can arrange packages for its guests. This inn is right on Canning's Main Street. Call (800) 928–4346 or (902) 582–7900, or visit www.farmhouseinn.ns.ca.

Pause at a point on Route 358 called *The Lookoff,* high on North Mountain, for a spectacular view of *Minas Basin,* site of the highest of the Bay of Fundy's record-breaking tides. There is adequate space here for parking, as well as washrooms and picnic tables, so you can take in the scenery while you munch. Sprawling below like a scattered bouquet you can see apple orchards, woods, lazy cows drifting through fields of clover, old farmhouses, and, farther back, spread out like a brown carpet, the muddy waters of the basin.

From this point continue a little past *Scots Bay,* where a walk of slightly more than 5 miles (8 km) begins. In June the red trillium blooms along this path. Far below you can watch eagles and hawks soar above the sea.

There is another hike in this area, slightly more than 10 miles (16 km) long. This hike starts at the campground at *Cape Blomidon,* atop the eroding sandstone cliffs, and then backtracks in a loop through woodlands.

Like the Cape Split hike, this trail demands extreme caution, as erosion is slowly claiming the cliffs. The edge of the headland is dangerous; no barriers are there to protect people from falling to the beach 330 feet (100 m) or so below the footpath. Several times along this path, the trail diverges to the edge, so the incautious could plunge to their doom.

Whatever you do, don't whiz past this area after your Cape Split excursion or a visit to Blomidon. Since it is set deep in the heart of a rich agricultural area, with trendy cuisine inspired by the population drawn to the local university, the stretch of road from Kentville to Wolfville has much to offer the gourmet.

If you are there at the right time of year—that is, the third weekend in May—you must take in the Annapolis Valley's **Apple Blossom Festival.** Even if you hardly take in any of the festival events, the scenery here at the end of May is breathtaking. There will be mile after mile of orchards in full bloom and beautiful spring weather. You can also enjoy an assortment of stately old homes for bed-and-breakfasting, as well as gourmet restaurants in the college town of Wolfville. The **Tattingstone** is particularly noteworthy.

The Glooscap Trail

From this point in the valley, you can easily drive back to Halifax via **Windsor,** home of nineteenth-century novelist and Windsor native Judge Thomas Haliburton—the Mark Twain of Canada. His creation, Sam Slick, the Yankee clock peddler, was an unparalleled smooth talker, whose colorful aphorisms live on to this day. Among Haliburton's pithy clichés are: "Facts are stranger than fiction," "raining cats and dogs," "quick as a wink," "barking up the wrong tree," and "circumstances alter cases."

You can visit this famous wit's Windsor home, **Haliburton House,** since it has been a branch of the Nova Scotia Museum for many years. The house and its lovely grounds can be found just off route 101 and are clearly marked from the road. The house contains a number of items of local historical interest and effects related to the life of the town's famous author. If you are interested in reading more, get a copy of *The Clockmaker.*

If you have already visited Halifax and are heading out of the province, you may want to try following a route referred to as the **Glooscap Trail.** This nears the shores of Minas Basin, the inner arm of the Bay of Fundy. It is a pretty, unspoiled area, accessed by leaving Highway 101 at exit 5 in Windsor and driving along Trunk Highway 215.

It is with this routing that I will take you out of the province. (If you drive back to Halifax, you can always rejoin the Glooscap Trail in Truro 60 miles/100

trivia

The originator of the expression, "A nod is as good as a wink to a blind horse," was Thomas Haliburton, creator of the literary character Sam Slick.

Giant Pumpkins and Their Seeds

Peter Peter Pumpkin Eater must have lived in **Windsor** once. Howard Dill, a resident of Windsor, is internationally famous for breeding the world's biggest pumpkins year after year, earning Windsor the name of "Pumpkin Capital of the World." The genetics hobbyist took many years to come up with his own patented strain of giant pumpkin seeds, and even when his own pumpkin doesn't win the Giant Pumpkin weigh-ins, you can bet that it was a Howard Dill seed that gave the champion life. Mr. Dill explained his practical method of selective breeding to my son, comparing it with growing good kids. "You start with healthy parents, and go from there."

You can drop in at **Howard Dill's Farm and Visitor Centre,** and buy yourself a packet or two of giant-pumpkin seeds, while you are in Windsor. My favorite time of year to come is in early fall, when the pumpkin patch is overrun by excited children who climb the mountainous fruit (yes, pumpkins are fruit!) to get their pictures taken. Dill's best pumpkins can still make a preteen look like a dwarf. Needless to say, I had to buy a much humbler specimen to fit into my trunk.

You can visit this shrine to the Giant Pumpkin, at 400 College Road. The field is overlooked by King's Edgehill School, a private school for which the town is well known. To get there take a left at exit 5 off Highway 101, drive 2.5 miles (4 km), and then turn left onto College Road. You can also call the Giant Pumpkin patch at (902) 798–2728.

There are destinations off the beaten path, and then there are destinations that are offbeat. This next event, the **Pumpkin Regatta,** falls into this category. Held in Windsor's Lake Pizaquid, it generally takes place the second Sunday in October. It's one of the wackiest events in the Maritimes and a big hit with the kids. It starts with a parade of suitably equipped pumpkins, which have been hollowed out in preparation for the race. Accompanying them on their floats are the paddling crews in equally laughable costumes.

The race then gets under way, with a number of heats run throughout the afternoon. Amazingly, quite a few of the giant pumpkins do manage to reach the finish line before sinking. Needless to say, a carnival atmosphere reigns. For details, call (902) 798–2728.

---

km, past Halifax toward New Brunswick). To do this take exit 14A or 15 off Provincial Highway 102 outside Truro to Route 2.

If you travel the considerably less-traveled Route 215, you will be edging the area of the world's highest tides, which reach their peak of 53 feet (16 m) at Burntcoat Head near Noel. Just a few minutes' drive farther down the road, and you will reach **Maitland,** the entry spot for ***rafting on the tidal wave.*** This wave is otherwise known as a tidal bore, a scientific term for a wall of water created when a large volume of water from the oncoming tide is forced into a much smaller channel. The resulting tidal bore will push passengers up the Shubenacadie River for 18 miles (29 km) aboard Zodiacs—big, inflated dinghy-type boats. The entire trip takes half a day, during which time you are pushed by "roller-coaster" rapids of 3 to 10 feet (1 to 3 m). Lunch is included.

Several outfits take rafters on this trip. I'll name the top three here, followed by their phone numbers and Web sites. They are all reliable, experienced, and similarly priced at around $40 per person. Remember that departure times vary depending on the day's tides, which are given on the Web sites. The rafting companies are Shubenacadie River Runners Ltd. (800–856–5061 or 902–261–2770, www.tidalborerafting.com); Shubenacadie River Adventure Tours (888–878–8687 or 902–261–2222, www.adventure@shubie.com); and the Shubenacadie Tidal Bore Rafting Park (800–565–RAFT or 902–758–4032, www.tidal boreraftingpark.com). Tours, with this last group, end with a barbecue.

If you haven't arrived at the right time for the day's tides, or if you expect you'll be too wet and tired to leave afterward, you can find reasonably priced accommodations at the renovated home of a former sea captain. *The Captain Douglas House Inn and Restaurant* is right on Highway 215. The municipal Heritage property dates back to 1860 and has a country restaurant on site. For reservations, call (902) 261–2289. Rates are standard to moderate.

The *Shubenacadie Tidal Bore Rafting Park,* mentioned above, is a short distance from the intersection of Route 215 and Highway 102 (marked on the map at exit 10). It features fully equipped housekeeping cottages right on the Shubenacadie River, as well as rafting packages. Call toll-free at (800) 565–7238 or (902) 758–4032.

The first highlight of the road after Truro is in *Portapique,* where you can pay a visit to the studio and gallery of noted artist Joy Laking. You may have seen some of her prints in other areas of the province. Laking's work is composed of watercolors and serigraphs of a decidedly nostalgic nature—sunny front porches on hazy summer afternoons, lady's slippers and trilliums, and kitchen curtains blowing softly in a summer breeze—all painted with delicacy and liveliness. The *Joy Laking Gallery* is indicated by several signs along Highway 2. You will not see the gallery itself from the road. A driveway leads to a home and the studio, in a separate whimsically decorated outbuilding. The gallery is open year-round. June to August it is open Monday to Saturday from 9:00 A.M. to 5:00 P.M., Sunday from 1:00 to 5:00 P.M. At other times, you can arrange an appointment to visit by calling ahead at (902) 647–2816. The artist also produces serigraphs of her charming works, which may better suit a souvenir hunter's budget than an original watercolor. In Portapique you will also find the remains of an Acadian dike, along the salt marsh that edges the shore.

Just after Portapique you will come to **Bass River.** Don't be fooled by Bass River's deceptively small size: It is the home of the Bass River chair, an elegant oak rocker with a press-back floral design. These are sold in furniture shops throughout the region. Keep your eyes peeled for the **Dominion Chair Company's** retail outlet right on Highway 2, on the right side of the road as you drive north along Minas Basin. Although Bass River is a small community, the shop is often open late.

Apart from its obvious appeal to beachcombers, the rugged Fundy shore of Nova Scotia has much to offer would-be geologists and other rock hounds. The areas of coastline that front the Bay of Fundy contain a wealth of prehistoric fossils just waiting to be gathered like so many wild berries.

If you take a close look at your official "Scenic Travelways" map (available at any tourism information booth), you will note the fossil icons that dot the shores of the Bay of Fundy. They indicate the richest areas for fossil exploration.

Roughly 350 million years ago, long before dinosaurs began decorating kids' pajamas, this area was teeming with life. Lying near the equator, it was wedged between North America and Africa, in the middle of the supercontinent called Pangaea. As the continents started drifting apart, huge rift valleys formed, of which the Bay of Fundy is one. As the tides coursed through this cleft in the continents, water eroded a huge cross section, revealing a window into the world of 200 million years ago and beyond.

The area of the Bay of Fundy is noted as the world's best site of continuously exposed Late Carboniferous Age rocks. Along these same shores are exposed sea cliffs that reveal ancient treasures from the Triassic and Jurassic geological periods. And you would never think of Nova Scotia as a place full of volcanoes, but along these shores you will quite unexpectedly come across rock formations created by ancient lava flows.

The fossilized legacy of some of the world's oldest terrestrial reptiles and the oldest land-dwelling snails have been found along here. Two hundred million years ago, some of the planet's first dinosaurs roamed the desert that was Nova Scotia. And 70,000 years ago mastodons were here. Bones of two mastodons, including a baby, were recently found in a gypsum pit near Halifax.

Apart from rugged basalt cliffs and fossils, the area has other geological delights, noted and treasured for centuries by the native peoples. Mi'Kmaq legend has it that the mighty Glooscap lived across the narrow neck of the Minas Basin, in the area of Blomidon and Cape Split, the breathtaking promontory that overlooks the spot where tides reach 50 feet (16 m) and more. From there the great god of the Mi'Kmaq looked over his children.

Once he was mocked by an animal spirit named Beaver, and his anger caused him to scoop up land from the gorges and fling the clods of earth at the mocking spirit, creating islands that now comprise *Five Islands Provincial Park* (near Economy) and scattering the jewels, known today as jasper, agate, onyx, and amethyst. To this day the legendary gifts of Glooscap draw rock hounds from around the world to the shores of the Bay of Fundy. The park is open from mid-May to September.

At Five Islands Provincial Park, on Route 2, you will find camping, a beach, and, of course, five islands: Moose, Diamond, Long, Egg, and Pinnacle.

The picnic areas and the *Estuary Nature Trail* in this park are marked with interpretive displays explaining the geology of the site.

In the *Parrsboro* area you'll run into a lot of geology buffs and rock hounds. The pleasant little town of some 1,600 persons is actually the biggest community along this route, so this is the place to stock up on film or food before exploring the area's coastline. The rock hounds you will meet will be looking for zeolites—semiprecious stones such as amethyst and agate.

From the *Fundy Geological Museum,* on Two Island Road in Parrsboro, paleontologists lead daily tours to the site of the biggest fossil find in North America. Every tide brings more erosion, exposing two different prehistoric periods, the Jurassic and Triassic, 200 million and 350 million years ago, respectively.

There are two types of guided collecting tours: One explores mineral sites; the other, fossil sites. You can generally count on one of these tours occuring daily, but not both. If you have a particular interest or preference, call (902) 254–3814 to confirm the tour's planned itinerary. Tour departure times are dictated by the tides, which can reach as high as 44 feet (14 meters). Less-mobile or rainy-day visitors can opt to cut and polish semiprecious stones at a lapidary workshop at the museum.

If you do go on a tour, be sure to wear a hat and effective sunscreen. The constant breezes can fool visitors into thinking that the sun is not very strong here, but the reflection off the basalt rock can cause a brutal sunburn.

Visitors are prohibited from removing any fossils from the rock face, and no one is allowed to use hammers on the outcrops. There are many loose fossils to be found, however. Every fossil is carefully examined by the tour leader, whose expertise is really needed for identification of each specimen.

The tours cost $7.00 per adult and $3.00 per child, ages six to seventeen. Families with two adults pay $12.00. If you are touring the beach areas, pack a sweater, because when the fog rolls in the temperature can drop quite suddenly.

The museum recently added a 10-foot-long, 200-million-year-old prosauropod dinosaur to its collection. This herbivore was discovered encased in sandstone, gradually unearthed, and assembled at the museum over the course of several years. The museum also features some interesting workshops during the

A Visit to Wasson Bluff

On a tour led by Ken Adams, a curator of the Fundy Geological Museum, I visited the site known as *Wasson Bluff,* a pebbly beach at the foot of an eroding cliff. The mouth of the brook that cuts through the bluff is made of reddish-brown, 300-million-year-old sandstone and shale beds, where visitors regularly find footprints of ancient amphibians, ancestors of the dinosaurs.

Turning west across a fault line—a fracture in the earth's crust—the rock suddenly changed to a deep greenish-gray basalt and purple sandstone. The basalt is volcanic rock that in places looks like it was squeezed out of a toothpaste tube. Roughly 200 million years old, it was part of a massive lava flow that reached as far south as Boston and created both Brier Island and Grand Manan Island farther out in the Bay of Fundy.

One layer under this lava flow marks the period when almost half the earth's prehistoric animals were suddenly rendered extinct. As the lava cooled, little bubbles formed, and in these bubbles, minerals known as zeolites were formed. Fragments of these zeolites were scattered along the beach. Beyond this point, the fault line forked. The fossils unearthed here come from the Jurassic period and include tiny dinosaur footprints, as well as dinosaur bone fragments.

These volcanic cliffs look much as they did in the Age of Dinosaurs. The remains of the animals that made these cliffs their homes are found in the red-and-orange sandstone, now packed into cracks left by the volcanic rock. Because the faults move slightly over time, these fossils are often crushed into fragments, which visitors find scattered in the sandstone like chocolate bits in scoops of Rocky Road ice cream.

summer and an elderhostel geological safari in early October. If you want to plan ahead to join one of its programs, visit http://museum.gov.ns.ca/fgm/ for information. This site, although a little overwhelming, has a link listing events for all the provincial government museums. You will discover listings for beginner, intermediate, and advanced silver-making workshops, for example, at the end of which you will have a piece of jewelry made by your own hands.

The museum is open daily year-round, June 1 to mid-October, from 9:30 A.M. to 5:30 P.M. Winter hours are Tuesday to Saturday 9:00 A.M. to 5:00 P.M. and Sunday afternoon from 1:00 to 5:00 P.M.

The other highlight along this coast is *Joggins,* which can be reached via two routes after Parrsboro. Route 2 turns inland, leaving you with the choice of taking a small highway (209), which skirts the remainder of the Fundy Coast, or traveling inland along Route 2 and either skipping Joggins altogether or backtracking to Joggins via exit 4, some 13 miles (20 km) from Amherst, and then driving to Joggins on Highway 242. Along this road you can take a break to stretch your legs at **Cape Chignecto,** a wilderness area that includes a number of nature trails. Admission is $3.00. The park is open from mid-May to mid-October.

Joggins is a must if you want to get to the bottom of fossils' mysterious appeal. When you reach the village, turn onto Main Street in beautiful downtown Joggins (population 491), where you will find the **Joggins Fossil Centre. Guides** here will take the time to explain the origins of the area's many 350-million-year-old fossilized trees, ferns, insects, amphibians, and animal tracks. The center is open from June 1 to the end of September and has an extensive collection of fossils on site. For more information, write to the Joggins Fossil Centre, Main Street, Joggins, NS B0L 1A0; or call (902) 251–2727 in season or (902) 251–2618 off-season. Admission is $5.00 for adults, $3.00 for children ages eighteen and younger.

After Joggins you have merely a 12-mile (20-km) drive to the New Brunswick border, where your travels through mainland Nova Scotia will be complete.

Places to Stay in Western Nova Scotia

ANNAPOLIS ROYAL

King George Inn
548 Upper St. George
(902) 532–5286
This is one of those massive homes previously owned by a sea captain. Dating back to Confederation, this antiques-filled inn is close to all the town's best sights. Standard.

BRIER ISLAND

Brier Island Lodge and Restaurant
(800) 662–8355 or
(902) 839–2300
You'll love this place as much for its location as its ambience. Good seafood. Standard to moderate.

CALEDONIA

Whitman Inn
Route 8
(2.5 miles/4 km south of Kejimkujik National Park)
(800) 690–INNS or
(902) 682–2226
A good place to stay if you don't want to leave civilization behind but still want to enjoy the national park. Breakfast for guests. Standard.

CANNING

The Farmhouse Inn
9757 Main Street
(902) 582–7900
Charming country setting amid miles of apple orchards. Four-star bed-and-breakfast with assorted packages. Standard.

DIGBY

The Pines Resort Hotel
The Shore Road
Digby County
(877) 375–6343 or
(902) 245–2511
Luxurious Norman-style chateau resort overlooking the water. Tennis, golf, and other amenities available. One of the province's poshest places. Deluxe.

MAITLAND

Captain Douglas House Inn and Restaurant
8842 Highway 215
(902) 261–2289
Former sea captain's home, now a Heritage property, featuring in-house restaurant.
Standard to moderate.

MAITLAND BRIDGE

Mersey River Chalets
Route 8
(902) 682–2443
Year-round rustic cottages overlooking Mersey River, offering abundant outdoor activities and proximity to national park.
Moderate to deluxe.

MAVILETTE BEACH

Cape View Motel and Cottages
Near Salmon River, off Route 1
Yarmouth County
(902) 645–2258
Best location near spectacular beach.
Also has a diner.
Standard.

PARRSBORO

Parrsboro Mansion
15 Eastern Avenue
(902) 254–2585
An Italian-style mansion on park grounds.
Central location.
Standard.

PORT WILLIAMS

Planter's Historic Inn
Highway 101, exit 11, then Route 358
(902) 542–7879
The oldest building in Nova Scotia, this English manor-style house seems straight out of *Pride and Prejudice*.
Standard to moderate.

SANDFORD

Churchill Mansion
Route 1
Yarmouth County
(888) 453–5565 or
(902) 649–2818
You'll find quirky charm in this "haunted" Heritage property. An excellent value.
Standard to moderate.

SANDY COVE, DIGBY NECK

Olde Village Inn
Route 217
(800) 834–2206
Housed in a nineteenth-century building, this antiques-filled inn is tucked away in Digby Neck.
Moderate.

SMITHS COVE

Mountain Gap Resort
off Highway 101, exit 24 or 25
Digby County
(800) 565–5020
Great setting.
Moderate.

WOLFVILLE

The Blomidon Inn
127 Main Street
(800) 565–2291

Places to Eat in Western Nova Scotia

ANNAPOLIS ROYAL

Leo's
222 Lower Saint George Street
(902) 532–7424

Newman's
218 Lower Saint George Street
(902) 532–5502

DIGBY

The Pines Resort
Shore Road
(902) 245–2511

WOLFVILLE

Blomidon Inn
127 Main Street
(902) 542–2291 or
(800) 565–2291

Tattingstone Inn
434 Main Street
(902) 542–7696

Cape Breton

Home of the Ceilidh

Linked to the mainland of Nova Scotia by the world's deepest causeway since 1955, Cape Breton remains very much an island, in every sense of the word.

Here "bilingual" could just as easily mean Gaelic and English as French and English, although all these cultures plus Mi'Kmaq are strongly evident on Cape Breton Island. The Mi'Kmaq, of course, have been here for more than ten thousand years. Today visitors will spot posters proclaiming "The Champion Returns," meaning fiddle champion Lee Creemo, a Mi'Kmaq from the shores of the Bras d'Or Lake.

Scots came in two basic waves of immigration. After the failed rebellion of 1745, many Highlanders chose Cape Breton as their exile and refuge. Then, in the 1820s, many landlords drove the Scottish tenants off their land and took it over as sheep pasture. The landless Scots left for Cape Breton and points beyond in search of a place where they could continue to live as their ancestors had.

The French actually settled Cape Breton before the Scots but were exiled after the fall of Louisbourg, their stronghold.

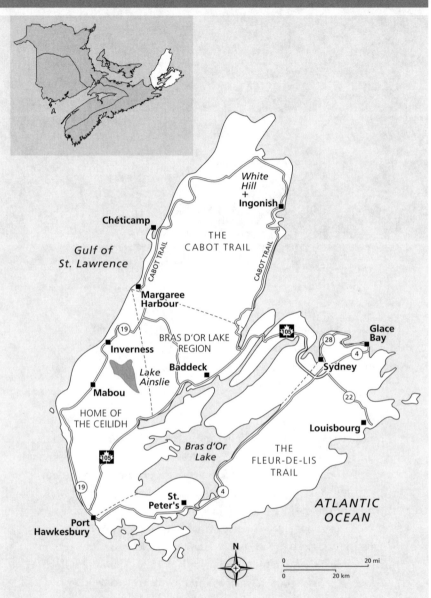

White
Hill
+
Ingonish

Chéticamp

THE
CABOT TRAIL

*Gulf of
St. Lawrence*

CABOT TRAIL

CABOT TRAIL

**Margaree
Harbour**

BRAS D'OR LAKE
REGION

105

19

Inverness

Baddeck

*Lake
Ainslie*

**Glace
Bay**

28

4

Sydney

Mabou

HOME OF
THE CEILIDH

105

*Bras d'Or
Lake*

22

THE
FLEUR-DE-LIS
TRAIL

Louisbourg

19

**St.
Peter's**

4

*ATLANTIC
OCEAN*

**Port
Hawkesbury**

N

0   20 mi

0   20 km

Many of them returned to France but came back to Cape Breton a few years later and settled in communities only a few miles from the Scots.

At every gas station and rest stop on Cape Breton you will see locally produced books, stories of the first Scottish settlers or the French. Among the stacks of videotapes, heavily in demand by visitors awed by the island's spectacular scenery, will be those that focus on Cape Breton's native sons and daughters who have managed to carve out their own niche in the music industry with a blend of Celtic traditional and modern rock ballads.

You will be shortchanging yourself if you do not take the time to enjoy firsthand the music and arts that have kept a love of Cape Breton culture foremost even in the hearts of the island's economic exiles who have drifted off to central Canada in search of opportunity.

Eleanor Mullendor, Mabou innkeeper as well as the neighbor of the musical Rankin family, points out that there is a local festival somewhere on the island at least once a week all summer long. Along the boardwalk that skirts the waterfront of Chéticamp, near the start of the Cabot Trail, one has a chance of catching live performances three times a week. If you happen to spend any length of time in one place you may also be lucky enough to get invited to a traditional Gaelic party, or ***ceilidh*** (pronounced *kay-lee*), at someone's home. If this happens, you're in for a treat, a holdover from the descendants of the hardy group of pioneers who left the difficult times and persecution of Scotland to establish a New Scotland for themselves on Cape Breton Island.

With that in mind, the very first thing to do once you cross the causeway is buy a copy of the local paper, *The Cape Breton Post,* turn to the entertainment

TRUDY'S FAVORITES

Alexander Graham Bell Museum,
Baddeck

Amoeba's Sailing Tours,
Baddeck

Cape Breton Highlands National Park,
from Chéticamp to Ingonish

Fortress Louisbourg,
Louisbourg

Keltic Lodge,
Middle Head

LeNoir Forge Museum,
Isle Madame

Scarecrow Village,
Cap Le Moine/Monk's Hat

Sunset Art Gallery,
Chéticamp

Wallace MacAskill Museum,
St. Peter's

section, scan the listings, and plan your itinerary accordingly. Then fill up your tank before leaving Port Hastings and turn left onto Route 19 to head north along the scenic western coast.

In short order you will come to *Judique* (the Judiques, to be exact, since there are supposedly ten of them, including North Judique, South Judique, Big Judique, and Little Judique, not to mention the Centre, Banks, Chapel, Ponds, and Rear and Intervale Judiques). Along the shore road in this area you will find a number of wharves where you can purchase lobsters straight from the boats.

A short drive farther up Route 19 will bring you to a sign indicating a left turn to get to Port Hood, where a public wharf serves more lobster fishermen. If you continue on Route 19 from this junction, you will soon come to *Mabou,* home of the Rankins, who achieved international recognition for their singing, songwriting, and animated performances. Several of them have gone on to successful solo careers. They still retain strong links to the area.

The pride that Mabou's inhabitants feel in the singers' success is at least partially due to their skill in taking Gaelic singing to the masses, once again putting the spotlight on Mabou as a center of Gaelic language and traditional culture.

In a small part-time museum called *The Bridge,* or, in Gaelic, *An Drochaid*, eager youngsters line up for fiddle lessons. Located near the bridge on the only piece of highway in the village, the museum also offers day-camp courses in Gaelic, with children from far afield taking the opportunity to learn the ancient language, which reportedly is spoken by more people here than in Scotland. Formerly a general store, *An Drochaid* also houses artifacts, genealogical and historical records, research, and local music. Admission is free. The little museum is open year-round (upon request). If you don't find it open, you can call locally at (902) 945–2311 or (902) 945–2790.

Mabou is a small place, with a population just over 300, and so serene that it seems quite likely that very little has changed here in the past several decades. It is peaceful, restful, and unhurried.

For a village this size, one can find a remarkable chowder, along with other typical Maritime delicacies, at *The Mull,* situated on the main road. The settlers of this area came from the Isle of Mull in Scotland, and near here you will find the Mull River. A random sampling of chowders from throughout the island came up with the Mull's chowder as the top choice. The restaurant also sells big rings of Mabou cheese and other local products. (For more about this, read on.)

The Mull was started by innkeepers Eleanor and Charles Mullendor several years before they opened the **Duncreigan Inn.** The Mullendors hail originally from Connecticut. They discovered the spot when they came north for a holiday. Before long they bought a 120-acre farm nearby, settled there, and became citizens. They bring their love affair with their chosen homeland into their work, filling the inn with local handicrafts, along with paintings by the province's artists; some of these items are for sale.

The inn itself is a modern building, with all the newest comforts, although it was designed to incorporate features of the original farmhouse the Mullendors bought on their land. At one time it was a charming old home, say the innkeepers, but it had reached the point where, as the locals put it, the building was "after falling down."

At one point the Mullendors headed the local arts council for the Inverness area. They have developed considerable contacts with area artists. In every room in the inn, you will find old-time Chéticamp hooked rugs colored with organic dyes in the traditional manner. They also prepare special meals for their guests, including local Mabou cheeses and *maraq,* also known as "poor man's haggis," a combination of suet, onions, and oatmeal done up like sausage meat in a cow's intestine. Reportedly, it's not a process for the unambitious cooks among us. For reservations call (902) 945–2244 or write to Box 59, Mabou, NS B0E 2T0. Rates are moderate.

Take a look at Mabou from the front deck of the Duncreigan Inn (located just south of the village proper and across the bridge from the community). One has a view of the tiny village church, reflected perfectly in the still water. It is easy to imagine a life where time stands still, even though the village has international recording stars living next to the bald eagles and the moose. Innkeeper Eleanor Mullendor sometimes organizes a *ceilidh* for her guests at the inn, inviting local performers and Gaelic-speaking seniors for a "milling frolic," so it's worth asking if one of these events is being planned.

Mabou pioneers were determined not to yield to persecution in their homelands. The Scottish settlers who came to this end of Cape Breton and succeeded in making a life of it were of the most hardy stock. Think of it as pioneers' Darwinism: Those who did not succeed moved on. At one point 800 of the Scottish pioneers left Cape Breton en masse for New Zealand. Those who remained and thrived were the toughest of the lot.

Their memory is preserved in the **Our Lady of Seven Sorrows Pioneers Shrine,** which looks for all the world like a simple country church from the patio of the Duncreigan Inn. It's a surprising optical trick. From the outside it seems almost too small to accommodate the congregation. But inside, the Douglas fir timbers used to make columns and the skillfully constructed archways make it look like a tiny cathedral.

You can trace the roots of this region's Scottish settlers at the same *An Drochaid* where fiddle lessons are held. It houses the **Mabou Gaelic and Historical Society Museum.** Admission is free. For information about hours, call (902) 945–2311.

There are several interesting walks in the area. If you turn toward the sea just before crossing the bridge to exit the village, you can follow the Harbour Road to **Mabou Harbour Mouth.** At the tip of land you will find the tiny, pretty lighthouse at **Mabou Mines.**

From here, provided it hasn't been too rainy, you can walk along the shore for a good distance north. Once-thriving Mabou's mines eventually had to be abandoned when the ore that could be reached safely was depleted and digging under the water became impossible. For the vigorous among you, the walk is 7 to 8 miles (11 to 13 km) and will take you to Sight Point, where you can rejoin a road that leads north to Inverness.

Another good hike, this time inland, is in a protected stand of forest wilderness owned by a local historian. The **MacFarlane Woods Nature Reserve** was settled by the MacFarlanes in the 1820s, but they never cut the trees on the hilltop. There you will find a mature maple, beech, and yellow birch forest of a type that covered much of this area before the arrival of the white man.

bonappétit!

Many visitors get a little queasy when it comes to eating haggis, the ultimate Scottish food. The problem is knowledge out of context.

Haggis is made from the heart, lungs, and liver of a sheep or calf. The organs are mixed with suet, chopped onions, and oatmeal, boiled in a sheep's stomach and, voilà! Haggis. Sounds terrible, doesn't it? Actually, it's not much different from sausage, which is traditionally made from spiced (and sometimes smoked) organ meats that are dried or cooked and then inserted in animal intestines. The methods used for making both haggis and sausage were developed to preserve meat in the days when the only things refrigerated were your toes on a cold winter night.

Now that you realize that you've been eating similar stuff all along, next time a Cape Bretoner offers you a plate of the dreaded haggis, dig in!

To get to the woods, cross the village's bridge in the direction of Port Hood, and take the first left along the Mabou Ridge Road. A sign will direct you to **Glencoe Mills Hall.** The woods are marked. An access trail leads up to the top of the hill, where you will see trees, some of which are as big as 3 feet

TOP ANNUAL EVENTS

Big Pond Summer Festival,
Big Pond (mid-July to month's end);
no phone

Highland Village Day Concert,
Iona (first Saturday in August);
(902) 725–2272

Cape Breton Fiddlers' Festival,
St. Anns (second to last
weekend in August);
no phone

Fête de St. Louis,
Louisbourg (late August);
(902) 733–2630

(1 m) in diameter and 100 feet (30 m) high. In early summer you will find rare wild orchids, along with wood sorrel, starflower, and bunchberry. Later in the season the ground will be dotted with wild mushrooms.

When you return to Mabou, you can detour to the ***Mabou Pioneers Cemetery*** by turning left instead of right at the intersection of Route 19 and the Mabou Ridge Road and then turning right at the West Mabou Road. Just after the West Mabou Sports Club and Hall, turn right toward ***Indian Point,*** which overlooks the harbor. Here you will find the old graveyard of the village's pioneers, punctuated by a cairn (a traditional stone marker) and neat rows of headstones of the area's founders, who came here in the early 1800s. The church in the village originally stood here; it was moved to its current location in 1967.

When it's time to leave Mabou, return to Route 19, head north, and follow the signs for ***Inverness.*** Ever want to explore the mysteries of Scotch whisky, or perhaps just want an excuse to taste-test quite a lot of it? En route from Mabou to Inverness you will come to the ***Glenora Inn and Distillery,*** which offers you a unique opportunity. This is the only single-malt whisky distillery in North America and is strikingly similar to distilleries in the old country. The whisky is produced in the traditional copper-pot stills, but cannot be called Scotch unless it is produced in Scotland. Glenora's brew, named Glen Breton Rare Canadian Single Malt Whisky, is available in provincial liquor stores, as well as places as far away as Bermuda, Mexico, Switzerland, Ireland, France, and the United States. The micro-distillery is limiting production to only 2,000 dozen-bottle cases a year to maintain quality. (The brew is also aged at least eight to ten years). A whisky museum is part of the distillery tour. Every day the distillery offers tours from 9:00 A.M. to 5:00 P.M. The 600-acre property is also home to an inn and Celtic pub, so you could just decide to explore Scottish culture in more depth. The inn has nine bedrooms and six chalets. The

Scottish-style Glenora Pub showcases musicians several times daily. The dining room specialty is salmon smoked in a whisky barrel. For information, call (800) 839–0491 or (902) 258–2662, or visit www.glenoradistillery.com. Rates are moderate. Just outside of town you will see a sign indicating a provincial picnic park. Just after this the road passes over two rivers. The second of these is fed by **Glenora Falls,** a walk of 0.2 mile (.4 km) in from the road.

After a brief drive you will come to Inverness. You will notice that after several miles of driving in the interior, you are now along the coast again, and even though you have stayed on the same stretch of highway, you will have made a right turn just as you entered the village.

To your left is a pristine but exposed beach overlooking the Gulf of St. Lawrence, reached by a small boardwalk. On the other side of the street are a number of craft shops, featuring items from as far away as Chéticamp and Judique; they range from tartans to hooked rugs.

To stock up on film or medical needs before your next scenic excursion, you will find a pharmacy on your right almost as soon as you enter "town," which basically consists of a small stretch of Route 19 that runs along the coast. People in town will direct you to **Freeman's Pharmacy.** The pharmacy is fascinating. There is a large stock of books on local Gaelic culture and history as well as volumes of scenic photography. CDs and cassette tapes of all the fiddling greats are on the counter next to the cash register.

Backtrack about a block from the intersection that brought you into town and then drive down toward the government wharf. You will notice a small, old-style railway station that has been converted into the **Inverness Miners' Museum.** Outside you will see a cairn, upon which are noted the names of men who died in various local mine disasters before mining was completely abandoned in the 1940s. Admission is $1.00 for adults, 50 cents for students. It is open mid-June through September from 9:00 A.M. to 5:00 P.M. On weekends, the museum opens from noon to 5:00 P.M.

The railway station was built in 1901, during Inverness's salad days, when mining was the town's economic mainstay. In 1977 the village's historical society turned it into a museum. It also contains a small archive and displays artwork and photography on a rotating basis.

If you happen to be in Inverness on a Thursday in July or August, take a room in any of the establishments that line the road on the beach side of town and attend the *ceilidh* at the fire hall, which starts at 8:00 P.M. The last week in July, there is always the Inverness Gathering, where the *ceilidh* spirit will prevail.

After years of active involvement in the community arts scene, the **Inverness County Centre for the Arts,** a wonderful new arts center, was opened in Inverness in 2003. Along Route 19 in the north end of Inverness, it's on the opposite side of the highway from the Inverness Beach Village. Open from June 1 to the middle of September, the center's hours are 10:00 A.M. to 5:00 P.M. Monday through Friday, open two hours later on Thursday, and open after 1:00 P.M. on the weekends. The center houses the work of local and international artists, as well as special events, workshops, and performances. Details of their schedule can be found on their Web site at http://invernessarts.ca, or you could call (902) 258–2533.

Leaving Inverness, continue for a short way along the coast on Route 19. You'll come to a fork in the road at Dunvegan. From here you have the option of continuing along the scenic coastline on a secondary highway, Route 219, or traveling the more modern stretch of highway that leads to **Southwest Margaree.** There are a number of Margarees in this area of beautiful rolling hills and meadows, and the scenery is just as lovely as it is along the coastline.

Of note is the **Margaree River,** which in 1991 was designated as a Canadian Heritage River. It is excellent for salmon fishing. You'll see many anglers as you drift along its banks, should you decide to hike in this area. If you want to make an entire vacation of fishing, the Margaree would fit the bill very well.

Continue inland from Margaree Forks into Northeast Margaree. There you can explore the collection of angling and salmon paraphernalia at the **Margaree Salmon Museum,** to find out just how special the river is for fishing. For information call (902) 248–2848. The museum is just 0.2 mile (0.3 km) off the Cabot Trail.

Something happens on this stretch of highway. Within a few miles the family names change from MacDonald and MacMaster to Doucet and LeBlanc. Gaelic heritage starts to give way to French Acadian and, just at the Margarees, the transition seems to be at its high point.

It's surprising when you think of it: Two generations ago, just south of Margaree, people lived and worked in Gaelic. To this day their children learn the traditional songs and attend Gaelic classes. And then, just a short stretch of road away, the language changes to French. How can it have happened that these two cultures managed to survive in a largely English-speaking province?

One gentleman I met provided a few clues. Back in the days of one-room schoolhouses, before buses brought children to their classes, a young pupil's study was at the mercy of the elements. As soon as the bad weather commenced, many children couldn't manage the walk of several miles to the school. So they kept speaking only the language of their forefathers, being educated largely at home during the long winter months. In the space of a few miles one would find areas so heavily populated by transplanted highland

Scots that you would swear you were in Scotland, and then, isolated by rough roads and bad weather, another whole community of people who continued to speak the French of their ancestors.

Any way you look at it, the impact is a rich cultural stew.

The Cabot Trail

Continue along Route 19 north after Margaree Forks until you rejoin the Cabot Trail at **Margaree Harbour.** (If you took the coastal route, you're already there.) On both sides of this harbor are pleasant, uncrowded beaches. Beyond the harbor is a small bridge that promptly brings you to **Belle Côte.** From here on you will encounter a string of thriving Acadian communities.

Just after the road passes a piece of coast that appears to jut out into the gulf, look to your right. A weathered "old barn," which appears to be propped up on one side by poles, has an unusual group of individuals standing around not doing anything in particular. These are the scarecrows of **Cap Le Moine** (on some maps this appears as its English translation: "Monk's Hat").

There are more than one hundred scarecrows in all, including a golfer. The proprietor of this **Scarecrow Village** has capitalized on these cool lawn ornaments to draw business for a take-out and gift shop that he runs on the same site. It's worth stretching your legs to take a look around, but if you're busy looking at the coast, you could easily miss it.

Continue up the road for a few minutes and you will come to **St. Joseph du Moine.** In this little village you will notice a small art gallery named, imaginatively, **La Bella Mona Lisa.** You can't miss it: The facade is decorated with a massive folk-art painting of a cow in red sneakers. Inside, there are all manner of tongue-in-cheek objets d'art, a lot of them involving cows. There are also gift items such as wind chimes and locally made duck decoys that are too pretty to use.

A short drive from here is **Chéticamp,** population 979. It is the largest Acadian community in the area and the location of the hospital and other essential services such as a pharmacy. Because of this, it seems much more of a town than a village. During the summer months large numbers of French-speaking visitors come here from the rest of the Maritimes. Roughly 20 percent of its total visitors come from Quebec. In summer this influx of French-speaking visitors gives Chéticamp the atmosphere of a surprisingly cosmopolitan village.

The origins of Chéticamp are not entirely straightforward. Although unmistakably French in character, the village's earliest settlers were actually from the

French-speaking Channel Islands, under the British Crown. Following the Treaty of Paris in 1763, the French lost fishing rights in the Gulf of St. Lawrence.

Quickly filling the vacuum was Charles Robin, a French Huguenot from the Isle of Jersey. And at about that time, exiled Acadians were starting to come back to these shores. The exiles had been packed off to St. Malo in France, a port just south of Jersey. Robin offered them work, and soon a thriving community of returned Acadians sprang up. For many years afterward the people of Chéticamp were tied to the fortunes of the Robin family. (They weren't the only Acadians to have dealings with the Jersey "French": On the southeastern coast of Cape Breton, you will find other relics of the Jersey connection in St. Peter's and Arichat.)

You might want to visit a replica of the Robin Company Store, re-created to evoke the year 1896, a time when the economic well-being of the village's fishermen depended on the whim of this solitary, family-run company. This is located in a new complex, completed in mid-2002, called *Musée La Pirogue* ("Pirogue Museum"), at 15359 Cabot Trail Road. The museum is a reproduction of an old Acadian homestead and features demonstrations on the making of lobster traps, and the characteristic Chéticamp rag rugs. Admission is $5.00 for adults, $4.00 for children ages six to twelve, and free for children under six.

Just before reaching Chéticamp proper, you'll see a sign indicating *L'Auberge Doucet,* or "Doucet Inn," which is set far back off the road at the end of a massive sloping lawn that would make a good bunny slope at a ski school. Just behind the inn is an unspoiled view of the Cape Breton Highlands. This is your best bet for a quiet place to stay in Chéticamp, which is less than a mile (1 km) farther down the road. Rates are standard to moderate. From the patio that separates the two parts of the inn, you can see a small inlet, and off in the distance, Chéticamp Island. For information call (800) 646–8668 or (902) 224–3438.

The *Coopérative Artisanale de Chéticamp Ltée* is the first eating establishment that you will encounter as you enter Chéticamp. It is marked by three flags outside: the Canadian maple leaf, the Nova Scotian St. Andrew's cross, and the Acadian tricolor with a star, which you have no doubt seen all over New Brunswick.

Here you can eat a traditional Acadian meal (such as a meat pie) and then check out the craft co-op on the other wing of the same building. On display are excellent examples of Chéticamp hooked rugs. These are so intricately executed that they look more like needlepoint than the usual hooked rug one finds in hobby shops.

The morning that I visited, a lady named Claudette Leblanc demonstrated the rug-hooking technique that developed in Chéticamp as a way of covering the cold wooden floors of the simple Acadian homesteads. As sometimes happens when necessity and isolation conspire, an original art form developed from the use of objects at hand. At first women used burlap potato sacks, stretched out on a frame and pulled tight. Starting with rags and then moving on to wool yarn, the women drew the fabric through the holes in the burlap, forming a loop. They followed a pattern that had been drawn or stamped on the bags. When the intricate pattern had been filled in, the stretcher was loosened and the burlap relaxed. This caused the wool loops to be tightly enclosed by the burlap, and a beautifully patterned rug would result.

Several decades ago some women from New York discovered the Chéticamp rugs and started buying them for resale in the United States, where they gained considerable popularity.

There is an amusing story about the start of the hooked-rug cottage industry. One of the early developers of the technique was a woman who was quite noted for the designs she stamped on the burlap backing. As a young girl she had made her materials from rags that she cut from family clothing. Eventually, the industry became lucrative and her entire family became involved in it, sons as well as daughters. But as the matriarch who started the rug business aged, she became more and more determined to produce the rag carpets, so much so that the family had to hide all scissors and fabric from her. She passed away at age eighty-nine, still eager to cut rags at every opportunity.

The home she spent her life in is a Heritage property, out of which a craft shop called **Le Motif** operates. It is painted a deep blue and is located at the northern end of town. The specialty here, not surprisingly, is rag rugs.

trivia

Caid Mile Failté is Gaelic for "100,000 welcomes."

Fishermen call an undersized lobster a tinker.

Several restaurants operate down along the boardwalk that follows the waterfront from the government wharf to the end of the village's main drag. You can sit in the **Harbour Restaurant** and watch the lobster boats drift off to cast their traps.

Just past Le Motif you will notice that the village is thinning out as you head north. At this point, on your left, you will see a large, brightly painted sign for the **Sunset Art Gallery** and an arrow indicating a small wooden building across the street. This is the studio of Bill Roach, one of the province's most noted folk artists. You can't miss his calling: He has a fence made out of people who resemble giant clothes pegs. In the back of the studio, it looks like someone is splitting wood for the fire. A stout woman, carved from a substantial tree trunk, seems ready to shake your hand. Inside, the brightly colored ornaments most frequently are animal friends.

Roach's works have been displayed at the Nova Scotia Art Gallery. One was sent to the Canadian Embassy in Washington, D.C., for a six-month period. His wife, Linda, runs the gallery, and she proudly displays photographs of his many commissions, some of which have been sent as far away as Australia.

One woman had the master craftsman produce likenesses of all four of her dogs from detailed photographs that she had sent him of their front, side, and back views. Then she decided to have her husband done, but all she provided

Folk Art at Sunset Art Gallery

of her spouse for Roach to produce this work of art was a single wallet-size snapshot. Judging by the photo of the final product, it was enough for a lively depiction of the fellow.

You might also want to visit ***Chéticamp Island.*** For many years this island was in the hands of the Robin family (known locally as "the Jerseys"), until in 1893 a priest and activist, Father Pierre Fiset, arranged the purchase of the island. This was one of many actions undertaken by Fiset in his struggle to lessen the hold of the Robin merchant family on the village.

From the road that runs along the harbor side of Chéticamp Island, you can get a charming view of the village, punctuated by the large church of St. Pierre, all set against the backdrop of the highlands. The view of the village and the church (built under the direction of Père Fiset) is well worth the trip to the island, where you can also hike and view eagles, cormorants, cliffs, moorlands, a lighthouse, and beaches.

Apart from checking out the village's thriving crafts and arts community, a warm summer day in Chéticamp is best spent strolling along the boardwalk, where there are free concerts three times a week in summer. Once you've fulfilled your need for human company, follow the road leading out of the village at its northern end, toward ***Cape Breton Highlands National Park.*** Be sure to bring something along to munch and drink, because eating establishments are few and far between along the route you will follow; you may find yourself

The House That Sank

There are only a few houses and cottages on *Chéticamp Island,* but some of them have an unusual history, recounted to me by Wilbert Aucoin, the owner of one of them. Aucoin is a friendly gentleman who, after retiring from the Royal Canadian Mounted Police, returned to his native Chéticamp. The house he bought after his retirement had at one time been located in the area designated in the 1930s to become the Highlands National Park. At that time, it was decided that all the houses in the area had to be moved, by barge, up the Chéticamp River and into Chéticamp village. Just as they were pulling one house into the harbor, a big gust of wind blew up, followed by a large wave. The house, which may not have been very securely tied, went under the water. Aucoin remembers watching, along with most of the village, as the house was hoisted out of the water and deposited on the island. Many years later he bought the very same house that had sunk during moving.

getting hungry several hours before you reach the next restaurant, unless you curtail all stops. The park is located along the **Cabot Trail,** named for explorer John Cabot, who sailed into Aspy Bay, near Dingwall, in 1497, only five years after Christopher Columbus visited the Caribbean. Soon after Cabot's discovery of this neck of the woods, European fishermen and fur traders began visiting these shores, eager to make their fortunes from the natural bounty of the area.

The main interpretive center is at the park entrance. In the same building is a bookstore. Apart from the maps and information for sale or offered there, you'll have a chance to explore what has to be the most extensive collection of naturalist books you may ever see.

The park is full of natural wonders—from huge, 300-year-old sugar maples, yellow birch, and beech trees, to waterfalls rushing down rugged mountainsides, to eagles soaring gracefully in their wilderness refuge, to the black bear, which will tolerate no insult from human intruders who roam the park's interior. Take heed and use a telephoto lens to photograph any bears that you may happen to spot. You may also see a moose along the road in the park, so drive cautiously.

The park has been carefully mapped out with twenty-eight suggested trails—some challenging overnight ones, and some just twenty minutes long and on level ground. There are also plenty of places to stop and park so you can get a panoramic view of the ocean or river rapids far below the road, which winds its way around the highlands. Pick up a detailed map at the park entrance, as well as the booklet entitled *Walking in the Highlands,* which outlines the many hikes and has them conveniently arranged with numbers corresponding to indicators on the map.

Soon after you've entered the parkland itself, you will come to an area inhabited at one time by French Acadians. Several trails along the Chéticamp River are reminders of this area's first European settlers. If the long hike to **Pleasant Bay** is not your style, you can still get excellent views of the coastline from several lookout points along this part of the route.

On a very clear day it is worthwhile to make a stop at the **Fishing Cove Lookoff.** Cast your gaze northwest into the St. Lawrence. The islands you will see are 50 miles (80 km) away: Quebec's Magdalene Islands.

Try to imagine the intense isolation of this area of Cape Breton in the 1920s. The ice forms for miles out to sea in the winter. Before the minister of highways of the time conceived of the idea of building the road from Chéticamp to Pleasant Bay and beyond, and then turning the area into parkland, it was virtually impossible to make one's way beyond the next farmhouse during the many winter storms.

From the park entrance to Pleasant Bay takes about an hour by car if you stop only a few times to look around. This little village is just outside the national park, because the highway meanders outside park boundaries temporarily. During the summer months you may be able to dine at one of the few restaurants that operate as part of the motels.

Just north of Pleasant Bay, in the direction of Red River, a **Buddhist monastery** was established, after its founder, a Tibetan lama, believed the environment was suitable for contemplation. Once you've roamed around the Cape Breton Highlands for a while, you'll understand why.

When you exit Pleasant Bay along the Cabot Trail you will return to official national park territory within a few minutes. You will then steadily climb uphill while making a number of turns. Be on the lookout for a sign that indicates **Lone Shieling** and parking. If you don't grab a chance to park at this spot, it will be too late to look at Lone Shieling, except for a perfunctory glance as you whiz past in your automobile.

Once you do park, you have before you one of the most pleasant and interesting short walks that the park has to offer. The loop takes about a quarter hour, if you don't count the time you spend at the replica of a Scottish crofter's hut. The building was erected at the request of a man named Donald MacIntosh, a native of Pleasant Bay and a professor of geology at Dalhousie University. He donated one hundred acres (forty hectares) to the government in the area of Pleasant Bay in 1934, including some virgin forest. (The park has 80 percent of the province's remaining virgin forest.) After the land was absorbed into

Lone Shieling on the Cabot Trail

the budding national park, the government built this replica of the Lone Shieling, a crofter's hut like those on the Isle of Skye, the home of this man's ancestors. It's a cleverly constructed little shelter; one can well imagine a shepherd huddled in here with his sheep when storms made the out-of-doors unpleasant.

After viewing the hut descend a small set of steps and walk along a woodland path in an area of tall, ancient yellow birch and 350-year-old sugar maples, accompanied by interpretive park signs. The trail ends with another set of stone steps leading up to the parking area.

Another few minutes' driving time from here will take you high up into the mountains, to a point where scenic views are around every corner. The best panoramic shots are cleverly designated by small lookout symbols and a widening of the road that permits parking. From one of these lookouts (indicated on the park map), you can see in the distance **Beulach Ban Falls,** which can be reached by a trail at the base of the mountain.

To get to the falls, follow the directions to the Aspy Trail; the entrance is at a turnoff just after the warden station. Take note that while the first part of the trail is accessible by vehicle, the road requires a high wheelbase and good suspension in the spring.

After the trail to the falls, the road once again exits official park territory and leads through a stretch of rural Cape Breton where you won't have an opportunity to eat for miles and miles, until at long last you come to **Cape North** and **Dingwall.** Here, finally, the hungry traveler can find several promising spots at which to eat.

At Cape North the road forks, with the left turn leading to the pretty coastal communities of Bay St. Lawrence, Capstick, and Meat Cove. Then the road stops. If you want to see more of the rugged coast, you can take a whale-watching cruise aboard a Cape Islander boat owned by Captain Dennis Cox in **Capstick.**

For information call (888) 346–5556 or (902) 383–2981. In addition to the frequent sightings of whales on this cruise, you'll stand a good chance of seeing eagles, cormorants, lots of puffins, moose, bear, waterfalls, and sea caves.

After experiencing Capstick you have no choice but to turn your car south and backtrack to the fork in the road at Cape North. (Take note that on a really foggy day, you may as well pass up this detour altogether, because you'll hardly be able to see anything.) If you take the right instead of the left road, and then drive for a moment, you will come to the turnoff for Dingwall, which is precisely 2 miles (3 km) after Cape North.

This road will take you to ***The Markland Coastal Resort*** in Dingwall. The Markland is considered by some to be the rival of the Keltic Lodge, which is a posh government-run resort in Ingonish. The Markland features rustic, Scandinavian-style pine chalets spread out over seventy acres (twenty-eight hectares) overlooking the ocean. A long, secluded, sandy beach here is complemented by a stretch of inland waterway suitable for water sports. For details call (800) 872–6084 or (902) 383–2246. Rates are moderate to deluxe.

During the summer months the Markland also operates a gourmet restaurant; this is virtually the last place to eat until you get to Ingonish. The restaurant is open only from late June to mid-October.

There are two options for heading southeast out of Cape North: You can drive through official park territory, or take the scenic route along a coastal road

Celtic Colors

Fall foliage season is glorious on Cape Breton. A visit at this time will yield lots of choices for pleasant outdoor recreation, stunning scenery, and the ***Celtic Colours International Festival.*** This great event brings together entertainers from Scotland and Ireland as well as other parts of Canada and the United States. In its ninth year in 2005, Celtic Colours has grown in popularity every year. In a typical year the festival entertains more than 8,000 persons attending close to three dozen concerts held in more than twenty-six communities all over Cape Breton. Needless to say, if you don't book well in advance, you'll have to scramble to get tickets. While you're booking your show tickets, be sure to reserve a hotel room, since accommodations too, will be in short supply. The festival is striving to maintain its rural emphasis, so many performances are held in cozy communities featured elsewhere in this book, with lots of other things to see and do while you are there. The festival kicks off on the Canadian Thanksgiving weekend, which for Americans is Columbus Day weekend. For details of the upcoming festival, call (902) 562–6700 or visit www.celtic-colours.com.

from Effies Brook to New Haven. Although the scenic route takes a bit longer, it's well worth it. There is a potential picture postcard around every bend.

This loop ends at the tiny community of **Neils Harbour,** which has a lighthouse and a picnic area where you can stretch your legs and roam around amid fishing shacks and lobster traps. Then it's back into the park for another stretch of hilly driving until you reach Ingonish and then **Middle Head,** which is lumped in with Ingonish whenever anyone talks about it as a destination.

Middle Head is the site of **Keltic Lodge,** not Ingonish, as you might hear. Keltic is the granddaddy of all Cape Breton resorts, perched majestically on a high promontory overlooking Ingonish Beach. Even if you don't stay here, it is worth your while to roam the grounds and enjoy the setting and view before moving on down the trail.

Keltic Lodge is in a lovely setting, and takes a fabulous picture. The restaurant at Keltic, the posh **Atlantic Restaurant,** is probably the only one on the island that requires male patrons to wear a jacket to dinner. Keltic is adjacent to an eighteen-hole golf course. To one side of Ingonish Beach is a freshwater lake with supervised swimming. For information call (800) 565–0444. Rates are deluxe.

Continuing along the Cabot Trail in the **Ingonish** area, you will soon see a sign on the right for **Lynn Gorey's Craft Shop and Art Gallery.** This is a must-see. "Lynn" is the wife of widely acclaimed artist Christopher Gorey, whose work is displayed in this shop (as well as at the Art Gallery of Nova Scotia in Halifax).

Along with wonderful, full-size original watercolors, which can be had for a few hundred dollars, Gorey has limited-edition reproductions in sizes that pack easily, unframed, for under $50. Gorey, whose studio is located in the back of the art gallery, depicts life on this coast with a special sensitivity for his medium. The shop is open mid-May to mid-October. For details call the gallery at (902) 285–2845.

From Ingonish you'll return briefly to the national park to climb one last mountain along a winding road. This is where the advice to travel the trail clockwise from Chéticamp to Ingonish comes in handy: If you went in the other direction, you would be "cliffside" on the road.

Die-hard cyclists love to "do" the Cabot Trail; often you will see one pedaling away in his or her lowest gear up **Cape Smokey.** If this is the case, exercise extreme caution, because cyclists often need considerable leeway on the road and cannot stop quickly. (My husband has cycled the trail five times, and he assures me that brakes won't work on the descent, even if you want to use them.)

A pleasant stretch of coastal road awaits you after leaving the national park for good. This area is sometimes referred to as *St. Ann's Loop.* Here there is an eclectic mix of artists and craftspeople who have been drawn to the area by its bucolic charm.

In *Indian Brook* you'll notice a rustic wooden home and shop called *Leather Works* on the right-hand side of the road. Operated by John Roberts, the store features historic reproductions of traditional

trivia

When it was founded in 1939, St. Ann's became the first Gaelic college in North America.

leather goods, including leather buckets, which modern-day owners use to chill champagne or as elegant flower pots. Leather buckets are lighter than wooden ones, so back in the days when brigades of men passed water buckets hand over hand to fight fires, these were the type used. Pitch was used to make them watertight.

The owner of Leather Works, a former Ontario resident, specializes in leather reproductions for national parks and museums across the country. For example, when you visit the Fortress Louisbourg, farther along in Cape Breton, take note of the fire brigade's leather buckets. These reproductions were made by Roberts.

Along with the buckets and belts, purses, and shoes at Leather Works, you will find tavern-style aprons in supple leather that are *très chic.*

A few moments' drive after Indian Brook will bring you to a tiny ferry crossing at Jersey Cove. Here you have the option of driving to South Gut St. Anns at the head of St. Anns Harbour, or taking a car ferry across the narrow harbor. Cars and passengers cross for a small fee.

Bras d'Or Lake Region

On the other side of the harbor is *Englishtown,* which has the distinction of being the birthplace and final resting place of a famous Cape Breton giant and one-time P.T. Barnum circus performer, *Angus MacAskill.* Just a minute after you drive off the boat, you will spot a small graveyard where the 7-foot-9-inch (2.4-m), 425-pound (193-kg) giant is buried. Not surprisingly, his is the biggest headstone.

Five minutes' drive farther down Route 312 will bring you to the *Giant MacAskill Museum,* which contains all sorts of memorabilia. A sign on Route 312 indicates the museum.

Open from mid-June to mid-September, the house contains artifacts—big ones, like massive boots and the giant's chair. These items from MacAskill's life and times provide a fascinating picture of one of the most unusual people of his day. A full-scale model of the giant (at one time displayed at the Halifax Citadel) gives you a good idea of the commanding presence of the man. For information, call (902) 929–2925. There is a small admission charge.

From here the drive to **South Gut St. Anns** is quite straightforward. Route 312 ends momentarily at junction 12, where you will join TCH Highway 105, headed south. Follow this route for 3.5 miles (5 km) until you reach exit 11. If you take this exit, you will find yourself in front of the **Lobster Galley at Harbour House.**

Complete with its own lobster pound at the inner limit of St. Anns Harbour, you can guess what the specialty is at the restaurant. (A waitress here, however, noted that they also serve vegetarian and macrobiotic items, and she estimated that one-eighth of their customers request vegetarian fare. Word of mouth has been sufficient to bring in large groups of Buddhist monks on the way to the abbey in Pleasant Bay.) The Lobster Galley has also added some Japanese items to their menu: tempura, samurai scallops, and appetizers. Sushi is available if you call ahead. The Harbour House also has a gift shop.

Right next door is the **Gaelic College of Celtic Arts and Crafts.** Locally known as St. Ann's Gaelic College, it is a place where visitors can explore the legacy of Scottish settlers to North America at the "Great Hall of the Clans." There is also a museum and craft shop. For information, call (902) 295–3411. Reach the craft shop at (902) 295–3441.

A Gaelic Language Primer

(Adapted from the Harbour House menu)

A nice touch on the Harbour House's menu is the "Gaelic Language Primer," complete with pronunciations. The English translations alone sound typical of Gaelic speakers, since they use colloquialisms and a sentence structure not wholly English.

Gaelic has only eighteen letters in its alphabet, but it has sounds unheard of in English due to the unusual combination of letters. Here are a few essentials:

Ciamar a tha thu-fhein, pronounced "Kimmer uh ha oo haen?" meaning, "How's yourself?" (It's their translation, not mine.)

De do naigheachd, pronounced "Jae daw neh ochk?" meaning, "What's new?"

Se biadh math a bha sin, pronounced "Sheh bee ugh ma uh va shin," meaning, "That was a lovely meal."

Am feum mi na soithichean a nighe? pronounced "Um faem nuh seh eechyun uh nee uh?" meaning, "Must I wash the dishes?"

Now the center of Gaelic education on the island and, in fact, host to visiting students from the Old World, St. Ann's has an interesting story attached to it. In the last century a group of 800 Scottish settlers decided that life in Cape Breton was just too hard, the soil too unyielding, the winters too long. Led by a Presbyterian minister, they pulled up stakes and moved to New Zealand. Today thousands of New Zealanders can trace their roots to one-time Scottish settlers in this area of Nova Scotia.

trivia

The world's tallest true giant (that is, not due to pathological causes) was Angus MacAskill, who at 7 foot 9 inches, or 236 cm, put the tiny village of St. Anns, Cape Breton, on the map.

Who could have predicted that a century after the Scottish settlers had abandoned their homes in St. Anns, the village would be the center of Scottish revivalism? One thing is certain: The story of the exodus to New Zealand does not get much play at the Gaelic college.

The first Scottish attempt at settling Cape Breton was in 1629, when a baronet named Lord Ochiltree promoted Cape Breton and its qualities. The king had established an order of baronets five years earlier, who were to promote and oversee the settlement of 3-by-6-mile (5-by-10-km) tracts of land along the coast. The rough equivalent of modern-day real estate developers, these baronets were gambling not just their personal fortunes, but also their lives.

Soon after Lord Ochiltree landed at Baliene, on the island's east coast, he discovered French fishing vessels in what were supposed to be British waters. The baronet sent a ship to tell them they could stay to fish and trade with the Mi'Kmaq if they paid him 10 percent of their earnings. Ochiltree and his soldiers then took the first mate hostage and kept three cannons as collateral until the French captain was able to pay.

At about this time yet another declaration of peace was being signed between France and England. Meanwhile, another sea captain named Daniels arrived from France, landing at St. Anns, where some French settlers told him about the Scottish pioneers at Baliene. Peace declarations aside, Captain Daniels determined to teach Ochiltree a lesson, gathered together his hardiest men, had scaling ladders constructed, and went to make a neighborly call on Ochiltree. Once inside Scottish walls, Daniels captured Ochiltree. His men subdued the baronet's armor-clad soldiers. Once again a French flag flew over the island. Baronet Ochiltree was taken prisoner along with all his men and brought to St. Anns, where the most able Scotsmen among them were set to work building the French a fort, chapel, and magazine. By November 1629, Captain Daniels sailed for France with his captives, a number of whom died en route and were thrown overboard. Our hapless land speculator ended up in France, where he made unheeded appeals to the Court of Admiralty in Dieppe. Finally, Captain Daniels sailed off on another adventure, and Nova Scotia's unfortunate baronet was released. The entire misadventure had cost him £50,000 and thirteen men.

From St. Anns drive south back along the same stretch of highway and you will again reach exit 11, which brings you to the TCH. Follow it south until exit 10, which is the junction leading to *Baddeck,* your next destination, and the perfect spot for exploring the beauty of the *Bras d'Or Lake.*

Nova Scotia is home to one of the highest concentrations of *bald eagles* in North America. There are an estimated 250 nesting pairs of eagles, found for the most part along the shores of the Bras d'Or Lake. Incidentally, this isn't really a lake at all, but an inland sea with mildly salty water, at 5 percent salt content, sufficient to keep a lobster fishery going. Its total area is 450 square miles (1,165 sq. km).

Because it has virtually no tide, the saltwater arm of the sea freezes solid in winter. During July and August you'll have ample opportunity to see the eagles in their native environment. The birds are sufficiently plentiful and healthy that some newborn eagles are being exported to the United States, especially to the Quabbin Reservoir area of central Massachusetts.

Reproduction problems were experienced by many birds in the 1960s, due to DDT and other chemical insecticides in the food chain. In the isolation of the Nova Scotia coastline, these problems did not arise, leaving the province with healthy communities of raptors, including ospreys, hawks, and owls.

Several suggested routes to take to get a better look at the eagles include Highway 223, through the central Bras d'Or Lake district, and TCH 105, which skirts the northern outer rim of Bras d'Or. Pay particular attention to the "Scenic Travelways Map," available at all the province's tourism information booths. Along the map's outline of the lake are symbols of bald eagles, marking the best places for viewing them.

Several sailing tours are available in the area, as the lake is a haven for sailors. (Boats can get in from the northern inlet that you recently crossed by ferry or through St. Peters Canal, at the southern tip of Cape Breton. If it were not for a short strip of land now traversed by the St. Peters Canal, Cape Breton would really be two islands, not one.)

One recommended tour is with *Bird Island Tours Ltd.,* found at 1672 Old Route 5, Big Bras d'Or Lake, on Hwy 105, at exit 14. This two-hour narrated tour in a covered boat takes you to see the Bird Islands. These are abundant with puffins, other seabirds, eagles, and seals. Tours depart rain or shine daily. Reservations are recommended. This company also runs a gift shop and a campground and rents cottages. They are open mid-May to mid-September. Call toll-free (800) 661–6680.

Helen Sievers, co-owner of **Auberge Gisele's Inn** in Baddeck, capitalizes on the beautiful natural setting of the village by referring guests to a local naturalist who leads them out on wild mushroom hunts. Chanterelles are one find that the inn's chefs freeze and use in their scrumptious meals. In fall, they even find delicious boletes, which are also used in the inn's cuisine, along with fiddleheads, when in season.

The inn now has an art gallery featuring the work of many local artists who depict the beauty of Baddeck and its environs.

Gisele's has a long, sweeping lawn built up a hill, giving such a picturesque view of Baddeck that painters sometimes set up their easels there. For reservations, call (800) 3040–INN or (902) 295–2849; fax (902) 295–2033. Rates are moderate to deluxe.

Also in the Baddeck area you can visit the **Alexander Graham Bell Museum and National Historic Site.** Bell spent summers here for many years and quite a bit of time in the winter as well. Displays on his many inventions tell his life story.

Bell was initially involved in speech therapy, as were his father and grandfather. His mother was partially deaf, and Bell eventually married one of his deaf students. His work on the telephone came as a result of his intense interest in communications technology. Along with inventing the phone at age twenty-nine, he worked on airplane development, building the Silver Dart, which was flown over Bras d'Or Lake. (He used the frozen lake as his tarmac for takeoff and landing.) He also built a hydrofoil, the original HD–40 version of which is on display at the museum. Of course, you also get to see lots of early telephones. Admission is $4.25 for adults, $2.25 for kids. It is open year-round with some reduced services and early closing in the off-season. It's open in June from 9:00 A.M. to 6:00 P.M., July and August from 8:30 A.M. to 7:30 P.M.

trivia

Cape Breton Island comprises one-third of the entire area of Nova Scotia.

Baddeck is an anomaly: This tiny village with a population of slightly more than a thousand souls swells to several times this number in the summer without being frazzled. The result is a collection of good eateries along the waterfront and a number of interesting things to do. The community even has a ferry that takes people over to nearby **Kidston Island**'s beach for free.

The **Bell Buoy** provides scrumptuous desserts, delicious seafood, and a great view of the lake, including the little lighthouse on Kidston Island, which is just facing the restaurant. You'll also see a lot of yachts. Since it's a charming little community with a good marina, it has become a haunt of yachters who love the Bras d'Or for its excellent sailing.

Bell's stately summer home overlooks the inlet where the village is nestled, just across from a small island and lighthouse. The home's setting couldn't be prettier.

Another cozy restaurant operates out of the *Telegraph House,* which has been an inn for more than a century. In the late 1880s it was the home-away-from-home of Alexander Graham Bell before his mansion was built on the stretch of headland overlooking the lake. The building also housed the telegraph office at one time. Today it is owned and operated by the fourth and fifth generations of the Dunlop family. Room number one, Bell's room, has been left in very much the same state as when he used it.

The Victorian home was built in 1861 and has hosted dinner for Prince Michael, brother of the Duke of Kent, and a prince and princess of Japan, photographs of whom are displayed at the inn.

The place is utterly charming, right down to the fireside armchairs and grandfather clock. For information, call (902) 295–1100. Rates are standard.

Moving from the Baddeck area into the forest hinterland, you can take the time for one of the most scenic walks in this end of the country, culminating at *Uisage Ban Falls,* Gaelic for "white water." To get there you will have to backtrack about 1 mile (1.6 km) to the Cabot Trail (which terminates at Baddeck) on Route 105, just after the TCH junction leading to Baddeck.

A sign indicating a left turnoff will direct you to the falls. Follow the signs to a parking lot, where you can leave your vehicle and proceed on foot up a moderately steep incline for about 1 mile (1.6 km), past a stream that runs through a thick stand of birch and evergreens. At the end your reward will be the sort of astoundingly beautiful, ice-cold waterfall that could have appeared in a Robin Hood movie.

Once you're on the road again and have left Baddeck behind, turn south on Route 105 in the direction of Little Narrows. From here you can take another little ferry across a narrow arm of the lake onto a small patch of land, the *Washabuck Peninsula,* which is practically an island itself.

You will have a choice of two directions as soon as you get off the ferry. Choose the road to your right, the southern end of Route 223. This road will take you through rolling hills that yield a beautiful view of the lake, an area that seems completely untouched by the modern world. It is a likely setting for the *Highland Village,* in *Iona,* just before the recently built bridge that spans the Barra Strait.

Just before you approach the bridge, turn right and follow the shore road a short way. High on a hilltop overlooking the Bras d'Or, you will find a replica of an old Scottish pioneer village. There are homes from 1830, 1865, and 1900, as well as a thatch-roof Hebridean Black house, of the type used by the earliest settlers, and a log house. There are also a school, forge, carding mill, and barn. Costumed guides will show you around. On the first Saturday in August each year they hold Highland Village Day, with traditional Scottish music. Admission is $7.00 for adults, $2.00 for children ages five to eighteen, families $14.00, seniors $6.00. For information call (902) 725–2272.

Iona is also one of the venues for the ***Celtic Colours International Festival***, held the second week in October. Over the years the little village's Legion Hall has been the stage for performers from Scotland and Ireland, as well as local entertainers. Ticket information for this particular concert is available by calling the number for the Highland Village listed above. For the rest of the Celtic Colours Festival tickets, call (800) 565–9464 or (902) 564–6668. Tickets go on sale in mid-August, and I would strongly advise you to book well in advance.

From Iona drive across the bridge to ***Grand Narrows.*** This is a wonderful, unspoiled spot worth your time. There is good swimming with warm water at ***Pipers Cove,*** just after Grand Narrows.

You can take either Route 223, along St. Andrews Channel on the northern end of this peninsula, or the southern route past Eskasoni, a large Mi'Kmaq community. Regardless of which end of highway you choose, head to Sydney so that you do not find yourself trying to get to Louisbourg on secondary roads with rough patches.

Sydney, population 26,000, is a good spot for a rest stop. There are a number of interesting things to see here. You will enter the city on Route 4, which quickly becomes King's Road, until you reach the city center. This is a city built by the coal and steel industries of the past century. These days there is a small university here, and the city serves as a service hub for the island.

A number of historic buildings can be found here. ***Cossit House,*** reputed to be the oldest building in Sydney, dates back to 1787. You will find it at 75 Charlotte Street. It's part of the Nova Scotia Museum Complex. Carefully restored to its original condition, it includes furnishings listed in an

trivia

To put it delicately, Alexander G. Bell liked to relax *in puris naturalibus,* meaning he was a nudist.

During the Second World War, a passenger ferry on the Sydney–Port aux Basques route was sunk.

Bran Bonnach

You may be wondering what kind of food the early settlers ate. Here is a recipe for bran bonnach (pronounced *ban-auch,* with a hearty gutteral ending), as made by the highland Scots. Similar to biscotti, a bonnach is a flat homemade oatcake sometimes cooked on a griddle. The recipe is courtesy of the Highland Village, in Iona.

1 egg

1 cup bran (softened in warm water and drained)

⅓ cup brown sugar (optional)

¾ cup rolled oats

1 cup buttermilk

½ cup melted bacon fat or lard

2½ cups flour

3 teaspoons baking powder

1 teaspoon baking soda

1 teaspoon salt

Preheat oven to 400°F (182°C). In a large bowl, lightly beat the egg and add bran. Add brown sugar (if desired), rolled oats, buttermilk, and melted bacon fat. In another bowl, mix together flour, baking powder, baking soda, and salt and add to mixture. The dough should have the texture of lumpy biscuit dough. Roll out on a floured board. Take care when rolling: The rolled dough should be the thickness of scone or biscuit dough. If rolled out too flat, the oatcakes will be hard and dry. Mark with a fork, and place on a nonstick baking sheet (or brush with butter). Bake for 40 minutes.

inventory of the building in 1815. Cossit House was the home of the island's first Anglican minister.

To get to Cossit House, continue along King's Road until it becomes the Esplanade. This ends at the corner of Prince Street, which is also, mysteriously, named Route 4. Follow the waterfront for 4 more blocks and then turn right onto Charlotte Street.

Cossit House is 1 block from the river. In addition to the costumed guides and antiques, it has a pretty garden. It is open only June 1 to October 15 from 9:30 A.M. to 5:30 P.M., Sunday from 1:00 to 5:30 P.M. For more information, call (902) 539–7973.

Also on Charlotte Street, and just a stone's throw away at number 54, is ***Jost House.*** It gives one a good idea of how homes evolved on Cape Breton over the years and offers a look at artifacts related to old-style cooking and baking. Jost House is open June 1 to late August from 9:30 A.M. to 5:30 P.M. and September and October from 10:00 A.M. to 4:00 P.M. For information, call (902) 539–0366.

One other particularly noteworthy historic house is now a country inn with a renowned restaurant. *The Gowrie House,* at 139 Shore Road in Sydney Mines, is a three-and-a-half-star establishment set in a home dating back to 1834. To visit you'll have to detour across the harbor to Highway 223 northbound, to Sydney Mines. There is only one seating for dinner, at 7:30 P.M. To reserve ahead, call (902) 544–1050.

The Fleur-de-Lis Trail

Once you've seen enough of Sydney, take Highway 22, which runs straight off George Street downtown. Highway 22 is the most direct route to take to see Fortress Louisbourg, North America's largest and most authentic historical restoration, but there are many other routes.

Highway 22 takes you across the *Mira River,* which has been immortalized by one of Cape Breton's most popular ballads. (If you're in the Maritimes for any length of time, you're bound to hear "Song for the Mira.")

Just 2 miles (3 km) east off Route 22 at exit 17 in *Albert Bridge,* you will find the *Mira River Provincial Park,* where there are facilities for swimming and picnicking. Because the land at this part of the river forms a peninsula, there are several little coves and secluded swimming areas as well as launch sites for canoes. Many locals have summer cottages along this river and in Catalone, just 2 miles (3 km) farther along Route 22.

Back on Route 22, just before you reach Louisbourg, you will come to the old *Sydney and Louisbourg Railway Museum.* It features two wonderful, full-size, turn-of-the-century railway coach cars in mint condition, a caboose, an oil car, and a freight car—sufficient paraphernalia to satisfy any railway buff. The museum also chronicles the salad days of Louisbourg, when shipping, mining, and the railway made this excellent harbor a thriving community. The building that houses what is left of the railway is the station, which, along with the freight shed, was constructed in 1895, an era when this little stretch of rail had more than four million tons of coal a year hauled across its ribbon of steel.

Sadly, the original roundhouse is gone. But an exact replica has been constructed and is used to house the rolling stock during the winter. For more details on the local area, visit the railway museum information center.

Along with railway memorabilia, the museum has many photographs chronicling the three transatlantic Marconi wireless stations established by

Italian inventor Guglielmo Marconi. At the turn of the century, Marconi spent several years near Glace Bay setting up his wireless stations.

Just after the railway museum, you'll arrive in **Louisbourg,** whose tiny downtown area seems to be thriving with businesses catering to summer visitors to the **Fortress Louisbourg.**

It's an amazing turn of events, when you consider the unfortunate location of the original fortress. It lay on windswept land, surrounded by hills that left it quite exposed to attacks, so barren that it was difficult to cultivate food for the fortress inhabitants. It was located here because the magnificent harbor had been discovered by Europeans by 1713, leading to the founding of a town. It soon became the East Coast's third-busiest seaport. Because it was far closer to France than the scattered settlements along the St. Lawrence River, no price seemed too high to pay in the defense of the "Gibraltar of the North."

The restoration has been arranged to re-create life in the town during a summer's day in 1744, the peak of French power in the New World. Along with a garrison of 600 soldiers was a permanent population of approximately 2,000 administrators, clerks, innkeepers, cooks, artisans, and fishermen. The restored fortress includes fifty buildings (one-quarter of the original town). Local residents, many descended from the original French settlers, portray the residents of the French garrison town.

When you arrive at the fortress gate, you are immediately accosted by a French "soldier," who demands to know your business there. One hundred interpreters in full costume explain intricate details of life at Louisbourg in 1744.

In the chapel, an impressive church that is part of the fortifications, tiny model ships hang in the window. These traditionally were built by fishermen as a way of expressing their gratitude to God for a good catch. Only the elite sat in the church; all others stood, so it held hundreds at a single mass.

The governor's wheelchair in his chambers dates from that era. His room is adorned with carefully reproduced portraits and period furniture.

Take note of the open fireplaces, where meat was roasted on spits. Cooks would turn a mechanical device, which would evenly rotate the spit, untended for a half hour or so before the cook had to attend to the basting.

Ultimately, the location that made winters severe and cultivation difficult also led to the downfall of the fortress. In 1745, one year after the summer's day you see reenacted, an expedition of New England volunteers laid siege to Louisbourg's barely complete defenses. The fortress garrison held out for several weeks.

During the following winter, 900 of the victorious New Englanders died of cold and starvation. The dead had to be buried under floorboards until the spring thaw.

Finally, the New England soldiers mutinied and drowned their sorrows in drink. When reinforcements arrived, the new British governor ordered their rum confiscated. A total of 64,000 gallons was seized.

Three years later, Louisbourg was briefly returned to the French. In 1758, a year before the fall of Quebec, a force of 15,000 British soldiers and more than 150 ships attacked, blowing the fortress to smithereens.

For years afterward Louisbourg was nothing more than a source of cut stone and hardware for buildings as far away as the newly founded Halifax. Eventually, because the fortress did not have a modern city constructed over it, the ruins allowed for an amazingly authentic restoration.

Admission to tour the site is $13.50 for adults, $11.50 for seniors, and $7.00 for students and children. Children ages five and under are free. For information, call (902) 733–2280.

After Louisbourg you have no option but to return almost to Sydney on Highway 22, then exit to Highway 4 southbound, just outside the city. From here you will skirt the southern end of the Bras D'Or Lake until you reach *St. Peter's.*

The reward of this slight backtracking to Highway 4 will be self-evident: The road passes through breathtaking scenery, particularly late in the day as the sun sets over the lake.

In St. Peter's the land narrows so much that, for want of a few inches of water, Cape Breton would consist of two major islands instead of one. One hundred and forty years ago, the opportunities presented by this geographic fact led to the building of the *St. Peters Canal.* Before that time, the area was the haunt of French fur trader and adventurer Nicolas Denys, who eventually became the governor of New France in the late 1600s.

Lobster Boat in St. Peters Canal

Everything there is to see in St. Peter's is within walking distance of the rustic log structure of the charming **Bras d'Or Lakes Inn,** which fronts the lake. If you stay at the inn, take note of the log-construction hardwood chairs and furnishings. These were made by a local furniture artisan.

trivia

The Bras d'Or Lake isn't really a lake at all. It's an inland sea, with a saline level of roughly 5 percent.

It is open year-round. Rates are moderate. For reservations call (800) 818–5885 or (902) 535–2200.

A short walk from the inn will take you to the canal, along which you can walk for a considerable distance. On the north side you will find **Battery Park,** a pleasant place where you can stroll around the point of land or turn southward and cross the canal along walkways that form the top of the locks.

Between the lake and the ocean there is a differential of 8 inches (20 cm) of water, between high and low tides. Because of the calm seas, it is a haven for pleasure boaters, many of whom use the canal to enter the Bras d'Or.

On a hill overlooking the south side of the canal is the **Nicolas Denys Museum.** The building is a modern reconstruction of an old-style French fur-trading post, of the sort historians think was used at the time of Denys's stay in Cape Breton. In the 1650s, shortly after his time in Miscou and before he decamped to Bathurst, Denys had a post here. It's a small museum, but it does recount the life of one of the most exciting and adventurous explorers of the French colonial era. It is open from June 1 to the end of September. There is an admission fee of 50 cents for adults, 25 cents for children. For more information call (902) 535–2379.

Another worthwhile stop in St. Peter's is a short walk from the canal. Situated on Main Street (Highway 4) is a small, unassuming, 120-year-old house, the birthplace of one of the country's most famous photographers. The **Wallace MacAskill Museum** contains well over one hundred photographs, many of them hand-tinted, as well as biographical material of the famous marine photographer.

MacAskill literally made Peggys Cove into the tourist icon it has become. His photographs from the 1930s, when it was depicted as the ultimate sleepy little fishing village, set the stage for the growth of the tourist industry in this province. His most famous photograph is accessible to millions: Just reach into your pocket and pull out a Canadian dime. That's a MacAskill of the original *Bluenose.* The museum is open in July and August and on September weekends from 9:30 A.M. to 5:30 P.M. Admission is free; donations are welcome.

With St. Peter's your tour of Cape Breton is almost complete, except for a stop at the ***LeNoir Forge Museum*** on ***Isle Madame***. Leaving St. Peter's, you can continue along Highway 4 or take Highway 104. Either way, to visit Isle Madame you will have to turn off at exit 46, near Louisdale, and drive to ***Arichat***. Here again you will find an Acadian community, many of whose residents are descendants of exiled Acadians who returned to these shores.

Added to this mix is the trail of Jersey Island money and investors in the fishing industry who moved into the area as soon as the land was ceded to England. Arichat may seem like a sleepy little village now, but 200 years ago it was one of the continent's biggest fishing boomtowns. In the 1700s at the height of this fish-based economic boom, a stone blacksmith was set up right along the shoreline for the purpose of forging whatever tools were needed. You will find this impressive restored stone smithy harborside, just 1 block off Route 320 in Arichat. Admission is free, but it is frequently closed when it ought to be open, so call ahead to confirm times if your sole purpose in visiting Arichat is to see the blacksmith shop. The phone number is (902) 226–9364.

If you have visited Isle Madame, you will need to return to exit 46 via either Highway 206 or 320. From exit 46 southbound you can take either Highway 104 or the slightly more scenic Highway 4 to Port Hastings, the Canso Causeway, and beyond, bringing to a close your tour of Cape Breton.

Places to Stay in Cape Breton

BADDECK

Auberge Gisele's Inn
Shore Road
(800) 304–0466 or
(902) 295–2849
Nice rooms and excellent restaurant.
Moderate to deluxe.

CHÉTICAMP

L'Auberge Doucet Inn
Cabot Trail
(800) 646–8668 or
(902) 224–3438
View of Chéticamp Island on one side and Cape Breton Highlands on the other. Nice rooms. Standard.

DINGWALL

The Markland Coastal Resort
(3 miles/5 km off the Cabot Trail)
(800) 872–6084 or
(902) 383–2246
Excellent outdoor setting. Rustic Scandinavian-style cabins set amid beaches, mountains, and dunes.
Moderate to deluxe.

GLENVILLE

(midway between Inverness and Mabou)

Duncreigan Country Inn
Route 19
(902) 945–2244
Intimate setting overlooking picturesque Mabou Harbour. Open year-round.
Moderate.

MABOU

Glenora Inn and Distillery
Route 19
(6 miles/9 km north of Mabou)
(800) 839–0491 or
(902) 468–6516
Moderate to deluxe.

ST. PETER'S

Bras d'Or Lakes Inn
Route 4
(800) 818–5885
Pleasant inn with log cabin-style dining room. Adjacent to St. Peters Canal. Within easy walking distance to park and nature trails. Standard.

Places to Eat in Cape Breton

BADDECK

Telegraph House
Chebucto Street
(902) 295–1100
Charm dating back to Alexander Graham Bell.

CAPE NORTH

Morrison's Pioneer Restaurant
The Cabot Trail
(902) 383–2051

INGONISH BEACH

The Keltic Lodge
Cabot Trail
Middle Head Peninsula
(800) 565–0444

MABOU

The Mull
Route 19
(902) 945–2244

MARGAREE VALLEY

The Normaway Inn
Egypt Road
(exit 7 off Highway 105)
(800) 565–9463

ST. ANNS HARBOUR AT SOUTH HAVEN

The Lobster Galley
(exit 11 off TCH 105, 12 miles/19 km north of Baddeck)
(902) 295–3100

SYDNEY MINES

Gowrie House
139 Shore Road
(902) 544–1050
Historic setting.

Index

About the Author

Trudy Fong has worked as a journalist in Canada and in Southeast Asia. For a time she was a reporter for the *Hongkong Standard,* and then she turned to magazine writing. Before she settled into a steady job, she traveled around the world for three years with her husband, Greg, during which time she visited and wrote about more than twenty-five countries. Trudy speaks several languages, including French, which was especially useful while researching this book. She lives in Nova Scotia with her three sons and her husband, who owns the Garden View Restaurant (famous for its all-meat egg rolls), on Main Street in Dartmouth. If you happen to find her there, be sure to ask her to autograph your book for you, and give her an update on your own travels to these shores.